Object-Oriented Development
THE FUSION METHOD

PRENTICE HALL
OBJECT-ORIENTED
SERIES

B. MEYER
Eiffel: The Language

D. MANDRIOLI AND B. MEYER (EDS.)
Advances in Object-Oriented Software Engineering

B. HENDERSON-SELLERS
Book of Object-Oriented Knowledge

M. LORENZ
Object-Oriented Software Development: A Practical Guide

P. J. ROBINSON
Hierarchical Object-Oriented Design

R. SWITZER
Eiffel: An Introduction

B. MEYER AND J-M NERSON
Object-Oriented Appications

J-L KNUDSEN, M. LOFOREN,
O. LEHRMANN-MADSON, AND B. MAGNUSSON
Object-Oriented Software Development

K. LANO AND H. HOUGHTON
Object-Oriented Specification Case Studies

D. COLEMAN ET AL.
Object-Oriented Development: The Fusion Method

Object-Oriented Development

THE FUSION METHOD

Derek Coleman

Patrick Arnold

Stephanie Bodoff

Chris Dollin

Helena Gilchrist

Fiona Hayes

Paul Jeremaes

 Prentice Hall, Englewood Cliffs, New Jersey 07632

Object-oriented development : the fusion method / Derek Coleman . . .
[et al.].
p. cm. - - (Prentice-Hall object-oriented series)
Includes bibliographical references and index.
ISBN 0-13-338823-9
1. Object-oriented programming (Computer science) 2. System
analysis. 3. System design. I. Coleman, Derek. II. Series.
QA76.64.O247 1994
005.1'1- -dc20
93-2015
CIP

Publisher: Alan Apt
Production Editor: Mona Pompili
Cover Designer: Wanda Lubelska Design
Copy Editor: Andrea Hammer
Production Coordinator: Linda Behrens
Editorial Assistant: Shirley McGuire

©1994 by Prentice-Hall, Inc.
A Paramount Communications Company
Englewood Cliffs, New Jersey 07632

Printed in the United States of America

10 9 8 7 6 5 4 3

ISBN 0-13-338823-9

ISBN 0-13-338823-9
90000

9 780133 388237

PRENTICE-HALL INTERNATIONAL (UK) LIMITED, *London*
PRENTICE-HALL OF AUSTRALIA PTY. LIMITED, *Sydney*
PRENTICE-HALL CANADA, INC., *Toronto*
PRENTICE-HALL HISPANOAMERICANA, S.A., *Mexico*
PRENTICE-HALL OF INDIA PRIVATE LIMITED, *New Delhi*
PRENTICE-HALL OF JAPAN, INC., *Tokyo*
SIMON & SCHUSTER ASIA PTE. LTD., *Singapore*
EDITORA PRENTICE-HALL DO BRASIL, LTDA., *Rio de Janeiro*

*"Derek Coleman wishes to thank his wife,
Victoria Stavridou,
for all her patience, support, and encouragement
during the writing of the book and
the development of Fusion."*

Foreword

This book could have been entitled *Putting it all together*. There is no lack of publications on individual aspects of the object-oriented approach to software construction: how to structure systems, how to use inheritance, how to perform object-oriented analysis, and so on. The great merit of the method described here is that it starts at the beginning of the software construction process and accompanies the reader all the way to the end, while taking into account such concerns as reuse and management practices which extend across all life-cycle steps. So rather than being left with the task of reconciling a set of individually attractive but potentially incompatible concepts and techniques, readers are presented with a coherent approach to the analysis, design, and implementation of object-oriented software.

Another quality emanates from the presentation: practicality. The book has evolved from the authors' experience of using and teaching the method, an experience which has led to the eclectic case studies of chapter 7 and to the many examples scattered throughout the discussion.

Derek Coleman and his colleagues have done an equally thorough job of collecting useful information from the literature on object-oriented methodology and neighboring topics, so that in addition to the authors' own perspective you will get access to advice from many different sources.

Seldom then will have a name been better adapted. Welcome to the Fusion of some of the best in object-oriented methodology.

Bertrand Meyer

Preface

AUDIENCE

The target audience for this book is software engineers and project managers who have some familiarity with and *intend to try* the object-oriented approach. It could be used in courses on object-oriented software development as well as software engineering.

The reader should be acquainted with the concepts underlying the object-oriented approach and with software engineering terminology such as software life-cycle, requirements definition, and development process.

OBJECT-ORIENTED METHODS

Industrial software developers have come to realize the importance of having a systematic approach to the software development process. Initial attempts at introducing system development methods for object-oriented software used "structured" methods. The results were unsuccessful, mainly because of the mismatch between the object-oriented computational model and that assumed by structured methods. A key problem is that structured methods are of only limited use in describing the run-time behavior of object-oriented systems. In particular, support for designing and documenting how objects interact to satisfy functional requirements is essential for both developers and maintainers of object-oriented software.

Many object-oriented methods (e.g., Rumbaugh, Booch, Wirfs-Brock, Coad, etc.) were developed, aiming to remedy the situation. These initial offerings were enthusiastically received by object-oriented software developers. However, as vast differences in approach became apparent, the question as to which method was better was asked with increasing frequency.

From an industrial perspective, an object-oriented method must have a systematic process to support team management, must employ well-defined notations to aid team communication, and must cover the entire software development life cycle. While the available methods had relevant features, no one method met all these requirements.

The major deficiency of most methods is the weak process provided to guide the developer through the various phases of the development process. The methods often rely on a "bottom-up" approach, of focusing on identifying classes and (in our view, prematurely) their interfaces. Little connection is made between the functions required of a system and how the functions determine the class interfaces. Some methods provide little more than collections of heuristics to be applied in an indeterminate order.

Some problems with the notations employed include poor definition, neglecting the documentation of the run-time behavior of objects, and verbosity with a concomitant lack of scalability. Finally, few methods provide complete coverage of the software development lifecycle.

We have included a comparative analysis of the leading methods that we feel will be useful for evaluation.

FUSION METHOD

To address these problems, Fusion was developed to provide a systematic approach to object-oriented software development. The Fusion method has integrated and extended existing approaches to provide a direct route from a requirements definition through to a programming-language implementation. It also addresses the requirements of development *for* and *with* reuse and reengineering. Fusion represents the next generation of object-oriented software development methods.

Fusion is based on a concise but comprehensive set of well-defined notations for capturing analysis and design decisions. Starting from a requirements document, the analysis phase produces a set of models that provide a declarative description of the required system behavior. The analysis models provide high-level constraints from which the design models are developed. The design phase produces a set of models that realize the system behavior as a collection of interacting objects. The implementation phase shows how to map the design models onto implementation-language constructs.

The Fusion process is described as a sequence of steps within each phase. The steps order the significant decisions that have to be made at each step and the deliverables from each step explicitly feed into a subsequent step. Associated with each step, Fusion also provides rules for checking the consistency and completeness of the developing models.

TOPICS COVERED

The first part of this book is a technical presentation of the core of the Fusion method, and its approach to the software development phases of analysis, design, and implementation.

The first four chapters describe the modeling primitives and process comprising the Fusion method. The entire method is then illustrated in a case study. The last chapter provides exercises of varying difficulty.

The second part of the book focuses on the wider context of object-oriented technology and project management. It begins with a detailed assessment of the object-oriented software development methods that have had a major influence on Fusion. In the last two chapters, the role of the Fusion method in achieving reuse and management goals is considered.

The final part of the book contains reference material on the Fusion method: a summary of all the process steps, a notation summary, and a manual that defines the syntax and semantics of all the notations.

Derek Coleman
Patrick Arnold
Stephanie Bodoff
Chris Dollin
Helena Gilchrist
Fiona Hayes
Paul Jeremaes

Acknowledgments

During the development of Fusion we have had the support of many people in Hewlett-Packard. We especially want to thank our managers John Taylor, Virgil Marton, Ray Crispin, and Nigel Derrett.

Since the launch of Fusion in 1992, many people have been involved in promoting the method by providing training and consulting support. We particularly thank our colleagues in HP: Justin Murray, Claus-Dieter Kurzendoerfer, Wendell Fields, Todd Cotton, Kim Harris, Steve Bear, Rana Raychoudhury, Damian Black, Lisa Guinn, James Lancaster, Jean Rogers, Karen Thrasher, Philippe Schuler, Paul-Henry Ducroco, Russ Lash, and Edith Wilson.

We have also had support from many people outside HP. Ralph Hodgson of IDE (UK) has enthusiastically publicized Fusion since the early days. Dr. Anthony Lekkos and Diana Allen of ProtoSoft have given us valuable assistance by developing the first Fusion CASE tool.

Early adopters of the Fusion method have also played a crucial role in helping us to refine our ideas, in particular, Rolf Haas, Pia Landgraf-Hirschka, and Emmanuel Gayet.

Special thanks go to Alan Apt for his support and encouragement throughout the development this book and to Mona Pompili for coordinating the production so efficiently and cheerfully.

Contents

CHAPTER 1

Introduction

1-1 BACKGROUND

Software development is an exciting but messy business. Developers are expected to tackle increasingly complex problems, and the enormous flexibility of software means that it can be applied to a widening range of subjects. The abstract nature of most programming allows it to fit almost any domain, but it also deprives us of many intuitions that guide us in our interactions with the physical world.

Object orientation is one approach to programming that attempts to exploit those intuitions. The "atoms" of object-oriented computation, the *objects*, are likened to objects in the physical world. This produces a programming model markedly different from the traditional "functional" view. This difference is both a strength and weakness of the object-oriented approach. It is a strength because of its appeal to intuition, and because object-orientation is both theoretically and practically productive. It is a weakness because the older software development methods are mismatched to the new approach.

There are now many different development methods specific to object-oriented software. They may loosely be referred to as "first-generation" object-oriented methods, because they arose from applying the notions of object orientation to existing non-object-oriented methods. In this book we present *Fusion*, a second-generation object-oriented software development method. Fusion was developed to provide a systematic approach to object-oriented software development; it integrates and extends existing approaches.

To place Fusion in context, the rest of this chapter reviews some of the problems of software development. Solving these problems is the motivation for two kinds of techniques in software development: processes and tools. Under *processes* we discuss a model of software development that can be applied to many different kinds of programming, and explain the importance of early error detection and the benefits of a systematic development process. Under *tools* we outline the basis of object-oriented programming and describe its benefits.

We explain the difficulties of applying existing methods to object-oriented development, and introduce Fusion as a solution to those difficulties. We conclude by saying what Fusion has to offer and give an overview of the Fusion process.

1-2 SOFTWARE DEVELOPMENT

In this section we review some problems of software development. We describe a model of the software development process. We discuss how errors can be controlled and exhibit the advantages of having a systematic software development process.

1-2.1 Problems of Software Development

Many of the problems of software development have been recognized since the late 1960s, when the phrase "the software crisis" was coined. They include the following:

Poor predictability: Developers can have severe problems predicting how much time and effort is needed to produce a system satisfying the customers requirements. (Time and effort are not easily interconverted; see Brooks [15].) Systems are delivered long after the expected date.

Low-quality programs: Programs do not do what their customers have asked, sometimes crashing and losing data. This can be a consequence of rushing to deliver the software before it is ready. The original requirements might be incomplete, or self-contradictory, and this may not be discovered until late in the coding process.

High-maintenance costs: Maintenance can be *corrective*, when it fixes mistakes in the delivered system, or *enhancing*, when new features are added. Both are expensive when the original system has been built without a clear, visible architecture.

Duplication of effort: Projects often start "from scratch," sharing little code with earlier projects. Even within a single project, the same algorithms can be rederived for similar but different problems. It is difficult to share solutions or reuse old code because traditional languages make it hard to express the commonalities involved.

There are two approaches to controlling the complexity of software development. One is to improve the *tools* that the developer uses. The most obvious technical tools are high-level languages, which abstract away from the complexities of particular machines and allow code to be portable. Other technical tools include change-control systems, cross-referencers, editors, and debuggers.

The other approach is to improve the *process* by which software is developed. This includes various forms of project management: division of labor, estimation and planning, contracts, style guides, and education programs. The process may be broken down into parts, each done with its own techniques and managed in its own way.

The best results are obtained when tools and process support each other. (CASE tools are an approach where tools are provided to support the development process directly.)

1-2.2 Process of Software Development

One of the ways to manage software development is to divide it into several subtasks, called *phases*. Each phase addresses different problems, by having its own conceptual models, notations for these models, and heuristics to help the developer construct those models. The output from each phase is the basis for the next. There is broad agreement on the nature of the phases, although there is often dispute about their names and the exact placing of the boundaries between them. One model is shown in the V-diagram of Figure 1.1.

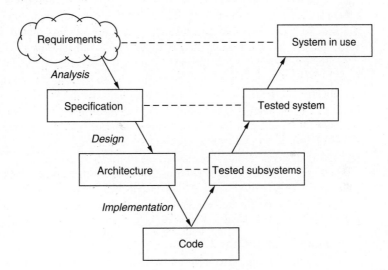

Figure 1.1   Phases of Software Development

The cloud represents the original requirements for the system to be produced. (Requirements documents are often not under the control of the software developer, that is, they may be supplied by a customer.) The boxes represent the outputs of the different development phases. Time runs from left to right; the downward flow on the left shows the stages from requirements to code (*production*), and the upward flow on the right shows the code being integrated and tested before delivery (*assembly*). The dashed lines indicate that the results of the integration phase on the right are matched to, and should satisfy, the requirements on the left.

The software is produced in three phases; each phase attempts to deal with a different aspect of the system being developed.

Analysis: Analysis produces a specification of *what* a system does. The intention is to provide a clear understanding of what the system is about and what its underlying concepts are. The result of the analysis phase is a *specification document*.

Design: Design takes the specification document as its base and defines how the specified behavior is obtained from implementation-oriented components. The output of the design phase is an *architecture document*.

Implementation: Implementation takes the design document and encodes the design in a programming language. The output of the implementation phase is *code*.

Code is produced in pieces, and these pieces must be tested and assembled together before the system can be delivered to the customer.

Controlling Errors.

Quality code should contain as few errors as possible. There is a fundamental difference in approach between the first part of development, producing code, and the second part, assembly and testing. The latter obtains quality by *detecting and removing* errors. The former obtains quality by *avoiding* errors.

Experience shows that the earlier an error is introduced, the later it is likely to be found and the more expensive it is likely to be to fix it. For example, an error in the specification of a module is likely to be relatively cheap to fix because it will probably be found when testing the module. However, an error introduced during analysis may not be found until the whole system is under test, thus potentially requiring all the intermediate steps to be reworked. So, at the end of each production phase, as few errors as possible must be passed on to the next phase.

A reliable method must both use techniques that are, in themselves, less likely to generate errors, and it should contain checks to eliminate errors that have crept in. Because it is more effective to avoid errors than to correct them, Fusion concentrates on the production side, rather than the assembly side, of the model.

Benefits of a Method.

A method designed to support the software development process should provide *systematic* analysis, design, and implementation phases. Because the most visible result of a software project is the working system, there is pressure to start coding as early as possible. This leads to programs that are difficult to maintain and that do not satisfy the customers' requirements. Systematic methods spend more time in the earlier phases of software development. Code takes longer to appear, so their benefits are not always appreciated. They include the following:

Requirements checking: The analysis process generates searching questions about requirements. System modeling is a good tool for catching omissions and ambiguities that have escaped detection in the requirements phase.

Clearer concepts: Analysis leads to a better understanding of the problem domain. This makes the resulting models more robust against changes in the requirements. It also allows the results from analysis to be reused against different requirements in the same domain.

Less design rework: The models and notations used in analysis and design allow problems to be explored at different levels of abstraction, before the details of the implementation intrude. Because alternatives can be studied before committing to a single design, that design is more likely to be suited to the problem.

Better factoring of design work: Large problems require team development; team development requires that the problem be decomposed into independent parts. Doing analysis and design makes it easier to see how the problem can be successfully decomposed.

Improved communications between developers: The notations of analysis and design allow engineers and others to communicate in a precise but abstract way. In particular, the analysis model can, and should, be shared between the analyst and the customer to check their understanding of the problem.

Less effort needed on maintenance: Software is often maintained by people other than the developers. Analysis and design documents help maintainers understand the code by providing an abstract framework within which the code resides.

1-3 OBJECT ORIENTATION

The previous section looked at the need for a systematic process of software development. This section considers a particular tool for software, the *object-oriented* approach, and contrasts it with the traditional, "function-oriented," approach. Then we explain the managerial issues introduced by object orientation and how these can be tackled.

1-3.1 Promise of Object Orientation

In the object-oriented approach, the atoms of computation are *objects*, which send each other *messages*. These messages result in the invocation of *methods*, which perform the necessary actions. The sender of the message does not need to know how the object organizes its internal state, only that it responds to particular messages in a well-defined way.

This model is illustrated in more detail in Figure 1.2. The large rectangles represent the objects, and the arrows between them represent the messages. The state of an object, represented by the ovals on the diagram, is concealed inside it. The only way to read or change object state is by sending messages, and each object "takes responsibility" for how it responds to a message.

Objects are grouped into *classes* when they share the same interface, that is, respond to the same messages in the same ways. This allows many objects to be described by only a few classes. Classes are the building blocks of most object-oriented languages.

While the system is executing, objects come into existence, perform actions, and then cease to exist or become inaccessible. The model is essentially dynamic.

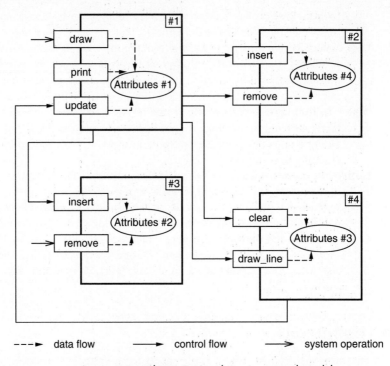

Figure 1.2 Object-Oriented Computational Model

Contrast this with the more traditional function-oriented approach to computation, pictured in Figure 1.3. Here the atoms of computation are the *functions*, which operate on a single, possibly heavily structured, shared *state*.

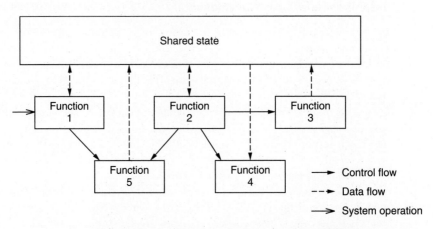

Figure 1.3 Function-Oriented Computational Model

The state is usually static, that is, its structure does not change over time, although the values in that structure (clearly) do. Any function may operate on any piece of the state. Even if the system can be divided into independent modules, each with control over some part of the state, the function-oriented approach has no underlying model to say how this division should be accomplished.

The advantages of object orientation are the following:

Data abstraction: The details of a classes representation are visible only to its methods; different implementations of a class can be used with no changes to code that uses that class. (Data abstraction is not unique to object orientation but arises naturally within it.)

Compatibility: Heuristics for constructing classes and their interfaces make it easier to combine software components.

Flexibility: Classes, or strongly related collections of classes, provide natural units for task allocation in software development.

Reuse: Bundling methods in with data representations to construct classes makes it easier to develop *reusable* software.

Extensibility: Software built using object-oriented techniques tends to be easier to extend. There are two reasons for this: Inheritance enables new classes to be built from old ones, while still participating in all the original relationships; and the classes form a loosely coupled structure that is easier to modify.

Maintenance: The natural modularity of the class structure makes it easier to contain the effects of changes, and the use of inheritance reduces the number of disparate concepts needed to understand the code.

Object orientation has proved to be both popular and effective. It has been embodied in several programming languages, the best known being C++, Eiffel, Smalltalk, and the Common Lisp Object System (CLOS).

1-3.2 Problems with Object Orientation

Object orientation as it appears in programming languages is only a *partial* solution to the software development problem. Although it makes the development of *programs* easier, there is more to developing a system than simply writing code. Its problems include the following:

Focus on code: The common emphasis in object orientation is on the programming techniques and languages, not on the development process. When expressed in programming terms, analysis and design models are not abstract enough.

Team working not addressed: Software is usually developed by teams, not individuals. Object orientation provides little help for this.

Difficult to find the objects: Finding the right objects and classes in an object-oriented system is not easy. This is partly due to the unfamiliarity of the approach, but it is also difficult in itself.

Function-oriented methods are inappropriate: When object orientation is introduced at the programming language level in a software development environment, the traditional methods of analysis and design *no longer work*. (This point is addressed more fully later.)

Management changes: As discussed earlier, the object-oriented approach is fundamentally different from the functional decomposition approach. Introducing new ways of working requires new ways of management.

Solving these problems is not just a matter of more powerful programming languages, or better programmer education. What is needed are development processes specific for object-oriented software.

1-3.3 Object-Oriented Development Methods

As mentioned earlier, traditional methods are inappropriate for object-oriented systems. Functional decompositions clash with the object structure of the implementation. A particular problem is that traditional function-oriented methods offer little help in understanding the run-time interaction between objects in object-oriented systems [29]. Also, methods are associated with pieces of state in the object model, but functions operate over the entire state in the functional model: If a function-oriented design is to be implemented in an object-oriented language, *all the object structure must be rediscovered or invented*.

Many first-generation object-oriented analysis and design methods have appeared aiming to remedy this mismatch. Although these extend object-oriented notions into the earlier parts of development, systematic evaluation [9] of several of the leading methods revealed several deficiencies. Two categories of deficiencies were identified. The first has to do with the *notations* used to capture the system under development. The second has to do with the *process* used to drive the development from a requirements definition to an appropriate implementation.

It was to address these problems that Fusion was devised. It builds on the first-generation methods by providing well-defined notations for its different models and by having a strong notion of process that reaches from analysis into implementation. A comparison of Fusion with other object-oriented methods is given in chapter 8.

1-4 WHAT IS FUSION?

Fusion is a software development method for object-oriented software. It is a full-coverage method, providing for all of analysis, design, and implementation. The notations of Fusion allow the systematic discovery and preservation of the object structure of the system. By integrating and extending existing approaches, Fusion provides a direct route from a requirements definition through to a programming language implementation.

Fusion is based on a concise but comprehensive set of well-defined notations for capturing analysis and design decisions. In this section we shall say what benefits Fusion has to offer and give a sketch of the Fusion development process.

1-4.1 What Fusion Offers

Fusion supports both the technical and managerial aspects of software development.

- It provides a process for software development. It divides this process into phases and indicates what should be done in each phase. It gives guidance on the order in which things should be done within phases, so the developer knows how to make progress. It provides criteria that tell the developer when to move on to the next phase.

- It provides comprehensive, simple, well-defined notations for all of its models. Because these notations are based on existing practice, they are easy to learn.
- It provides management tools for software development. The outputs of the different phases are clearly identified. There are cross-checks to ensure consistency within and between phases. Each phase has its own techniques and addresses different aspects of translating a requirements document into executable code.

In addition, Fusion can be *adapted*. A lightweight version can be used in projects that cannot afford the effort required to use the full version, or parts of the Fusion process or notations can be used within other development processes to address their weak points. This is discussed in detail in chapter 10. It is not restricted to the development of new systems; it can be applied in reengineering existing systems. Fusion explicitly addresses the issue of software reuse (see chapter 9).

Fusion can be used to develop sequential object-oriented systems and certain restricted kinds of concurrent systems. Because it is based on existing, well-known notations, much of it will be familiar to the experienced developer. Its adaptability allows it to be exploited without having to commit to the entire method.

1-4.2 Fusion Process

Fusion adopts the division of the development process into analysis, design, and implementation, which was discussed earlier. We now discuss each of the three phases of a Fusion development. Recall that requirements capture is usually performed by a customer, who will supply the initial requirements document, so Fusion has no requirements phase.

Analysis.

The analyst defines the intended behavior of the system. Models of the system are produced, which describe the following:

- Classes of objects that exist in the system
- Relationships between those classes
- Operations that can be performed on the system
- Allowable sequences of those operations

In contrast to some other methods, the analysis stage of Fusion does not attach methods to particular classes: This is done later. Analysis is described in detail in chapters 2 and 3.

Design.

The designer chooses how the system operations are to be implemented by the run-time behavior of interacting objects. Different ways of breaking up an operation into interactions can be tried. During this process, operations are attached to classes. The designer also chooses how objects refer to each other and what the appropriate inheritance relationships are between classes.

The design phase delivers models that show the following:

- How system operations are implemented by interacting objects
- How classes refer one to another and how they are related by inheritance
- Attributes of, and operations on, classes

Designers may need to investigate the substructures of some classes and their operations in more detail. They do so with *hierarchical decomposition*—applying the analysis and design techniques to those classes, regarding them as a subsystem. Design is described in chapter 4.

Implementation.

The implementor must turn the design into code in a particular programming language. Fusion gives guidance on how this is done.

- Inheritance, reference, and class attributes are implemented in programming-language classes.
- Object interactions are encoded as methods belonging to a selected class.
- The permitted sequences of operations are recognized by state machines.

Fusion also offers advice on performance issues, and suggests how traditional inspection and testing techniques have to be modified for object-oriented software. Implementation is discussed in chapter 5.

At the end of each phase, Fusion provides consistency checks to make sure that the models constructed agree with each other and with the results from the previous phase.

Fusion maintains a *data dictionary*, a place where the different entities of the system can be named and described. This is referenced throughout the development process. It is mentioned in chapters 2 to 5. Appendices A and B provide process and notation summaries, and appendix C is a reference manual for all the notations.

1-5 SUMMARY

In this chapter, we have reviewed the role of methods in software development, and the effect of object orientation on the software development process. We have described the Fusion process and its benefits.

- A software development process is necessary to reduce the number of errors that appear in the final product.
- Object orientation in programming languages has many advantages; traditional software processes are inappropriate for object-oriented development.

- Fusion is a second-generation method that builds on the successful parts of earlier object-oriented methods and addresses their weaknesses. It has three phases.

    - *Analysis*, which uncovers the objects and classes in the system, describes their relationships, and defines the operations that the system can perform.
    - *Design*, which decides how to represent the system operations by the inter-actions of related objects and how those objects gain access to each other.
    - *Implementation*, which encodes the design into a programming language.

CHAPTER 2

Analysis Models and Notations

2-1 INTRODUCTION

The Fusion method begins with analysis. The goal of analysis is to capture as many of the requirements on the system as possible, in a complete, consistent, and unambiguous fashion. Although there are many different requirements specification techniques [35], in practice the input to analysis is usually a natural language requirements definition document. Such documents usually contain a mixture of descriptions of what the problem is, what some solutions might be, and how a system that solves the problem ought to work. They often contains ambiguities and are at best only partially complete. At worst they can be internally inconsistent. Analysis strives to resolve these problems.

Analysis accomplishes this by constructing several models of the system. The models concentrate on describing what a system does rather than how it does it. Separating the behavior of a system from the way it is implemented requires viewing the system from the user's perspective rather than that of the machine. Thus analysis is focused on the domain of the problem and is concerned with externally visible behavior. The analysis phase of Fusion produces two models that capture different aspects of a system.

Object model: This model defines the static structure of the information in the system.

Interface model: This model defines the input and output communication of the system.

This chapter describes the notations used for the object and interface models. Chapter 3 explains how to develop the models and check them for consistency and completeness.

2-2 OBJECT MODEL

This section introduces the object model notation. The purpose of this model is to capture the concepts that exist in the domain of the problem and the relationships between them. The object model notation is based on extended entity relationship notation [22], [45]. It can represent classes, attributes, and relationships between classes. The extensions permit the use of aggregation and generalization.

2-2.1 Objects and Classes

Object-oriented analysis differs from other forms of analysis in that the notion of object is fundamental. In this section we explain the concept of object as it is used in the analysis phase of Fusion.

An *object* is a "thing" that can be distinctly *identified*. At the appropriate level of abstraction almost anything can be considered to be an object. Thus a specific person, organization, machine, or event can be regarded as an object.

In addition to being able to be identified, an object can have one or more values associated with it. For example, a person can have an address and an occupation as well as a name. In general an object may have a series of named values, called the *attributes*. A **person** object might have three attributes, **name**, **address**, and **occupation**, for example, ⟨**name:** Jack Smith; **address:** 33 Dove St., North City; **occupation:** taxi driver⟩.

The attribute values of an object can be changed, but the number and name of the attributes are fixed. The reader should note that, during the analysis phase, the values of attributes are not allowed to be objects. Attributes assume values from types such as integers, booleans, text, and enumerations. It follows that objects are more than tuples of values, because there can be many distinct objects with the same attribute values.

During analysis we are seldom interested in *how* an object can be identified from among all the other objects in the domain of discourse. There may be a special object identifier, or there may be some combination of the attributes that contain sufficient information to make identification possible. However, an object has two fundamental properties. First, it is always possible to distinguish distinct objects even if they have the same attribute values. Second, the identity of an object cannot be changed.

The analysis concept of object does not include any notion of method interface. Methods are the means whereby objects communicate to perform some task. In the analysis phase, we concentrate on specifying what tasks a system has to perform. Discussion of object communication is postponed until the design phase. Consequently, in the analysis phase, objects are similar to entities in traditional entity relationship modeling.

Objects are grouped into sets, called *classes*. A class is an abstraction that represents the idea or general notion of a set of similar objects. Associated with each class there is a predicate that defines the criteria for class membership. Thus we can always tell whether a given object belongs to particular class. For example, the **Professor** class comprises the set of all objects that satisfy the criteria for being professors.

Note that we adopt the convention that class names always start with an uppercase letter. When the class name starts with a lowercase letter, it denotes some member of the class.

The object model notation for a class is illustrated in Figure 2.1. Each class is represented by a box, with the name of the class at the top, separated from the rest of the box by a line. The attributes of the objects belonging to the class are named below the line.

Figure 2.1   Graphical Representation of Class

The figure shows a **Professor** class with the attributes **name** and **subject**. As an example, in a particular problem domain, the **Professor** class might comprise the objects shown in Figure 2.2.

Professor	
Name	*Subject*
George Lewis	French
Don Pullen	Math
Ann James	History
Jean Raoul	English

Figure 2.2   Professor Class Instances

As we shall see later in section 2.2.4, classes need *not* be disjoint, and one object may belong to more than one class. This enables us to model situations such as when a **professor** is also a student.

2-2.2 Relationships

In the real world associations exist between objects. An example is the relationship between professors and the courses they teach. A *relationship* is a tuple of objects, for example, ⟨ George Lewis; French Literature⟩. In general, depending on the relationship, any number of objects may be involved.

The object model shows classes, not objects. Thus we extend the notion of relationship to classes. In the object model a relationship is used to model the idea of association or correspondence between the objects belonging to classes.

A relationship between classes expresses only the *possibility* of a relationship between the objects of the classes involved. It does not imply that every object from one class is related to all the objects of the other classes. Thus formally, a relationship is a mathematical relationship between classes.

Diagrammatically, relationships are shown as a diamond joined to the participating classes by arcs. Figure 2.3 shows the **teaches** relationship between the **Professor** class and the **Course** class. The convention for reading relationships is to read from left to right, and from top to bottom. Thus in the example, a **Professor teaches** the **Course**.

Figure 2.3   The teaches Relationship

A relationship between two classes denotes a set of associated pairs of objects. Thus, if the **Course** class contains the set of objects with attribute **title** shown in Figure 2.4 then the **teaches** relation might be the set of tuples shown in Figure 2.5.

Course
French Literature
French Language
Algebra
Topology
American History
British History
Ancient History
English Literature
Modern Poetry

Figure 2.4   Course Class Instances

There is often a choice to be made as to whether a property should be modeled using a relationship or an attribute. Generally, using relationships is more flexible because attributes cannot have attributes themselves nor participate in relationships. In the **Professor** class using an attribute **course**, to model teaching would become a problem if it was required to model any specialist subject area within a **Professor**'s main subject.

Professor	Course
George Lewis	French Literature
George Lewis	French Language
Don Pullen	Algebra
Don Pullen	Topology
Ann James	American History
Ann James	British History
Ann James	Ancient History
Jean Raoul	English Literature
Jean Raoul	Modern Poetry

Figure 2.5   Teaches Relation Tuples

Cardinality Constraints.

The previous section describes how the object model represents relationships in a general way. Often we need to impose constraints on a relationship. A *cardinality constraint* restricts the number of objects which may be associated with each other in a relationship. Cardinalities allow the analyst to capture constraints such as each **Course** is taught by only one **Professor**, or that each **Professor** may teach zero or more **courses**.

Cardinalities are represented by annotating the arcs connecting the relationship to the classes. The annotations can take four forms: a number, for example, 10; a range, for example, 1..4; an asterisk, "*," denoting zero or more; and a plus, "+," denoting one or more. An arc without an explicit cardinality is given cardinality "*."

In general, not every object belonging to a class need participate in the relationship. This can be overridden by a *total marker*, ∎, on an arc, which indicates that all the objects in the adjacent class *must* appear in the relationship.

Figure 2.6 shows a simple object model with the cardinality annotations showing the relationships between **Student**, **Professor**, **Course**, and **Department** classes. It models the following situation:

- A student has to study between four and six courses, and at least one student has to study each course.
- A professor teaches zero or more courses, and every course must be taught by one professor.
- Each professor can head at most one department, and each department must have a head.

Invariants.

An *invariant* is an assertion that some property must always hold. Invariants are used to capture properties that cannot be modeled by cardinality constraints. They are expressed as textual annotations to an object model.

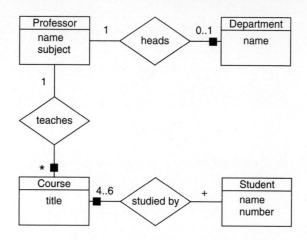

Figure 2.6   Relationship Cardinalities

As an example, consider the requirement that a head of department always teaches fewer courses than other professors. This cannot be expressed directly on an object model as it is a constraint that applies across two relationships, **heads** and **teaches**. However, it can be expressed as an invariant. Let **number_of_courses** be an attribute of **professor** objects that gives the number of courses that the professor teaches. Then the invariant, **heads have lighter teaching load**, can be defined by the following:

head.number_of_courses < non_head.number_of_courses

where

head is any **Professor** who heads a **Department**, and

non_head is any **Professor** who does not head a **Department**.

Roles.

The classes participating in a relationship have roles. Each role can be named by adding *role names* to the arcs connecting the relationship with the participating objects. The names for the roles in a relationship must be unique.

Role names are useful when it is unclear in which order to read relationship names. For example, consider the **child_of** relationship between two **Person** objects, shown in Figure 2.7. Without the role names **Parent** and **Child**, it would not be clear that it is a parent that can have many children and that it is a child that has exactly two parents. The total marker indicates that every **Person** has a parent, that is, must participate in the relationship as a **Child**.

Relationship Attributes.

Relationships as well as objects can have attributes. If we consider the **takes** relationship between **Student** and **Test** objects, we might want to record the **mark** a particular **Student** has for a particular **Test**. This value cannot be an attribute of the **Student** object, because a **Student** may take many **tests**. Neither can the value be an

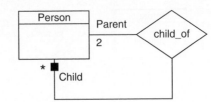

Figure 2.7 Relationship with Roles

attribute of the **Test**, because each **Test** may be taken by more than one **Student**. A solution is to make it an attribute of the **takes** relationship, thus allowing us to record the mark a particular **Student** and **Test** pair attain.

Relationship attributes are shown by including the attributes in the relationship diamond (Figure 2.8). These attributes are most common in many-to-many relationships, because in one-to-many relationships the attribute can sometimes be put into the singleton participant.

Figure 2.8 Relationship Attribute

Ternary and Higher Relationships.

The *arity* of a relationship is the number of separate objects that participate in the relationship. Many relationships in the real world are perceived as binary, involving two objects. Ternary relationships, as the name suggests, relate three separate objects. Relationships involving more than three objects are referred to as *n-ary* relationships. Ternary (and higher) relationships arise in similar situations to relationship attributes, for example, when one of the objects in the relationship is related to a specific pair of the other two objects.

As an example, consider the **takes** relationship between **Student** and **Test** from the previous section. Suppose that the requirement was modified so that now each particular **Student** and **Test** combination was to be associated with the room where the exam takes place. This can be modeled by a ternary relationship among **Tests**, **Students**, and **Rooms**.

Figure 2.9 shows the graphical representation of the example relationship. The participating classes are all connected by arcs to the relationship diamond. Arbitrary arity relationships can be denoted using this notation, although relationships of higher arities are difficult to understand and use.

2-2.3 Aggregation

Aggregation is a mechanism for structuring the object model. It permits the construction of an aggregate class from other component classes.

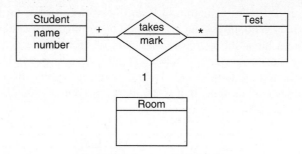

Figure 2.9   Ternary Relationship

The graphical representation of an aggregate object is shown in Figure 2.10. The aggregate object is a box with the usual class name. The component classes that make up the aggregation are shown nested in the box. The cardinality of each component in the aggregation is placed outside the component class. If the cardinality is omitted then it has default of one. An aggregate class can be treated in the same way as any other class, and may have attributes and participate in relationships.

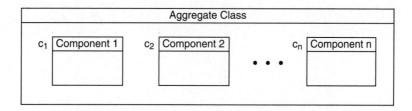

Figure 2.10   Graphical Representation of Aggregation

An aggregation can be used to model the notion of exam. Figure 2.11 defines the class **Exam** to be an aggregation of **Student** and **Test**. An **Exam** object contains some set of pairs of **Student** and **Test** objects.

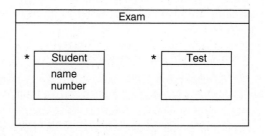

Figure 2.11   Exam as an aggregation of Student and Test

Aggregations are similar to relationships since both are formed by taking tuples of class instances. An aggregation can be used to "wrap up" a relationship. In this case the tuples of the aggregate class must respect the contained relationship. In

Figure 2.11, the definition of **Exam** is too loose since an **Exam** object can contain arbitrary **Student-Test** pairs. This can be rectified by including the **Student takes Test** relationship in the aggregate. In Figure 2.12 **Exam** objects may only contain pairs that satisfy **takes**. This allows **takes** to be treated as a class which is related to the **Room** in which the **Exam** is held. The figure also illustrates that an aggregate class, **Exam**, can have an attribute, that is, **duration**, and that a component of an aggregate, **Test**, can participate in a relation.

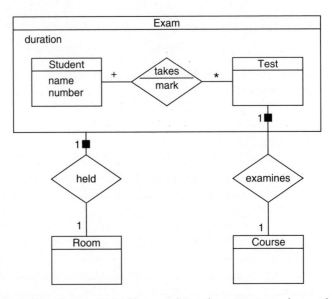

Figure 2.12   Aggregation Allows a Relationship to Be Treated as a Class

      Aggregation allows ternary (and higher) relationships to be factored into binary ones. In the previous section a ternary relation in Figure 2.9 is used to model a **Student** taking an **Exam** in a **Room**. The use of an aggregation, as shown in Figure 2.12, makes the model simpler to understand because of the separation of concerns. In many cases this also makes it easier to decide appropriate cardinality constraints and role names.

2-2.4 Generalization and Specialization

      Generalization allows a class, called the *supertype*, to be formed by factoring out the common properties of several classes, called the *subtypes*. *Specialization* is the converse case in which a new subtype is defined as a more specialized version of a supertype. For simplicity we will refer to generalization in the text.

      In a generalization, the attributes and the relationships of the supertype are "inherited" by all the subtypes. Each subtype may have additional attributes and participate in additional relationships. Generalization has the important property that all the objects of a subtype also belong to the supertype.

The notation for a generalization is a filled triangle connecting a supertype to its subtypes. Figure 2.13 shows a simple example of generalization. **Course** is a supertype with two subtypes **Undergraduate Course** and **Postgraduate Course**.

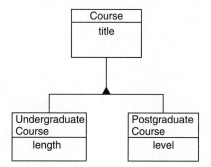

Figure 2.13   Disjoint Subtypes

The subtypes *partitions* the supertype, that is, the subtypes are disjoint, and their union is the supertype. In the example a **Course** object must belong to one of the two subtypes, **Undergraduate Course** or **Postgraduate Course**.

Partitioning can be too strong a requirement. An empty triangle is used to indicate that the subtypes overlap or that there are objects of the supertype that are not members of a subtype. In Figure 2.14 the subtypes do not partition the supertype because a **Department Head** may also be **Permanent Professor**.

The objects of a subtype only extend the properties of the supertype; they cannot alter them. Therefore a subtype object can always be freely substituted for a supertype object. This is important because it simplifies reasoning; whatever can be deduced about the superclass also holds for its subclasses. Inheritance in object-oriented programming languages does not enforce this restriction. In the interests of implementation efficiency, a subclass is allowed to overwrite parts of the super-class. Consequently the substitution property cannot always be guaranteed. The reader should be aware therefore that generalization corresponds to a *restricted use of inheritance.*

Multiple specialization.

Multiple specialization allows a new subtype to be defined as a specialization of more than one immediate supertype. This permits information to be mixed from more than source. The subclass inherits the attributes and relationships of all its superclasses.

The example, Figure 2.15, models the situation in which a trainee member of staff is a member of staff who is also a student. Thus a **Trainee Staff** object has a **name** attribute and two number attributes. The two numbers can be disambiguated by appending the class name, that is, **number@Student** and **number@Staff**.

Staff and **Student** are both generalizations of **Trainee Staff**. *Multiple generalization* is the process whereby some class is broken into two or more superclasses.

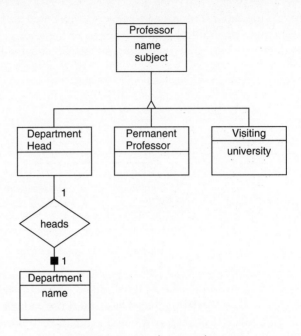

Figure 2.14 Nondisjoint Subtypes

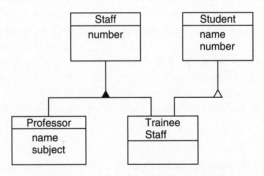

Figure 2.15 Multiple Specialization

2-3 STRUCTURING OF OBJECT MODELS

Diagrammatic notations can be difficult to understand if the diagrams get large and sprawl. The object model notation is no exception, so we allow a diagram to be broken into several subdiagrams. The complete object model is just the union of all the subdiagrams.

If two class boxes, with the same name, appear in the same object model, they denote the same class. The attributes of the class are formed by taking the union of all the attributes of the individual boxes. Thus each appearance need only contain the attributes needed for its immediate context.

Relationships are treated in a similar way. Two diamonds with the same name, connecting the same classes, and with the same role names denote a single relationship that is formed by taking the union of all the attributes.

Figure 2.16 illustrates that aggregation provides a means of *leveling*, or abstracting detail out of, the diagrams, because the components of the aggregation need only be shown once. All other occurrences can omit the details.

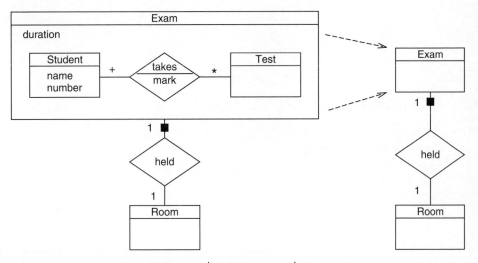

Figure 2.16   Leveling Diagrams with Aggregation

2-4 SYSTEM OBJECT MODEL

An object model presents a model of the problem domain. Thus the classes and relationships can specify concepts belonging to the environment of the system as well as to the system itself.

A *system object model* is a subset of an object model that relates to the system to be built. It is formed by excluding all the classes and relationships that belong to the environment. Thus a system object model contains a, possibly redundant, set of classes and relationships for modeling the states of the system. The boundary between the system and its environment is shown by a closed dashed curve on an object model. Note that a system object model must be a well-formed object model; consequently if any relationship is in a system object model, then all the classes that have a role in the relationship must also be in the system object model.

Clearly the extent of the system object model depends on the functionality of the system. Figure 2.17 illustrates how system functionality relates to the system object model. A system for calculating exam results and awarding degrees and doing room scheduling would have boundary A, whereas a system to do just room scheduling would need boundary B.

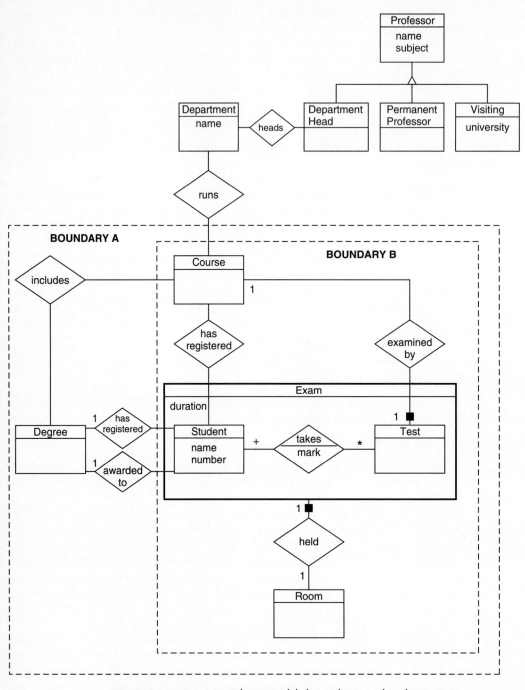

Figure 2.17 A System Object Model shows the Boundary between System and Its Environment

If the system object model is the entire object model for the problem domain, then the system must be a closed world that does not interact with its environment; in other words, the system is a simulation.

2-5 INTERFACE MODEL

The system object model describes the structure of a system, but not its behavior; this is the purpose of the interface model. The description is in terms of events and the change of state that they cause. A system is modeled as an active entity that interacts with other active entities called *agents*. Agents model human users, or other hardware or software systems. The important characteristics of an agent are that it is active and that it communicates with the system. The *environment* is the set of agents with which a system communicates. In fact, the system is just the name for the agent that is being analyzed.

An *event* is an instantaneous and atomic unit of communication between the system and its environment. An *input* event is sent by an agent to the system; an *output* event is sent by the system to an agent. The communication is *asynchronous*, as the sender does not wait for the event to be received. The sender may supply data values and objects with an event.

When a system receives an event it can cause a change of state and the output of events. The effect of an event is determined by the values that are supplied with it and the state of the system when it is received. An input event and the effect it can have are called a *system operation*. At any point in time only one system operation can be active.

The *interface* of a system is the set of system operations to which it can receive and the set of events that it can output. Figure 2.18 shows a simple banking system.

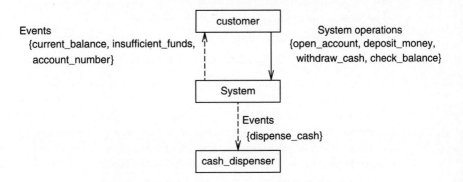

Figure 2.18   Agents Involved in Banking Example

The system operations are

{open_account, deposit_money, withdraw_cash, check_balance}

and its output events are

{account_number, dispense_cash, current_balance, insufficient_funds}

The **customer** is an agent who invokes all the system operations and also receives the **current_balance**, **insufficient_funds**, and **account_number** events. In this simple example, the only other agent is the **cash_dispenser** who receives the **dispense_cash** event.

In general, a system cannot participate in arbitrary patterns of interaction with its environment. The allowable sequences of communication are called the *life cycle* of the system. For example, the life cycle of the banking system might reasonably require that a **withdraw_cash** can only occur after **deposit_money**.

An interface model uses two models to capture different aspects of behavior:

Operation model: This model characterizes the effect of each system operation in terms of the state change it causes and the output events it sends.

Life-cycle model: This model characterizes the allowable sequencing of system operations and events.

The next two sections introduce the notation for each part of the interface model.

2-5.1 Operation Model

The operation model specifies the behavior of system operations *declaratively* by defining their effect in terms of *change of state* and the *events that are output*.

In the analysis phase, the *state of a system* is modeled as a set of objects that participate in relationships. The system object model determines the relationships and the classes to which the objects belong. The actual composition of the system state at any instant depends on what system operations have been invoked. A system operation may

- Create a new instance of a class.
- Change the value of an attribute of an existing object.
- Add or delete some tuple of objects from a relationship.
- Send an event to an agent.

The operation model specifies operations using preconditions and postconditions, as in Figure 2.19. The precondition characterizes the conditions under which the operation may be invoked. The postcondition describes how the state of the system is changed by the operation and what events are sent to agents. The preconditioners and postconditions are written as a series of descriptive clauses that have to be either **true** or **false**, that is, logical predicates. Thus, during analysis, system operations are treated like black boxes.

The operation model specification says nothing about the intermediate states through which the system passes while the operation is active. These states are dependent on the way the operation is implemented and are therefore not the legitimate concern of the analyst.

Before   After

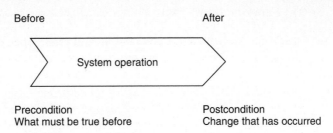

System operation

Precondition   Postcondition
What must be true before   Change that has occurred

Figure 2.19   Black-Box Specification of System Operation

The next section explains the syntax and semantics of the notation for the operation model.

Operation Model Schemata.

The operation model is expressed as a series of schemata. There must be at least one schema for each system operation. Schemata are structured text; their syntax is shown in Figure 2.20.

Operation:	*Name*
Description:	*Text*
	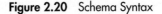
Reads:	*Items*
Changes:	*Items*
Sends:	*AgentAndEvents*
Assumes:	*Condition*
Result:	*Condition*

Figure 2.20   Schema Syntax

We consider the semantics of each of the clauses in turn.

- **Operation:** *Name*

  Name is a unique identifier for the system operation. Intuitive and free-format identifiers are preferred. Restrictions such as those found in programming languages are unnecessary.

- **Description:** *Text*

Text is an informal and concise description of the operation.

- **Reads:** *Items*

Items is a list of all the values that the operation may access but does not change. Each *Item* is the typed identifier of an object, attribute, or relationship belonging to the system state. The keyword **supplied** preceding an *Item* indicates that the identifier is a parameter of the operation. Relationships cannot be supplied values.

- **Changes:** *Items*

Items is a list of all the values that the operation may access or change. Each *Item* is a typed identifier of an object, attribute, or relationship belonging to the system state. The keyword **new** preceding an object identifier indicates that the system operation creates a new object in the system state.

- **Sends:** *AgentAndEvents*

AgentAndEvents is a list of all the agents and the events that the operation may send them. Each *AgentAndEvent* comprises the name of an agent and all the events that may be sent to it by the operation.

- **Assumes:** *Condition*

Condition is a predicate defining the precondition. A predicate is a list of clauses. Each clause must be **true** for the predicate to be satisfied (i.e., they are combined using logical **and**). If any of the clauses is **false**, then the whole predicate is **false**. The effect of invoking an operation when the precondition is **false** is undefined. The *Condition* can only reference parameters and parts of the system state defined by **Reads** and **Changes**. Any function, predicate, or other term that appears in a clause must have a definitions. The **Assumes** clause may be omitted if the precondition is **true**, that is, the operation can legally be invoked from any state.

- **Result:** *Condition*

Condition is a predicate defining the postcondition. The postcondition relates the state of the system before the operation is invoked to the state on completion of the operation and specifies the events that are sent to agents. The keyword Initial, (respectively Final) preceding an identifier is used to indicate the value before invocation (respectively on completion). The postcondition should determine behavior for all the initial states allowed by the precondition.

Note that all the operations in an operation model act on the same global state. Thus the same identifier in different schemata refers to the same component of state. However, **supplied** identifiers are local to the schema in which they are used.

In some cases it is convenient to use multiple schemata to specify one system operation. Appendix C contains details.

Example.

To develop examples of schemata for the simple banking system introduced previously we give a system object model (Figure 2.21).

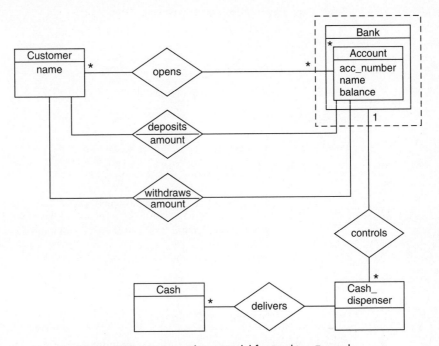

Figure 2.21   System Object Model for Banking Example

Figure 2.22 shows the schema for the **open_account** operation. The schema specifies that a **customer_name** has to be supplied to open an account. The result of opening an account is that new **Account** is created, which has name of **customer_name**, a zero **balance** and a unique **acc_number**. The **customer** is also sent the account number, **acc_number**.

The explicit typing of many identifiers can be avoided because of the convention that starting a class identifier with a lowercase letter indicates an instance of that class. Thus in the **Changes** clause **bank** is an object from the **Bank** class. This clause also specifies that a new **account** object is created.

In the **Results** clause the passive past tense, that is, "has been ...," is used to describe the state changes. This grammatical construction allows state changes to be described without detailing the order in which the changes occur. This is important because the operation model should be declarative.

Figure 2.23 specifies the system operation **withdraw_cash**. The **Reads** clause shows that the environment supplies two values, the number of the account to be accessed, and the amount of money requested.

Operation: open_account

Description: Opens a new account for a customer.

Reads: **supplied** name: customer_name

Changes: bank

           new account

Sends: customer: {account_number}

Assumes:

Result: An account has been added to the **bank**,

           account.balance has been set to zero,

           account.name has been set to **name**, and

           account.acc_number has been assigned a unique value.

           The account_number has been sent to **customer**.

Figure 2.22 Schema for open_account

The **Changes** clause shows that only the **account** is changed. The **Sends** clause shows that the **customer** and the **cash_dispenser** are the only agents that receive messages. The **Assumes** clause shows that it is the responsibility of the environment to ensure that the supplied **accountnumber** is valid and that the account is not overdrawn.

The **Result** of the operation is that if there are sufficient funds then the account is debited and an appropriate amount is sent to the **cash_dispenser**; otherwise a message is sent to the customer.

The example also illustrates two further conventions that can be used to simplify schemata.

- "⟨ id ⟩ with ... " can be used to provide a local name for an identifier satisfying some condition. In line (*i*), **account** is the local name for the account that has the appropriate account number.
- The present tense, "is," can be used to emphasize an invariant condition. Line (*ii*), the "account is not overdrawn" is **true** both before and after the operation is invoked.

Operation:	withdraw_cash
Description:	Requests an amount of cash to be taken from a given account. Cash is dispensed only if account has sufficient funds.

Reads:	**supplied** acc_number:accountnumber, **supplied** request:money	
Changes:	account with account.number equal to acc_number	(*i*)
Sends:	customer: {insufficient_funds}, cash_dispenser: {dispense_cash}	
Assumes:	acc_number is a valid account number, and the account is not overdrawn.	
Result:	If (Initial account.balance $\geq$ request) then account.balance has been reduced by request, and dispense_cash amount has been sent to cash_dispenser. Otherwise, insufficient_funds has been sent to customer. The account is not overdrawn.	(*ii*)

Figure 2.23   Schema for withdraw_cash

2-5.2 Life-Cycle Model

The life-cycle model is the second component of the interface model. An object model schema describes the behavior of an individual system operation, whereas the life-cycle model describes behavior from the wider perspective of how the system communicates with its environment from creation until its death.

A *life-cycle expression* defines the allowable sequences of interactions that a system may participate in over its lifetime. If at any point the system receives an event that is not allowed according to the life cycle, then the system ignores it and leaves the state of the system unchanged.

Figure 2.24 gives the syntax and semantics of life-cycle expressions. Life cycles are simple extensions to regular expressions or grammars [38]. A life-cycle expression defines allowable sequences of events in the same way that grammar describes the allowable sequences of symbols that are acceptable to a compiler.

Life-cycle expressions define patterns of communication. As an example consider the simple banking system. A very simple pattern occurs in response to balance inquiries. A check_balance event is always followed by the output of a current_balance event.

Enquiry = check_balance . #current_balance

- *Alphabet.* Any input or output event may be used in an expression. Output events are prefixed with *#*.
- *Operators.* Let x and y be life-cycle expressions, then

       $x.y$ denotes x is followed by y.
       $x|y$ denotes either x or y occurs.
       x^* denotes zero or more occurrences of x.
       x^+ denotes one or more occurrences of x
       $[x]$ denotes that x is optional.
       $x||y$ means arbitrarily interleaving the elements of x and y.

- *Substitutions.* An expression can be named in a substitution:

              Name = Life-Cycle Expression

Name may be used in other expressions, but substitutions must *not* be recursive.

- *Operator precedence.* In decreasing order the precedence is

$$[\,]\,,\,{}^*\,,\,{}^+\,,\,.\,.\,,\,|\,,\,||$$

Expressions may be bracketed to override default precedence.

Figure 2.24 Syntax and Semantics of Life-Cycle Expressions

There are two input events, **withdraw_cash** and **deposit_money**, that relate to cash transactions. A **withdraw_cash** must result in either **dispense_cash** or **insufficient_funds** being output. No events are output following **deposit_money**.

    Transaction = withdraw_cash . (# dispense_cash | # insufficient_funds) |
              deposit_money

In the simple banking system there is no provision for overdrafts. Consequently all **withdraw_cash** events should be ignored until a **deposit_money** event has occurred. However, any number of **Enquiries** may happen in the meantime.

    Initialization = open_account. #account_number . Enquiry* . deposit_money

This life-cycle expression makes explicit an important property of the system that would otherwise have to be deduced from a schema. However, not every property can be so conveniently expressed using a life cycle. For example, a life-cycle expression cannot be used to ensure that a later **withdraw_cash** event does not make the account overdrawn. This has to be captured in the schema for **withdraw_cash**, as in Figure 2.22.

The life-cycle of the whole system is defined by **Initialization** followed by any number of alternated **Transactions** and **Enquiries**.

---

lifecycle Banking_system: Initialization . (Transaction | Enquiry)*

Initialization = open_account. #account_number . Enquiry* . deposit_money
Transaction = withdraw_cash . (# dispense_cash | # insufficient_funds) |
                deposit_money
Enquiry   = check_balance . #current_balance

The life cycle ensures that one **Transaction** or **Enquiry** finishes before the next is started, even if it was later extended to contain several system operations; for example, the user may be required to enter an account number. Where operations from different parts of the life cycle occur independently, in any order, those parts should be interleaved. For example, suppose the banking system were extended to allow privileged access to accounts.

---

lifecycle Banking_system: Initialization . ((Transaction | Enquiry)* || PrivEnquiry*)

Initialization = open_account. #account_number . Enquiry* . deposit_money
Transaction = withdraw_cash . (# dispense_cash | # insufficient_funds) |
                deposit_money
Enquiry   = check_balance . #current_balance
PrivEnquiry = authorize. (#confirm | #deny).
                (inquire. #amount)* . finish

The steps of a privileged inquiry can proceed even when ordinary transactions and enquiries are happening. This allows sequences such as the following:

    authorize. #confirm. check_balance. #current_balance.
    inquire. #amount. deposit_money. finish

where a **Enquiry**, **check_balance**, and a **Transaction**, **deposit_money**, can occur while the **PrivEnquiry** is in progress.

Life cycles are intended as a convenience for making explicit those aspects of system behavior that may be troublesome or clumsy to express using the operation model alone. Life cycles are excellent for expressing ordering or repetitions dependent on the occurrence of input events; however, attempts to make them express behavior conditional on output events (e.g., by trying to prohibit **inquire** events when authorization has been denied) are rarely satisfactory. This kind of behavior is best expressed using operation model schemata.

2-5.3 Life-Cycle Model and Operation Model

The behavior of a system is described by the life-cycle model and the operation model taken together. The life cycle determines the acceptability of an event, whereas the precondition, that is, the **Assumes** clause, determines whether its effect is well behaved. The reader may wonder what happens if the life cycle ignores the event and the precondition is **false**. As Figure 2.25 shows, the life cycle takes precedence. An input event that is not acceptable to the life cycle is *rejected* (even if its precondition is **false**).

Precondition lifecycle	true	false
Accept	Operation invoked	Undefined
Reject	Ignored	Ignored

Figure 2.25   Preconditions and Life Cycles

Rejecting an input event means that, as far as the analyst is concerned, the state of the system must be unaffected. However, analysis uses an abstract notion of state, and the implementation is free to respond to the erroneous event, for example, with an helpful error message. Error handling and life cycles are dealt with in chapter 5. Appendix C describes more advanced ways of responding to rejected events.

When input events are considered as invoking system operations, the corresponding output events are bound to the operation that generates them. Thus, when interleaving, we regard the elements of the sequence as consisting of system operation names *and all the output events immediately following them.*

A system need not have a life-cycle model. In this case, there is an implicit life cycle in which any input event is always acceptable and there is no restriction on the order of output events. In these circumstances, the behavior of the system is then solely determined by the operation model.

2-6 SUMMARY

This chapter has introduced all the notation used to construct the analysis models.

- Analysis produces two models: the object model and the interface model.
- During analysis objects do not have a method interface.

- The object model is an entity-relationship diagram that captures the static structure of the problem domain. A system object model is a well-formed subset of an object model that defines the structure of the system state space.
- The interface model comprises the operation model and the life-cycle model.
- The operation model defines the behavior of individual operations, whereas the life-cycle model defines system communication over the lifetime of the system.

CHAPTER

3

Process of Analysis

3-1 INTRODUCTION

In this chapter we consider how to carry out an analysis. Of necessity, analysis is an iterative and incremental activity. An informal requirements document has to be turned into an unambiguous and precise set of models. Consequently decisions are continually subject to review and revision as all the implications of the requirements become clear. However, analysis is not an anarchic process; there is a definite sequence of steps that can be applied iteratively to produce a complete and consistent specification that captures the requirements. The process is defined as follows:

1. Develop an object model for the problem domain.
2. Determine the system interface.

    - Identify agents, system operations, and events.
    - Produce the system object model by adding the boundary to the object model.

3. Develop an interface model.

    - Develop a life-cycle model.
    - Develop an operation model.

4. Check the analysis models.

For all, but the most trivial, problems the process should be accompanied by the construction and use of a data dictionary.

The next section introduces the data dictionary. Later sections illustrate the Fusion analysis process and the role of a data dictionary by considering the *ECO Storage Depot*, a more substantial example than has been used previously.

3-2 DATA DICTIONARY

Throughout the phases of Fusion, it is necessary to construct and use a *data dictionary*. A data dictionary is a central repository of definitions of terms and concepts. Without it the Fusion models have little semantic content. It is only when every element of all the models has been fully defined that the whole constitutes a specification.

A data dictionary is a vital tool by virtue of its role as a *single* place to look up definitions. Defining dictionary entries encourages clarity of thought about why each concept or term is necessary. Once constructed, the dictionary plays a central role in cross-checking the models for completeness and consistency. A further important reason for having a data dictionary is that it helps someone unfamiliar with the development to understand it. Without a data dictionary the unfamiliar reader is often forced to rely on decoding "meaningful" identifiers. A short entry in the data dictionary is a far better way to make it clear what is meant.

Figure 3.1 shows the tabular format we use for the data dictionary.

Name	Kind	Description
Name of entry	*class, system operation agent, etc*	*Text defining or explaining the entry*

Figure 3.1   Data Dictionary Structure

Extra columns are introduced where necessary for specific kinds of entry. The actual format of the data dictionary is unimportant. Both manual and computer-based systems are acceptable. Regardless of which approach is taken, the following requirements should apply:

- Definitions should be readily accessible by name.
- Occurrence of aliases should be minimized.
- Entries should not duplicate information contained in the models.

The reader is referred to [37] for a fuller account of how to build and implement data dictionaries.

The next section introduces the requirements for the ECO Storage Depot problem. This example is used to explain and illustrate the Fusion process.

3-3 ECO STORAGE DEPOT

The ECO storage depot operates in accordance with the Environmental Protection Agency (EPA) regulations controlling the storage of environmentally damaging chemicals. The ECO depot is only licensed to store drums of chemicals classified as EPA hazard types 1, 2, or 3.

The drums are stored in special storage buildings; in the depot there are also buildings that house scientific and administrative staff. Each storage building is licensed to hold a maximum number of drums. Furthermore the EPA requires that types 1 and 2 must not be stored in the same building; however, type 3 may be stored with either types 1 or 2. If either of these regulations is violated, then the EPA will close the depot as unsafe, pending emergency action.

Management has decided to install a computerized system to manage and control the depot. It is of paramount concern that the system never allow the depot to become unsafe.

The ECO management is concerned about avoiding litigation from employees or the local council. They have introduced a company regulation that requires the depot manager to be able to monitor the state of the depot and to always be able to check if the depot is in a vulnerable state. The regulation states that a depot is vulnerable if any two neighboring buildings contain the maximum permitted number of drums.

When a truck arrives at the loading bay, the clerk enters the manifest accompanying the load and checks in the drums one at a time. As each drum is checked in it is allocated an identifier. Once all the drums have been checked in any discrepancies between the checked load and the manifest are notified to the loading bay clerk. The system then produces a drum-to-building allocation list that determines where each drum is to be stored. The loading bay clerk is notified of any drums that must be returned to the truck through lack of space.

Drum collections are initiated by the loading bay clerk inputing an order manifest for the number and type of drums that are required. The system identifies the drums that are to be retrieved from the storage buildings. A manifest for the order is sent to the loading bay clerk.

Because there is only one loading bay, it must be empty before a delivery or collection can begin. It is the clerk's responsibility to notify the system when the bay is empty.

3-4 DEVELOPMENT OF THE OBJECT MODEL

Getting started can often be the most difficult part of analysis. Probably the least effective first step is to take a pile of blank paper, and try and draw an object model directly from the requirements. It is better to use the requirements to brainstorm a list of candidate classes and relationships. The temptation to classify the entries should be avoided; concentration should be on producing a list of entries that might be useful. Here are some guidelines for finding classes and relationships. The examples are taken from the ECO Storage Depot problem.

Classes: Almost any noun, or noun phrase, can give rise to a class. However, to be included the noun should pertain to a concept that is important to an understanding of the domain. Physical objects, people, organizations, and abstractions are all possible sources of candidate classes including the following:

- Physical objects. For example, loading bay, drum.
- People and organizations. For example, clerk, manager, EPA.
- Abstractions. For example, discrepancies, allocation list.

Relationships: These model correspondences between objects. Communication, physical associations, containment, and actions are all possible sources for candidate relationships.

- Communication. For example, manager monitors state of depot.
- Associations. For example, a building is a neighbor of another.
- Containment. For example, drums in the loading bay.
- Actions. For example, drums are checked in.

At this stage, temporal properties associated with the relationship should be ignored.

It is more effective if the brainstorming process is carried out as a group exercise rather than by individuals working alone. The separation of concerns can be used to break a problem into cohesive and independent parts. The analysis should be started at a high level of abstraction. Only after its overall structure is judged to be satisfactory should the details be added.

Once the lists have been drawn up, they should be rationalized. Each entry should be considered, in its own right and also in relation to the other entries. Check that each entry is relevant, removing any that are clearly inessential to an explanation of the problem. Overlapping entries should be coalesced and misleading identifiers renamed. Always keep the most general candidates. Remember that the object model uses classes, whereas a requirements document is mainly expressed in terms of specific objects.

The lists must be checked for completeness by reexamining the requirements document to ensure that nothing has been omitted. The process should be repeated until the lists have stabilized. At that point, the classes and relationships can be used to start the data dictionary. Figure 3.2 lists some entries for the ECO Storage Depot problem.

Simultaneously with the entries being put in the data dictionary, a start can be made on producing a draft of the object model. The following guidelines may be helpful:

Generalization. Generalization models the "kind of" or *is-a* relationship. For example,

> The drums are stored in special storage buildings; in the depot there are also buildings that house scientific and administrative staff.

suggests that **Buildings** can have two specializations, **Store Buildings** and **Admin/Lab Buildings**. Generalizations should be introduced toward the end of constructing the object model. Premature use of generalizations based on plausible, but ultimately ill-founded, preconceptions, can distort the model by introducing inappropriate classes. It is better to examine the object model retrospectively to identify classes with common properties such as the same attribute or participation in the same relationships. The common attributes and relationships can be abstracted into a generalized object of which the original classes are specializations.

Name	Kind	Description
Loading_Bay	class	place in Depot where Drums are held temporarily
contains	relationship	Loading_Bay contains Drums during delivery and collection
Building	class	a structure in the Depot
neighbors	relationship	Buildings that are physically adjacent to each other
Admin/Lab Building	class	a Building that houses administrative or scientific staff
Store Building	class	a Building that is a permanent store for Drums
max capacity	attribute	EPA maximum permitted number of Drums in Building
holds	relationship	the Drums held in a Store Building
Allocation List	class	list of Drums held in Store Buildings
Manifest	class	document listing numbers of each Drum type
Discrepancy Manifest	class	Manifest used for listing excess or deficit Drums on delivery
documents	relationship	Manifest describes a collection of Drums
Drum	class	container for a chemical
chemical type	attribute	the EPA classification of Chemical

Figure 3.2 Example Data Dictionary Entries for ECO Storage Depot

Check that the specialization is well founded by ensuring that the subtype either has additional attributes or participates in extra relationships. Remember that there are two kinds of specialization, depending on whether the subtypes form a partition of the supertype.

Aggregation.   Aggregation models "part of" or *has-a* relationship. It can be used to model physical containment. Thus a Depot can be modeled as an aggregate of a Loading_Bay and some Buildings.

Aggregation can also be used as a convenient structuring device by treating a relationship as an entity. In these situations there need be no connotation of being physically part of. For example, the allocation of drums to buildings can be modeled by Allocation List, which is an aggregate of Store Buildings and Drums, even though an allocation list does not physically contain any buildings and drums.

Attributes.   These are best ignored during the initial brainstorming phase. Representing something as an attribute too early excludes adding more structure to that part of the model later. Any classes, which do not have any attributes, and which are related to only one other class, can be turned into attributes. For example, the different type of chemicals can be represented by a Drum attribute, rather than a class, because they are not involved in any other relationships.

Cardinalities.   Cardinalities should be decided at the time of defining relationships. Decide cardinalities by drawing up example sets of tuples for the relationship. Consider whether an object has to appear, and whether there can be a fixed, or arbitrary, number of corresponding objects. For example, Loading_Bay contains Drum is a one-to-many relationship because a loading bay can be empty or contain many drums, but a drum can only be in one loading bay.

Invariants.   Invariants may come to light at any time during the construction of the object model. They should be put in the data dictionary. For example, the **Depot** must always be safe. This constraint cannot be expressed using cardinality. The requirements also use the notion of the **Depot** being vulnerable. Both notions are defined and put in the data dictionary, as in Figure 3.3.

Name	Kind	Description
safe	predicate	Corresponds to EPA regulation that All **Store Buildings** must not exceed max capacity, and type 1 and type 2 **Drums** must not be stored in the same Building
Depot is safe	invariant	Depot must always be safe
vulnerable	predicate	true if any two neighboring **Buildings** contain their maximum number of **Drums**

Figure 3.3 Data Dictionary: Object Model Invariants

Derived Relationships.   These relationships can be defined in terms of more primitive ones. For example, an **ancestor** relationship is a derived relationship in the presence of the **parent** relationship. Derived relationships should not appear on the object model; important ones should be put in the data dictionary.

An object model is constructed by applying these guidelines. For convenience of presentation, the ECO Storage Depot object model is partitioned into three diagrams (Figures 3.4 to 3.6), each gives the classes and relationships for a different aspect of the domain.

In Figure 3.4, which deals with buildings and drums, the capacity of a **Store Building** and the type of a **Chemical** are represented by attributes as they do not participate in any relationships of their own. **Manifest** has three attributes giving the numbers of drums of each type. It also has a non-partitioning subtype, **Discrepancy Manifest**. The specialization is non-partitioning since there are **Manifest** objects which do not belong to the subtype. **Delivery Manifests** are used in figure 3.6 to report excess and deficits of drums on delivery. **Allocation List** has two subtypes, **Status Allocation List**, which details the contents of all **Store Buildings**, and **Delivery Allocation List**, which is used to allocate **Drums** to **Store Buildings** on delivery.

In Figure 3.5, a generalization is introduced for the two kinds of reports monitored by the manager. This is not a direct consequence of the requirements but is used as a stylistic convenience.

The clerk is involved in the collection and delivery process. The object model relating to collection and delivery (Figure 3.6), simplifies the model by using a single relationship, **collects**, to stand for all the relationships involved in collection. Delivery

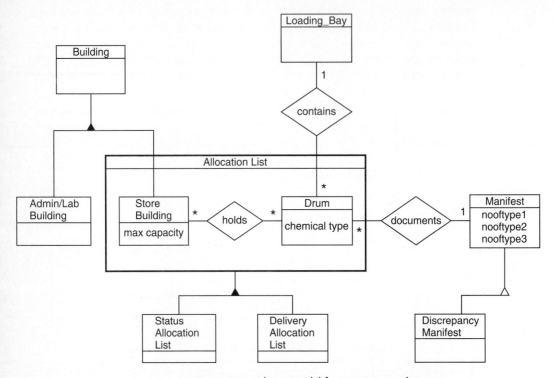

Figure 3.4   Object Model for Buildings and Drums

is treated in a similar fashion. The class **Delivery_Report** is an aggregate for the information that is associated with a delivery. In each delivery, there can be at most two **Discrepancy Manifests**, one for excesses and one for deficits, and at most one **Return List**, that is, set of drums that cannot be allocated. Finally there has to be a **Delivery Allocation List**. Coalescing relationships should be done with caution because it can be misleading.

After construction the component diagrams should be inspected for mutual consistency. The best safeguard is the conscientious use of the data dictionary. The models should also be checked for completeness against the requirements.

We conclude this section with some general remarks on building object models:

Object Modeling is not a precise science.   There is no perfect answer, so the result of analysis always depends in part on the experience, and even aesthetic tastes, of the analyst. As the analysis progresses it is likely that the model will have to be updated as further understanding of the domain is gained. Therefore the analyst should guard against spending too much time trying to get it exactly right. Constructing the operation model will help reveal any serious inadequacies and they can be fixed then.

Abstractions can be objects too.   It is important to remember that objects do not have to model things; they may also model abstractions.

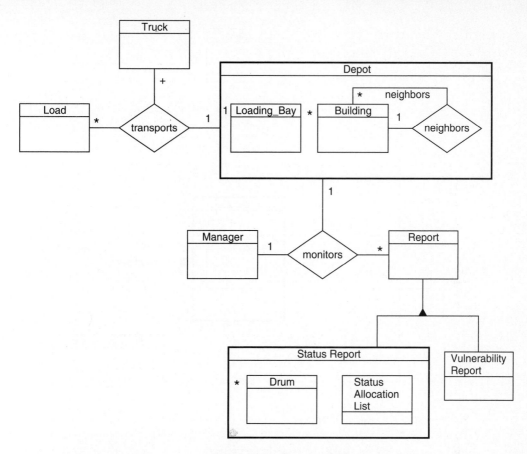

Figure 3.5 Object Model for Depot

If there is no extant real-world system on which to base the object model then analysis will necessarily involve inventing domain concepts. Even if systems already exist they may not appear very object oriented; for example, at first sight many computing applications, like compilers, do not seem to be very object oriented. In these circumstances, building the object model requires devising a set of abstractions whose properties model the problem domain. Thus in a compiler one might expect classes for abstractions such as **Parse_tree** and **Grammar_production**. Similarly, analyzing an oscilloscope will probably require abstractions such as **Waveform** or **Trace**.

Beware Data Flow Diagrams (DFDs).   Familiarity with structured analysis may cause class boxes to be misinterpreted as processes and relationships to be misinterpreted as data flows. The temptation is particularly great if many of the relationships actually model real-world actions. Explanations of the model should not rely on notions of temporal order and flow of data between "classes." Sentences such as "Customers insert a card into the automated teller machine (ATM) and type in their password, which the ATM then sends to the bank for checking" are a telltale sign of a DFD masquerading as a object model. Remember that relationships denote sets of

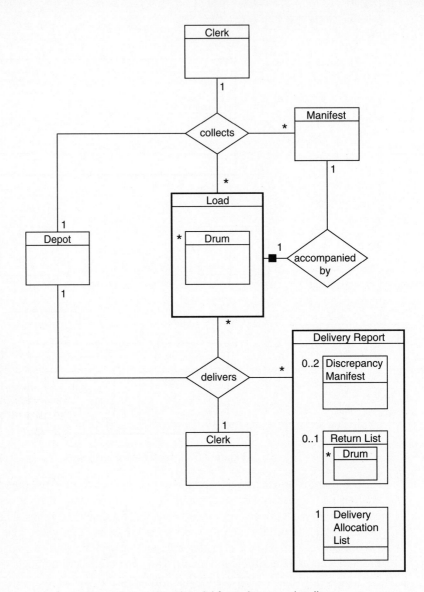

Figure 3.6   Object Model for Delivery and Collection

tuples of objects; therefore, do not invent a relationship unless such an ianterpretation make sense.

The initial object models make no distinction between the system and its environment. The next step is to determine the boundary between the two, that is, the system interface.

3-5 DETERMINATION OF THE SYSTEM INTERFACE

Recall that during analysis, a system is modeled as an active entity that cooperates with other active entities, called agents. The system and the agents communicate by sending and receiving events. When events are received by the system they can cause a state change and events to be output. An input event and its associated effect are known as a *system operation*.

The interface of a system is the set of system operations to which it can respond and the events that it can output. A system operation is always invoked by an agent, not an object; the analysis phase is *not* concerned with internal messaging between objects.

Defining the system interface may be nontrivial. Confusion can arise because the notions of operation and event are often closely connected with some relationship between classes. Another problem can be differentiating between internal operations and events, and those that communicate with the external environment.

A useful technique is to focus on scenarios of usage. A *scenario* is a sequence of events flowing between agents and the system for some purpose. Each scenario involves agents, the tasks they want the system to do, and the sequence of communications involved in getting it done.

A scenario is represented as a timeline diagram, showing the temporal ordering of system operations and events that flow to agents. Timeline diagrams cannot show alternative communication paths. In general, therefore, multiple diagrams may be needed for a single scenario.

In the ECO Storage Depot problem, the collection and delivery of loads are two distinct scenarios. In both, the clerk can be modeled as an agent who invokes operations such as checking in drums. Consideration of the collection and delivery tasks reveals that there must be another agent involved. Somebody, or something, must be responsible for moving the physical drums to and from the store buildings once they have been checked in. We model this by another agent, called **drum storage**. In reality, it may be the clerk who does the moving, but it is more general to assume the existence of a separate agent.

Figure 3.7 shows a scenario for collection. System operations are shown by solid arrowed lines and output events by dashed arrowed lines. The scenario assumes that the **drum storage** agent is perfect and unfailing. If requested to deliver the drums to the loading bay, it will do so without further intervention from the system. Without this assumption a more complex dialogue would be needed.

According to the requirements, delivery is more involved as the drums have to be individually checked in. Figure 3.8 shows a possible scenario for how delivery can be accomplished. The dotted portion of the timelines for the **clerk** and the system indicate that the **check_in_drum** and **drum_identifier** may repeat.

Similar scenarios can be constructed for the managerial reports on vulnerability and depot status. They are simple stimulus-response protocols and are omitted. All the system operations and the output events in the system interface must be entered

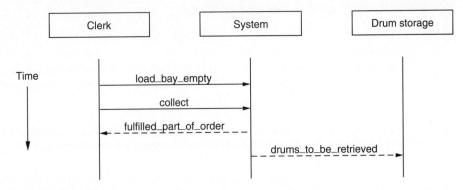

Description:
  The clerk informs the system that the loading bay is empty. The collection then starts with
  the clerk giving the system the manifest for the requested load. The system calculates what
  proportion of the load it can fulfill and informs the clerk. It also informs drum storage to retrieve
  the drums from the store buildings.

Figure 3.7   Scenario for Collection

into the data dictionary, as in Figure 3.9. The entries have an additional *Agents* column
showing the agents involved in the communication.

   Each agent should be documented by an entry in the data dictionary, as in
Figure 3.10.

Dealing with Concurrency.

   Although Fusion is a method for sequential systems, it can be applied to the
development of concurrent systems because many applications exhibit a very limited
form of concurrency in which

- Concurrency is provided by an operating system.
- Processes are sequential programs.
- There is a relatively small number of processes.
- There is very limited use of dynamic process creation.

   This kind of concurrent system can be viewed as a set of cooperating agents,
each of which can be developed using Fusion. In this context, scenarios are tools for
exploring the communication flows between processes, and the interface models can
be used to ensure that the processes have compatible interfaces.

   The task of designing concurrent system architectures lies outside the scope of
this book. A common approach is to base the design on an existing architecture.
Alternatively, there are several methods or techniques that can be used, e.g., [17], [31],
[48], [104].

Interface Design.

   The system interface determines how functionality is mapped to individual operations. The manner in which this is done enforces a protocol on any agent that

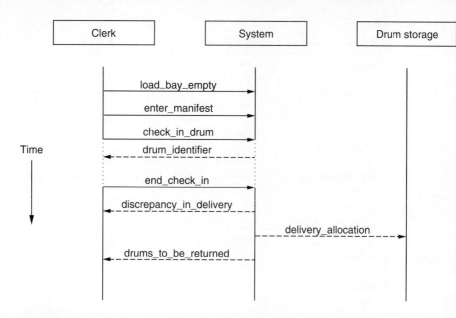

Description:

> The clerk tells the system that the loading_bay is now empty, so a delivery may begin. The clerk then gives the system the details from the manifest and starts checking in the drums. As each drum is checked in the system, an identifier for the drum is issued.

> When there are no more drums to be checked in, the clerk tells the system. The system then informs the clerk of any discrepancy in the delivery, vis-à-vis the manifest. The system computes in which store buildings the drums are to be stored and sends the allocation to Drum storage.

> Finally, the system tells the clerk, which, if any, drums cannot be stored and so must be returned from whence they came.

Figure 3.8   Scenario for Delivery

uses or communicates with the system. Consequently system interfaces have to be designed rather than discovered.

A major factor is the granularity of the data associated with operations. In the ECO example, a single operation, **collect**, processes a request for a set of drums in one go. In contrast, delivery is carried out in small steps, with each drum being individually checked in. Small grained operations lead to more responsive and interactive systems, in which errors can be handled, without having to abort the whole process. Large grain operations give rise to batch processing that does not require much interaction.

The extent to which a system is proactive in reporting its status is another issue in interface design. In the ECO example, a **vulnerability_report** is only output in response to specific requests. A different approach would be to have the status reported whenever an operation changes the depot status.

Designing the interface requires technical decisions concerning the amount of communication traffic and response times. For those parts of the interface that communicate with human users, their needs must be considered as well.

Name	Kind	Agent	Description
depot_status	system operation	manager	requests a status report on storage buildings and loading bay
is_vulnerable	system operation	manager	requests a report on vulnerability of depot
enter_manifest	system operation	clerk	initiates delivery of drums as specified in a manifest
check_in_drum	system operation	clerk	labels drum as it is put into the loading bay
end_check_in	system operation	clerk	informs system that all the drums have been checked in, and they are to be allocated to the storage buildings
load_bay_empty	system operation	clerk	informs system that loading bay is empty
collect	system operation	clerk	collects the drums specified in a manifest
status_report	event	manager	lists current contents of loading bay and allocation of drums to storage building
vulnerability_report	event	manager	whether depot is vulnerable or not
drum_identifier	event	clerk	unique identifier to label drum
discrepancy_in_delivery	event	clerk	any excess or shortfall between delivery manifest and checked-in drums
fulfilled_part_of_order	event	clerk	manifest for the drums that can be collected
drums_to_be_ returned	event	clerk	set of drums that cannot be stored in depot
delivery_allocation	event	drum storage	list of drums and the buildings to where they are to be delivered
drums_to_be_retrieved	event	drum storage	list of drums and where they are stored for retrieval

Figure 3.9   Data Dictionary: System Interface

Scenario timeline diagrams provide a tool for thinking through the consequences of the interface design and visualizing how the system behaves. They are useful when validating interface decisions with customers because they are simple and intuitive to understand. However, scenarios are limited because they provide only a snapshot of system behavior.

3-5.1 System Object Model

A system object model is a refinement of the object model developed in the first step of analysis. It uses the information about the system interface to indicate what classes

Name	Kind	Description
clerk	agent	loads drums from truck into loading bay and vice-versa; responsible for telling system when loading bay is empty
drum storage	agent	operates under direction of system; takes drums to and from loading bay and stores; guaranteed to operate perfectly
manager	agent	monitors status of depot

Figure 3.10   Data Dictionary: Agents

and relationships pertain to the state of the system, as opposed to its environment. A system object model is an object model that shows the system boundary. A class or relationship that lies outside the boundary is not needed to carry out the functionality of the system.

Figure 3.11 extends the object model presented in Figure 3.4. As can be seen, all the classes and relationships are inside the boundary. There is a further addition: **Drum** has an extra attribute, **identifier**. This is required because we now know that each drum in the system has an identifier, because all drums in the system must have been checked in.

Usually a system object model excludes part of an object model developed during the early stages of analysis. For example, classes that correspond to agents are usually not needed as part of the system. Likewise, the associated relationships that correspond to system operations or output events are also often not needed. Figure 3.12 is the system object model formed by drawing the system boundary on the object model for the depot (see Figure 3.5).

Thus **Manager** lies outside the boundary because it is represented by the agent, **manager**. Similarly the **monitors** is not needed because it is implemented by the system operations **is_vulnerable** and **depot_status**. However, the class **Report** lies inside the boundary because the system has to be able to generate **Report** objects.

In some circumstances a class may remain inside the system boundary, even if it corresponds to an agent. This happens if the system needs to record the occurrence of the system operation or output event. Thus if it was necessary for the ECO Storage Depot to keep track of the **is_vulnerable** requests that managers had made, then **Manager** and **monitors** would have to be inside the boundary.

Figure 3.13 shows the system object model dealing with delivery and collection. It is a refinement of Figure 3.6. Note that sometimes classes are excluded, even if they do not correspond to agents. For example, the **accompanied by** relationship between a **Manifest** and a **Load** is outside the boundary. This is because it is not needed by the system. It would not be harmful to include them, but it would be redundant. A system object model with redundant classes can be advantageous when developing reusable software.

The system object model is used by the operation model. After developing the schemata for each operation, it should be revisited.

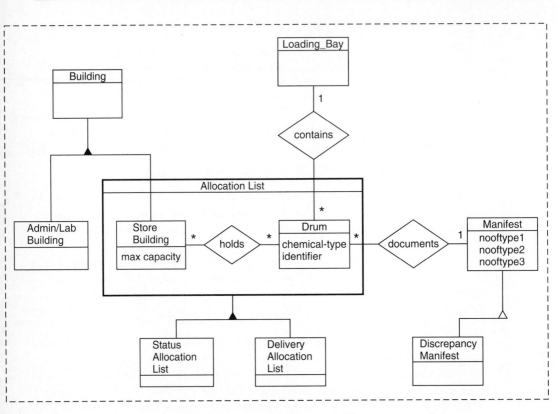

Figure 3.11   System Object Model for Buildings and Drums

3-6 DEVELOPMENT OF THE INTERFACE MODEL

The interface model comprises a life-cycle model and an operation model. The order of development is not fixed. However, it is better to start with the life cycle because the life cycle can be an aid to developing operation model schemata.

3-6.1 Life-Cycle Model

The life-cycle model is formed by developing life-cycle expressions that generalize the scenarios. Life-cycle expressions are more expressive than timeline diagrams, because they can express repetition, alternation, and optionality, as well as concatenation. A life-cycle expression can define a set of scenarios, whereas a timeline diagram can only show a single scenario. The process for forming the life-cycle model is

1. Generalize the scenarios to form named life-cycle expressions.
2. Combine the life-cycle expressions to form the life-cycle model.

Consider the scenario for collection, given in Figure 3.7; it can be translated directly into the following named life-cycle expression:

Collection = load_bay_empty.
   collect.
      #fulfilled_part_of_order.
      #drums_to_be_retrieved

Similarly the delivery scenario translates into

Delivery = load_bay_empty.
   enter_manifest.
   (check_in_drum.#drum_identifier)*
   end_check_in.
      [#discrepancy_in_delivery].
      #delivery_allocation.
      [#drums_to_be_returned]

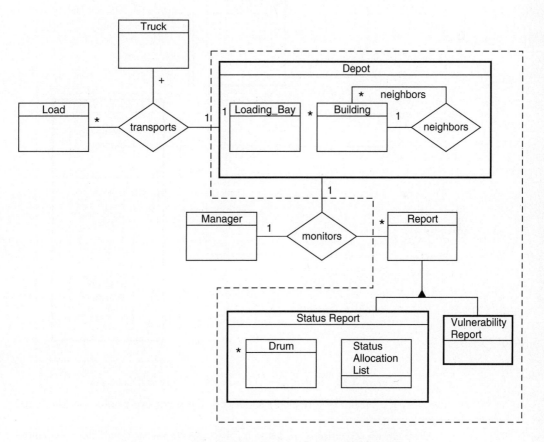

Figure 3.12   System Object Model for Depot

The use of the repetition **operator** , *, indicates that each invocation of **check_in_drum** results in a **drum_identifier** being output. Notice that invoking **end_check_in** is always

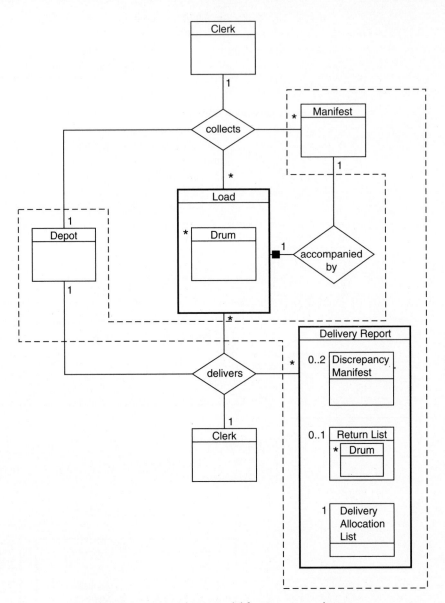

Figure 3.13   System Object Model for Delivery and Collection

followed by the output of a **delivery_allocation**; the other events are only produced in some circumstances.

Although no scenarios were given for the status requests, they have very simple life-cycles. Each request is always followed by the appropriate report event.

$$Status = depot\_status.\#status\_report \mid$$
$$is\_vulnerable.\#vulnerability\_report$$

After the life-cycle expressions have been produced for the scenarios, we need to consider their interrelationship. The life cycle is constructed by using the life-cycle expression operators to combine the individual named life-cycle expressions.

In the ECO Storage Depot there is only one loading bay, so a collection cannot happen while a delivery is in progress and vice versa. Consequently Collection and Delivery are alternatives. However they can be indefinitely repeated. Their combined life cycle is

$$(Collection|Delivery)*$$

Status can also be indefinitely repeated. In addition, a status request can happen even if a delivery or collection is in progress, because of a *company regulation that requires the depot manager . . . to always be able to check if the depot is in a vulnerable state*. Since the life-cycle expressions have disjoint alphabets they can be combined using the interleaving operator, ||. The lifecycle for the whole system is shown in Figure 3.14.

---

life-cycle ECOStorageDepot: (Delivery|Collection)*||(Status)*

Delivery = load_bay_empty.
             enter_manifest.
             (check_in_drum.#drum_identifier)*
             end_check_in.
                 [#discrepancy_in_delivery].
                 #delivery_allocation.
                 [#drums_to_be_returned]
Collection = load_bay_empty.
             collect.
                 #fulfilled_part_of_order.
                 #drums_to_be_retrieved
Status =   (depot_status.#status_report |
             is_vulnerable.#vulnerability_report)*

Figure 3.14   Life Cycle for ECO Storage Depot

3-6.2 Operation Model

The operation model defines the semantics of each system operation in the system interface. Each schema contains an informal precondition and postcondition specification, that is, the **Assumes** and **Results** clauses. Meyer [80] calls this kind of specification a *contract* between the operation and its users. The contract guarantees that the operation delivers a final state in which the **Results** clause is true as long as the operation is invoked with the **Assumes** clause satisfied. Thus it is the job of the analyst to draw up the contracts for the system operation such that they satisfy the customers requirements. The following sections illustrate how this can be done.

Figure 3.15 shows the schema for load_bay_empty. The **Results** clause promises to deallocate all the **Drums** in the loading_bay and to leave the loading_bay empty.

Operation:	load_bay_empty
Description:	Informs system that physical loading bay is empty.

Reads:	
Changes:	loading_bay, contains
Sends:	
Assumes:	
Result:	The identifiers of any **drums** in the **Initial** loading_bay are deallocated. The loading_bay has been initialized to empty.

Figure 3.15   Schema for load_bay_empty

A schema always refers to effects on the state of the system, not the real world. The object-oriented approach is based on real-world modeling, and the reader must bear the distinction in mind when reading and developing schemata. Thus it is the loading_bay object that is changed by the operation, not the physical loading bay. To be precise, it is actually the relationship, **Loading Bay contains Drums**, that is changed.

In general, developing the **Results** clause will require making decisions about the values to be *supplied* with a system operation. For example, a **Manifest** value has to be supplied with enter_manifest; this is recorded in the **Reads** clause of the enter_manifest schema in Figure 3.16.

The extra information discovered about each system operation must be recorded in the data dictionary. This can be done by adding a new column, *Arguments*, which gives the classes or types of the values. The modified entry for enter_manifest is shown in Figure 3.17.

Use of Life-Cycle Information.

The life-cycle model determines whether a system operation is required to send events to agents. From the **Delivery** lifecycle in section 3-6.1, it can be seen that a drum_identifier event has to be output following a check_in_drum system operation. Consequently, this event must appear in the **Results** and **Sends** clauses of the schema for check_in_drum (Figure 3.18).

The **Results** clause may also require decisions to be made about the types of the data output with each event. The **Results** clause of check_in_drum specifies that an identifier value has to be output with drum_identifier. This information also has

Operation:	enter_manifest
Description:	Start the delivery process by inputing the physical manifest.
Reads:	**supplied** manifest
Changes:	delivery_manifest
Sends:	
Assumes:	
Result:	The delivery_manifest has been initialized to the value of **manifest**, which accompanies the load.

Figure 3.16   Schema enter_manifest

Name	Kind	Agent	Arguments	Description
enter_manifest	system operation	clerk	Manifest	initiates delivery of drums as specified in manifest

Figure 3.17   Updated Data Dictionary Entry for enter_manifest

to be added to the data dictionary entries. Figure 3.19 shows the updated entries for check_in_drum and drum_identifier.

Development of Complex Results Clauses.

In general, **Results** may have several subclauses. Each subclause must be declarative and should describe one aspect of the effect of the operation. The meaning of the **Results** must *not* depend on the order of the individual clauses. There is *no* flow of control.

It usually takes several iterations to get the clauses right. Initial attempts often have too few clauses, making the behavior of the operation insufficiently constrained. It is usually the "minor," but potentially disastrous, issues that are omitted. In the case of the check_in_drum operation, it would be quite easy to forget that the identifier of the newly created drum, d, must be initialized. Omitting the requirement

Attribute d.identifier has been set to a unique value

would allow the implementation to assign whatever value it pleased to the attribute including an already allocated value. Consequently a **Results** clause should always be checked to see if it is strong enough. If it allows "incorrect" or unwanted values then the unwanted values must be excluded by the addition of extra subclauses.

Operation:	check_in_drum
Description:	Each drum delivered to the loading bay is labeled by a unique identifier.

Reads:	**supplied** drum_type
Changes:	loading_bay, **new** d: Drum.
Sends:	clerk:{drum_identifier}
Assumes:	
Result:	The loading_bay contains the drum d. The clerk has been sent drum_identifier(d.identifier). Attribute d.chemical_type of has been initialized to the drum_type of the physical drum. Attribute d.identifier has been set to a unique value.

Figure 3.18   Schema for check_in_drum

Name	Kind	Agent	Arguments	Description
check_in_drum	system operation	clerk	drum_type	labels drum as it is put into the loading bay
drum_identifier	event	clerk	identifier	unique identifier to label drum

Figure 3.19   Updated Data Dictionary Entries for check_in_drum and drum_identifier

The **end_check_in** operation (Figure 3.20), is considerably more complex than the previous examples. It will be developed incrementally to illustrate some further points about schemata.

As before, we start with the life-cycle model (Figure 3.14). The **end_check_in** operation sends **delivery_allocation** to **drum storage**. Furthermore, **discrepancy_in_delivery** and **drums_to_be_returned** are optionally sent to the **clerk**. Each output event is accompanied by some data values; for example, **discrepancy_in_delivery** is accompanied by two **Discrepancy Manifests**. These are the values of any excess, or deficit, between the actual delivery and the **Manifest** that was supplied by **enter_manifest**. This is captured in the **Results** clause. The data dictionary entries for the events have to be updated, as in Figure 3.21.

The schema illustrates some other issues that have to be considered. First, the system operations must respect any invariants on the system object model. Recall

Operation:	end_check_in
Description:	Informs system that all the actual drums have been checked in and are to be allocated to storage buildings.
Reads:	delivery_manifest, loading_bay
Changes:	store buildings in depot
Sends:	clerk: {discrepancy_in_delivery, drums_to_be_returned}, drum_storage: {delivery_allocation}
Assumes:	The depot is safe.
Result:	If there is a discrepancy between delivery_manifest and loading_bay then discrepancy_in_delivery(excess, deficit: discrepancy_manifest) has been sent to clerk. If there is capacity then all the drums in Initial loading_bay have been allocated to store buildings in depot otherwise as many as is possible of the drums have been allocated and drums_to_be_returned(return_list) has been sent to clerk. The delivery_allocation(delivery_allocation_list) has been sent to drum storage. The depot is safe.

Figure 3.20   Schema for end_check_in

that **depot is safe** is an invariant property (see Figure 3.3). Therefore it must be preserved by any operation, including **end_check_in**, that changes **store buildings in depot**. Consequently,

> The **depot** is safe

appears both as a precondition in the **Assumes** clause *and* as part of the **Results** clause.

Ensuring Satisfiable Specifications.

The main goal of **end_check_in** is to allocate drums to store buildings. At first sight, it might seem that

> All the **drums** in **Initial loading_bay** have been allocated to **store buildings** in **depot**

is an adequate clause to express this. Unfortunately, this is not correct because it would create an unsatisfiable schema. A schema is *satisfiable* if, for all initial values satisfying the **Assumes** clause, there exist final values that satisfy the **Results** clause.

Name	Kind	Agent	Arguments	Description
discrepancy_in delivery	event	clerk	Discrepancy_Manifest, Discrepancy_Manifest	any excess or shortfall between delivery manifest and checked-in drums
drums_to_be_ returned	event	clerk	Return_List	set of drums that cannot be stored in depot
delivery_allocation	event	drum storage	Delivery Allocation List	list of drums and the buildings to where they are to be delivered

Figure 3.21 Updated Data Dictionary Entries for discrepancy_in_delivery, drums_to_be_returned, and delivery allocation.

In the example, this is not the case because a **Depot** is finite and therefore there may not always be enough room to store the drums.

One solution is to strengthen the **Assumes** clause to exclude the undesirable case.

Assumes: Enough capacity is in store buildings for all drums in loading_bay.

Result: All the drums in Initial loading_bay have been allocated to store buildings in depot.

This is unsatisfactory because it makes the environment responsible for avoiding the problem and that may not always be possible. It is usually better to introduce a conditional expression to define the result in both the normal and exceptional cases. This is the solution adopted in Figure 3.20, the schema for end_check_in.

The **Assumes** and **Results** clauses should always be checked to see if they can be satisfied. If corresponding final states do not exist for *all* possible initial values, then the **Results** clause should be extended to deal with the exceptional cases, or conditions should be added to the **Assumes** clause to exclude problems.

Development of Reads, Changes, and Sends.

Once the **Assumes** and **Results** clauses are completed it is simple to extract the read and changed items, and the agents and events, and add them to the **Reads**, **Changes**, and **Sends** clauses. The purpose of these clauses is to scope a system operation by explicitly stating what objects and agents may be involved. Anything not identified in one of these clauses cannot affect the operation, nor be affected by it. These parts of a schema are particularly useful when considering the impact of modifications to systems, especially when carried out by someone other than the original analyst.

Overall Process.

The process for developing a schema can be summarized as follows:

1. Develop the **Assumes** and **Results** clauses.

    - Describe each aspect of the result as a separate subclause of **Results**.
    - Use the life-cycle model to find the events that have to be output in **Results**.
    - Check that **Results** does not allow unwanted values.
    - Add relevant system object model invariants to **Assumes** and **Results** .
    - Ensure **Assumes** and **Results** are satisfiable.
    - Update data dictionary entries for system operations and events.

2. Extract **Sends**, **Reads**, and **Changes** clauses from the **Results** and **Assumes**.

In the next section we provide some guidelines for checking the analysis models.

3-7 CHECKING OF ANALYSIS MODELS

It can be a major problem knowing when to stop doing the analysis. The dilemma facing the analyst is knowing when the analysis models are good enough to be used for the design. Perfection is unobtainable and is not usually required. A designer will probably not worry if a few trivial errors are found. However, a specification with gross errors cannot be used. It represents a waste of time and money.

In this section we suggest some checks that can be applied to the analysis models. The checks are not foolproof; if they fail, then something is definitely wrong and needs fixing. If they do not reveal any flaws then there can be some confidence that the analysis phase is complete and can be signed off. However, signing off a development phase is always going to require a cost-benefit judgment. There can be no guarantees.

There are two aspects to checking the analysis models. They should be *complete* and *consistent*. We consider each concept in turn.

A model is *complete* when it captures all the meaningful abstractions in the domain. Completeness is a relative concept. There has to be a defined notion of what it means for the analysis models to be complete. It can be measured against the requirements. This can be difficult, because the requirements document may be unclear. The analysis models must be tested against the requirements, and also the knowledge and expectations of the customers and domain experts.

A set of models is *consistent* when the models do not contradict each other, either explicitly or implicitly. A model should be checked for internal consistency and also for those areas where it overlaps with other models.

Explicit inconsistencies are relatively simple to find. They often show up when using the data dictionary. Inconsistencies that arise from the implications of a model are more difficult to find. To have a guarantee of consistency requires that it be possible to semantically check the models fully. This is not possible without the use of a formal specification language, such as Vienna Development Method (VDM) [63] or Z [99]. Unfortunately these techniques are only practical in safety critical and similar systems where defects must be avoided at all costs. In Fusion the semantics of the analysis models are defined, but only informally. This permits useful, but limited, consistency checking.

Checks.

In this section we present some guidelines for checking the analysis. The checks are not exhaustive but nonetheless useful.

1. *Completeness against requirements.* Reread the requirements document carefully. Resolve any outstanding issues with the customer. Clarify what the customer for the system wants. Then check that

   - All possible scenarios are covered by the life cycle.
   - All system operations are defined by a schema.
   - All static information is captured by the system object model.
   - Any other information (e.g., technical definitions and invariants), is in the data dictionary.

2. *Simple consistency.* These checks deal with the areas of overlap between the analysis models. Check that

   - All classes, relationships, and attributes mentioned in the operation model appear in the system object model. All other concepts (e.g., predicates), must be defined in the data dictionary or some referenced source.
   - The boundary of the system object model is consistent with the system interface given by the life-cycle model.
   - All the system operations in the life-cycle model have a schema.
   - All identifiers in all models have entries in the data dictionary.

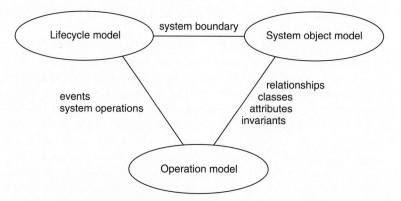

Figure 3.22   Check Intersections between Models

3. *Semantic consistency.* These checks attempt to ensure that the implications of the models are consistent.

   - *Output of events in life-cycle model and operation model must be consistent.* The schema for a system operation must generate the output events that follow it in the life-cycle model scenarios.
   - *Operation model must preserve system object model invariant.* If there is an invariant concerning a relationship or class, then any operation that can change it must respect the invariant in its schema (see section 3-6.2).

- *Desk-check scenarios using the schemata.* Choose examples of scenarios, and define the state change that each should cause. Then "execute" the scenarios, using the schemata to define the behavior of each system operation. Check that the result is what is expected.

The preceding checks can be applied in several ways. Ideally, they should be remembered during development. However, they are probably of most practical use as exit criteria for inspections [5], [43], [94].

3-8   SUMMARY

This chapter has described the process and heuristics for the analysis phase.

- Analysis is an incremental and iterative activity that formalizes the requirements. It can be carried out in a systematic manner.
- The Fusion process uses a data dictionary as a central repository.
- Checks should be applied to the analysis models to ensure they are complete and consistent.

CHAPTER 4

Design

4-1 INTRODUCTION

This chapter introduces the design phase of the Fusion method. During design, software structures are introduced to satisfy the abstract definitions produced from analysis. Recall that the *system object model* describes the classes in the system and the semantic relationships that must hold between them. This model is abstract, emphasizing what information is required and what relationships must be maintained. The output of design is an object-oriented software structure that contains the same information and preserves the relationships defined in the system object model. The *operation model* from analysis defines the expectations a user has of the system functionality. It is an abstract description of the effect of operations invocable by the user and environment on the system. The purpose of design is to define how that functionality is implemented. The output of design is a collection of interacting objects that realize the operation model.

There are four design models developed during this phase of the method.

- Object interaction graphs, describing how objects interact at run-time to support the functionality specified in the operation model
- Visibility graphs, describing the object communication paths
- Class descriptions, providing a specification of the class interface, data attributes, object reference attributes, and method signatures for all of the classes in the system
- Inheritance graphs, describing the class/subclass inheritance structures

These outputs provide the foundation for implementation, testing, and maintenance of the software system. In addition, the data dictionary documents the terms, concepts, and constraints built up during analysis and design.

Each of the design models will be introduced in separate sections. In each of these sections the notation's syntax will first be introduced followed by the design process, which explains how each design model is developed. Rules are then given to check the models for completeness and consistency at each stage of design. At the end of the chapter heuristics are given that provide guidance in producing high-quality object-oriented designs.

4-2 OBJECT INTERACTION GRAPHS

The first consideration in object-oriented design is the implementation of each system operation. The operation model declaratively specifies the behavior of these operations by defining the effect of the operation in terms of the change in system state and the output events. The purpose of this stage in design is to build the object messaging structures that realize the abstract definition of behavior. An *object interaction graph* is constructed for each system operation. We consider what objects are involved in the computation and define how these communicating objects are combined to satisfy the functional specification. The object interaction graph defines the sequences of messages that occur between a collection of objects to realize a particular operation.

Object interaction graphs are developed incrementally for each system operation. The goal is to distribute the functional behavior across objects in the system. As the design develops, the required method interface of objects in the system evolves. (Recall that objects do not have an interface defined during analysis.)

This section first describes the object interaction graph notation and then addresses how the graphs are developed during design. The process of hierarchical decomposition is also explained. Finally, rules are given for checking the design decisions against the system object model and operation model.

4-2.1 Notation

An object interaction graph is a collection of boxes that are linked by arrows. The boxes represent *design objects*, and the arrows represent *message passing*. Only one box, the *controller*, has an arrow coming into it that does not arrive from any other box; this arrow is labeled with the name of the system operation that the object interaction graph implements. The other boxes are called the *collaborators*. Every other arrow goes from one box to another. The graph is connected such that all boxes can be reached by traversing a path of arrows and boxes from the controller.

The sequences of messages between design objects determine the combined functional behavior of the objects declared on the object interaction graph. This defines the implementation of high-level functionality across objects for a system operation. Each object interaction graph also has associated descriptive text in the data dictionary, such as natural language narrative, pseudocode, or formal specification, to give meaning to the system operation and messages defined.

Design Objects.

The main components of the object interaction graph are design objects. A design object is an extension of the notion of object identified during analysis; it can be distinctly *identified* and can have *attribute* values associated with it. In addition, a design object has a *method interface*. Objects communicate via messages that invoke these methods to perform a task. The design object corresponds to a high-level design component, and it may undergo further decomposition and be implemented as a group of objects. The design object is, therefore, an abstraction and can be viewed as a black box with respect to its input and output behavior. Having made this distinction, design objects will simply be referred to as objects throughout the rest of the chapter.

Figure 4.1 gives an example of an object. The solid outlined box indicates a single object. The object in this figure has a name, **d**, which identifies it, and its class, **Directory**.

Figure 4.1   Object of Directory Class

Collections of objects of the same class can also be defined. An example is given in Figure 4.2, which shows a collection of files. For identification, the collection has a name, **files**, and each object in the collection has the same class, **File**. The dashed outline of the box indicates a collection or group of objects. Typical implementations of such collections will be lists or arrays.

```
┌ ─ ─ ─ ─ ─ ─ ─ ┐
│ files: File   │
│               │
└ ─ ─ ─ ─ ─ ─ ─ ┘
```

Figure 4.2   Collection of Objects of File Class

Note that a collection of a class is not a collection of *all* objects of that class, or a fixed subset. It is a relevant collection of objects identified in the design process. For example, the files in a directory as opposed to all files. The objects in a collection may change over time. More will be said about collections of objects in section 4-2.2.

Message Passing.

The only connection between objects is the labeled arrow representing message passing. Message passing is a directed point-to-point communication, and is realized as a function or method call. A message is denoted by a directed arrow from *sender* to *receiver* with a label indicating the message name. The sender is sometimes referred to as the *client* of the message, and the receiver is known as the *server*. A message may involve bidirectional data flow when the invocation of a method returns a value.

The existence of an arrow indicates that the sender *may* send the message, not that it *must* send it. When a message is sent, the receiver invokes the corresponding method in the interface. A message **m** to a server object of class **C** means that *all* objects of class **C** will include a method corresponding to **m** in the method interface. A description of the method is given by text in the data dictionary.

The example in Figure 4.3 shows an object interaction graph for an operation secure, which secures a named file by changing its access mode to a new value. The controller of the operation is the directory object **d**, and the file **f** collaborates to perform **secure**. When an operation is invoked, it is implemented by sending messages to the other objects. In the example, **d** may send a message **change_access_mode**, with actual parameter **newval** of type **Mode**, to the file. The notation defines the direction of the message, the sender and receiver of the message, its name, and its actual parameter(s).

A parameter consists of a *type* and an optional *name*. The type is the type of the argument required in the message. The name is required only to identify a particular value, in this case **newval**, to show that it is the same as another value in the object interaction graph.

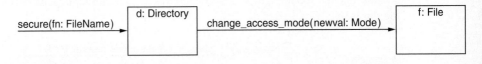

Description:
operation Directory: secure(fn: FileName)
   //protect the file with the name fn by changing its access mode
   Look up the file f with the name fn and change the access mode to the newval mode.

method File: change_access_mode(newval: Mode)
   Change access mode to newval.

Figure 4.3 Message Passing between Objects

When a message call delivers a result, the type of the returned value is shown after the parameter list. For example, if the **change_access_mode** method returned a status value, then the full label for the message arrow would be

change_access_mode(newval : Mode) : Status

A *name* can also be provided for the returned value, which can then be used as a parameter in later messages. For example,

s = change_access_mode(newval : Mode) : Status

Message Passing to Collections.

By default, when a message is sent to objects in a collection, all the objects in that collection receive the message. An example is shown in Figure 4.4 for an operation **secure_all**. This operation secures all the files in a directory. The directory object **d** is permitted to send the **change_access_mode** message to each file in the **files** collection. Hence, the messages sent to such a collection are in fact the messages permitted on each object in the collection. The messages are sent in an unspecified order.

```
                          ┌──────────────┐
secure_all( )  ──────────▶│ d: Directory │  change_access_mode(newval: Mode)   ┌┄┄┄┄┄┄┄┄┄┄┄┐
                          │              │ ──────────────────────────────────▶ ┊ files: File ┊
                          │              │                                     └┄┄┄┄┄┄┄┄┄┄┄┘
                          └──────────────┘
```

Description:
operation Directory: secure_all( )
  //secure all the files in the directory by changing the access mode.
  Change the access mode of all files in the files collection to the newval mode.

method File: change_access_mode(newval: Mode)
  Change access mode to newval.

Figure 4.4   Message Passing from Object to Collection

Messages sent *from* a collection form part of the behavior of each object in the collection and *not* the collection itself. The example in Figure 4.5 shows a modified **secure_all** operation. In this example each file in the **files** collection that executes the **change_access_mode** method is permitted to send a **mode_change_done** message to the directory.

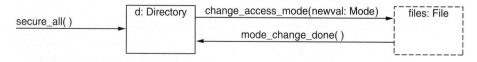

Description:
operation Directory: secure_all( )
  //secure all the files in the directory by changing the access mode.
  Change the access mode of all files in the files collection to the newval mode.

method File: change_access_mode(newval: Mode)
  Change access mode to newval.
  Notify directory that a mode change has been done.

method Directory: mode_change_done( )
  Notification that a file has changed its mode access.

Figure 4.5   Message Passing from Collection to Object

It is possible to specify that messages are sent to a subset of the elements in a collection. For example, sending the message **change_access_mode** to files in a collection that are executable is shown in Figure 4.6. The **secure_executable** operation only needs to change the access mode of files that are executable. The *select* predicate **executable** is included under the message name in square brackets. The message is only permitted on files in the collection for which the predicate is true. A *stop* predicate can also be specified within the square brackets after the *select* predicate.

[select predicate; stop predicate]

Any invocation that results in the *stop* predicate becoming true will prevent further invocations. An omitted *select* predicate defaults to true and an omitted *stop*

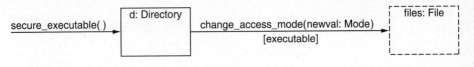

Description:
operation Directory: secure_executable( )
    //secure all executable files in the directory.
    Change the access mode of all executable files in the files collection to the newval.

method File: change_access_mode(newval: Mode)
    Change access mode to newval.

Figure 4.6 Message Passing to Subset of Collection

predicate defaults to **false**. Consequently, an omitted predicate annotation defaults to [**true, false**]. Only arrows leading to collection boxes can have predicates.

Message Sequencing.

When a message is sent to an object it results in the invocation of a method. The method call completes before control is returned to the caller. If the invoked method also sends messages to other objects, then the methods that are invoked must all complete before the initial invocation completes.

Sequencing information can be explicitly shown by introducing sequence labels in parentheses above the message name. For example, Figure 4.7 shows an object interaction graph for a system operation resize_view. This operation is designed to scale the components of a view window by first resizing the drawing area of the view and then adjusting the border, scroll bar, and title bar according to the new dimensions of the drawing area.

The message resize_area is first sent to the drawing area d. An invocation of this method in turn sends the dimensions message back to the controller v, with the new dimensions of the drawing area. The sequencing labels (1) and (1.1) on these messages indicate that the method invocation that results from the message (1.1) must complete before control is returned to the method invoked from resize_area (1). When the method resize_area completes, control is returned to resize_view, and the next message, setdimensions (2), can be sent.

Sequencers are ordered by lexicographic order. As shown earlier, the sequence labels are Dewey Decimal numbers. For example, (1) (1.1) (1.1.1) ... (1.2) ...(2) (2.1) and so forth. Decorations on sequencers (i.e., "'") specify additional constraints on invocations. For example, given the sequence labels (2) and (2'), the message with label (2') will not be invoked if message (2) is invoked and vice versa. This corresponds to a conditional selection in a method responsible for sending the message

if <condition> *then* (2) *else* (2')

A sequence label with an asterisk "*" indicates repetition of a message, that is, zero or more messages sent. By definition, sequence labels of messages to objects in a collection implicitly have an asterisk.

Note that messages labeled with the same sequence label occur in an unspecified order, considering the completion requirement on method invocation. Messages

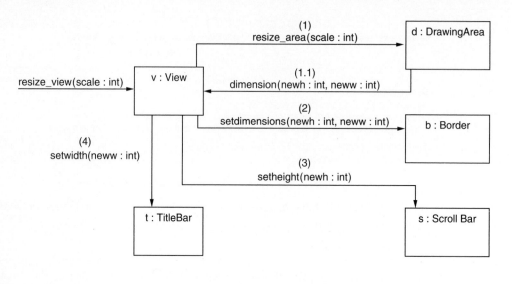

Description:
operation View : resize_view(scale : int)
  //resize all the components of the view by a scale factor.
  Resize the area of the drawing area, according to the scale.   (1)
  Set the dimensions of the border to the new height and width.   (2)
  Set the height of the scroll bar.   (3)
  Set the width of the title bar.   (4)

method DrawingArea : resize_area(scale : int)
  Resize drawing area by scale factor.
  Notify view of new dimensions of drawing area.   (1.1)

method View : dimension(newh : int, neww : int)
  Set the new height and width paramenters of view.

Figure 4.7 Message Sequencing Numbers

with no sequencer occur in any order. However, in both cases additional constraints may be specified by the associated method description or by pseudocode in the data dictionary.

Sequencing information is not intended to give full algorithmic control information for the design and subsequent implementation of methods. The textual description of each method in the data dictionary provides a more detailed explanation of its functionality.

Dynamic Object Creation.

The keyword **new** indicates that an object is created as part of the execution of an object interaction graph. The special message **create** must also be sent to every new object, with appropriate invocation parameters, to initialize it. Until this has been done, the object is in an undefined state, and no other messages should be sent to it.

The message **create** can only be sent to **new** objects. In Figure 4.8, for example, the operation **add_item** creates a new item to add to the list l.

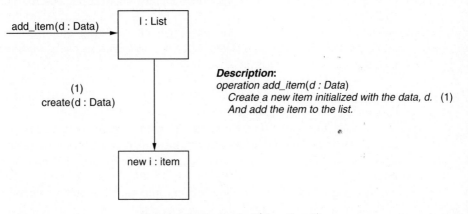

Figure 4.8   Dynamic Object Creation

To summarize, the objects declared on an object interaction graph can be combined by message passing. Each object interaction graph defines functional behavior that is distributed across the objects of the interaction. The messages sent to an object identify methods in the interface of all objects of the same class.

4-2.2 Development of Object Interaction Graphs

In this subsection we show how object interaction graphs are used in design. The purpose of this stage is to specify how the required system functionality, identified during analysis, is implemented by the objects in the system. Object interaction graphs are built for each system operation. This involves four main steps.

1. Identify the relevant objects involved in the computation.
2. Establish the role of each object.
   - Identify the controller (i.e., the object responsible for the system operation).
   - Identify the collaborators involved.
3. Decide on the messages between objects.
4. Record how the identified objects interact on an object interaction graph.

The first step is to identify the relevant objects, that is, those involved in the definition and hence implementation of the system operation. The schema from the operation model is used as the starting point for identifying the objects involved. The **Reads** clause of the schema provides a list of the objects that a system operation accesses but does not modify. The **Changes** clause lists the objects changed by the functional behavior. In addition to the objects listed explicitly in the schema, there may be other objects involved. For example, new objects may be introduced to represent abstractions of computational mechanisms not identified on the analysis models. The **Sends** clause of the schema, for example, lists output events to agents of the system.

Objects are required to deal with the interface to these agents. More will be said about introducing these objects in the examples given subsequently.

Second, the role of each object in implementing the operation must be decided. One distinguished role is that of the *controller*. The controller receives the request to invoke the system operation. The system operation is part of the method interface of the controller. The other objects involved, the *collaborators*, collaborate and cooperate with the controller to implement the system operation.

Next, the messages that are sent between the objects must be decided. Each object will provide different pieces of functionality. These pieces of functionality are composed by message passing between objects.

Finally, the distribution of functionality of the system operation is recorded on an object interaction graph. Each object provides a part of the functional definition of the operation, and this information can be extracted to define the object method interface. A textual description of each method is included in the data dictionary. This explains the meaning of the methods identified and provides the outline algorithm used to implement the system operation.

Example: Object Interaction Graph for is_vulnerable.

To illustrate the process outlined earlier, we now consider an operation from the ECO storage depot example, introduced in Chapter 3. One of the system operations in the interface model is **is_vulnerable**. The EPA regulations state that a depot is vulnerable if any two neighboring buildings contain the maximum permitted number of drums. The schema for this operation is shown in Figure 4.9.

Operation:	is_vulnerable
Description:	Requests a report on whether the depot is vulnerable.
Reads:	store buildings and neighbors of stores in **depot**
Changes:	
Sends:	manager: {vulnerability_report}
Assumes:	
Result:	A vulnerability_report, on the **depot**, has been sent to manager.

Figure 4.9 Schema for is_vulnerable

Step 1: Identify Relevant Objects.   The starting point for finding relevant objects is to look at the **Reads** and **Changes** clauses of the operation schema. We see that a depot and the stores in the depot are involved. A **depot** object and a collection of **stores** are introduced to represent these. The **Reads** clause also tells us that the neighboring store buildings of a store are involved in finding out if a depot is vulnerable. Another collection of store buildings is therefore introduced to represent the neighboring stores of a store. This collection is called **neighbors**.

Consideration also has to be given to the **Sends** clause. The manager has to be notified about the contents of the vulnerability **report**. A **depot_monitor** is introduced to deal with this output. Details of the monitor are not important at this stage of design, and it may later be implemented as a printer, terminal, and so forth. Note that the requirements for the ECO management system have not been precise about how the manager receives information about the vulnerability of the depot. This issue will have to be resolved with the customer.

For the **is_vulnerable** operation a **depot**, a collection of **stores**, a collection of **neighbors** of a store, a vulnerability **report**, and a **depot_monitor** are all potentially involved.

Step 2: Establish Role of Each Object.   A *controller* object, the object that is responsible for the **is_vulnerable** operation, has to be chosen. The agent responsible for requesting the operation is already known from analysis. Now it must be decided what object will receive this request and act as the controller. The **is_vulnerable** operation is allocated to the **depot** as being the most appropriate object to take on the responsibility to find out if the depot is vulnerable and to produce the vulnerability report. Note that we abstract away from the user input mechanisms that deal with how agents invoke system operations. More will be said about this in chapter 5. The only decision being made here is that the request from the depot manager to find out if the depot is vulnerable is dealt with by a **depot** object.

Step 3: Determine Messages between Objects.   We consider now all the collaborator objects and decide how they interact to carry out the operation. A **depot** is vulnerable if any two neighboring buildings contain the maximum permitted number of drums. One way to find this out is to check every store in the depot to see if it is at maximum capacity and, if so, to see if it has a neighboring store that is also at maximum capacity. If one store is vulnerable then the depot is vulnerable.

The solution is for the depot to send a message to every store to find out if it is vulnerable. A store would be responsible for finding out if it was vulnerable or not. This would involve checking the contents of the store to see if it was at maximum capacity and sending messages to all of its neighboring store buildings to find out if any were also at maximum capacity. If any store informs the depot that it is vulnerable then the depot itself is vulnerable, and the appropriate vulnerability **report** must be created and sent to the depot monitor.

Step 4: Record Interactions on Object Interaction Graph.   Figure 4.10 shows this design together with the data dictionary entries for the key methods identified.

Note the use of **new** in this example, which precedes the name of the **VulnerabilityReport**. This indicates that the object was created during the invocation of the operation. The **create** method initializes the vulnerability report to **true** or **false** as required.

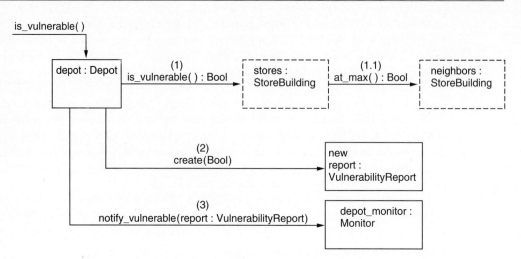

Description:
operation Depot : is_vulnerable( )
    Find out if there is a store in the depot that is vunerable.   (1)
        If there is, then create a 'true' vulnerability report.   (2)
        Else create a 'false' vulnerability report.
    Nofity the manager about the vulnerability report.   (3)

method StoreBuilding : is_vulnerable( ) : Bool
    If the store is at maximum capacity then
        Find out if a neighboring store building is at maximum capcity.   (1.1)
        If it is then return true else return false.
    Else return false

method StoreBuilding : at_max( ) : Bool
    If store is at maximum capacity then return true.
    Else return false.

Figure 4.10   Design for is_vulnerable

To review:

- The objects involved in the system operation have been identified: the **depot**, its collection of **stores**, the collection of **neighbors**, the vulnerability **report**, and the **depot_monitor**.

- Responsibility for the operation has been allocated to the controller object, **depot**.

- The system operation is decomposed into two key functional parts, **is_vulnerable** and **at_max**.

- The functionality has been distributed across the objects involved; **is_vulnerable** is sent to every **store** and **at_max** to each of its neighboring **stores** if the store is at maximum capacity.

During design, we apply the same process to each system operation. Object interaction graphs are used in this way to capture the skeletal structure of algorithms that satisfy the operation model specification.

4-2.3 Object Interaction Graph Refinement

The process of design is one of iterative development and hierarchical decomposition. Initial object interaction graphs are built for each system operation defined in the operation model. Each method identified in the interface of an object satisfies a functional definition, and entries are made into the data dictionary to provide a description of the algorithm used. Each method can then be considered in turn to design how it should be decomposed into suboperations.

Object interaction graphs provide a visual representation of the structure of algorithms. They enable experiments to be carried out with alternative designs and assist hierarchical decomposition. Both of these are discussed in more detail subsequently.

Alternative Designs.

Alternative designs are explored by developing object interaction graphs for the same operation, but with different objects chosen for controllers and collaborators, and with different messages passing between them. The consequences of these alternative designs can be clearly demonstrated, showing the run-time messaging that occurs for particular system operations.

Guidelines for the construction and evaluation of object interaction graphs are given in section 4-6. In this subsection an example is given to demonstrate the iterative nature of the design process.

Example: Choice of Alternative Controller.

To demonstrate the effect of changing the controller of an operation, we consider another operation from the ECO storage depot. The schema for the **depot_status** operation is shown in Figure 4.11.

Operation:	depot_status
Description:	Requests a status report on storage buildings and loading bay.
Reads:	stores and loading_bay of depot
Changes:	
Sends:	manager:{status_report}
Assumes:	
Result:	A status_report of the stores in the depot and the loading_bay has been sent to the manager.

Figure 4.11   Schema for depot_status

The objects involved in this operation are **depot**, a collection of **stores**, a loading_bay, an allocation_list, a status_report, and a depot_monitor to present the status report to the manager. Note that a status report consists of an allocation list of drums in the stores together with details of the drums in the loading bay.

First Design. The **depot** is identified as a controller for this operation. To satisfy the **Results** clause, an allocation list has to be constructed of the drums in all of the stores. Details of the drums in the loading bay also have to be obtained. A complete status report of the depot then has to be sent to the depot monitor for presentation to the depot manager.

Figure 4.12 provides one possible design. This requires that both loading_bay and the objects in **stores** have a method **contents** in the interface to return a collection of drums contained within. Note that the reserved word **col** is a type constructor for a collection type. The **depot** has responsibility for bringing together the drum collections from the stores to create the **allocation_list**. The **depot** then has to combine the **allocation_list** with the contents of the **loading_bay** to create the **status_report** that is sent to the **depot_monitor**.

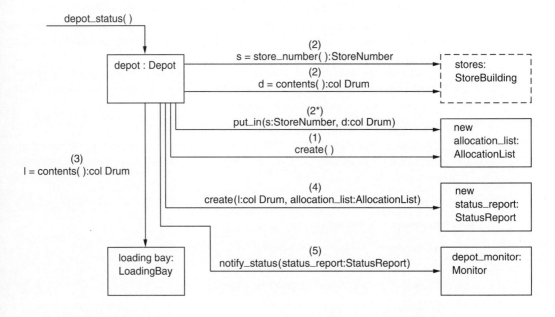

Description:
operation Depot : depot_status( )
*   Create a new allocation list.*   (1)
*   For all s in the stores collection put details of the store contents into the allocation list.*   (2)
*   Retrieve details of the contents of the loading bay.*   (3)
*   Create a new status report initialized with the loading bay contents and the allocation list*   (4)
*   Notify the depot monitor of the status report.*   (5)

Figure 4.12   depot_status Operation: Depot Takes Responsibility

Second Design.   We now consider the consequences of making the loading_bay the controller for this operation. The same approach is taken in coming up with an algorithm to produce a depot status report. The object interaction graph in Figure 4.13 shows a design with alternative messaging activity to realize the depot_status operation.

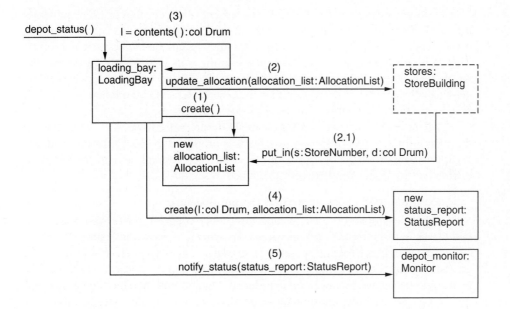

Description:
operation LoadingBay: depot_status( )   (1)
Create a new allocation list.   (2)
Get each store in the stores collection to update the allocation list.   (3)
Retrieve the contents of the loading bay.   (4)
Create a new status report initialized with the loading bay contents and the allocation list. (5)
Notify the depot monitor about the status report.

method StoreBuilding: update_allocation(allocation_list: AllocationList)
Put the store number and details of the collection of drums in the store in the allocation list (2.1)

Figure 4.13   depot_status Operation: More Responsibility to Stores

In this design, the loading_bay sends messages directly to the stores in the depot to get them to update the allocation_list. A store then has responsibility for putting its store number and collection of drums into the list. The depot does not collaborate at all to produce the status report. The new controller is responsible for bringing together the allocation information from the stores and the collection of drums in the loading_bay.

In the second design, the important change that has been made is to pass more responsibility over to the store buildings. Each store has to put details of the store contents into the allocation list. Another difference is that the depot is no longer involved in this operation. As the controller, the loading bay now has to be able to send messages directly to all the stores in the depot and take responsibility for producing the status report. It is up to the designer to decide if this is an appropriate solution. Criteria to help make these kind of decisions are given in section 4-6.

Hierarchical Method Decomposition.

A designer can reduce the complexity of an object interaction graph by postponing the decomposition of a method. This can be achieved by the use of an operation model schema to specify the method. Later in the design, the method schema can be used to produce an object interaction graph in the normal way. This structures the set of object interaction graphs as a hierarchy, with each postponed object interaction graph at a lower level of abstraction than the object interaction graph that uses it. This process is called the *hierarchical decomposition of methods*.

The first step is to specify *what* the method is intended to do. This is the same as the analysis of a system operation. A schema is produced to specify the precondition and postcondition of the method. An object interaction graph is then produced for the method using the same process as defined in section 4-2.2.

Example: end_check_in Method Decomposition.

As an example of method decomposition consider the system operation end_check_in from the ECO storage depot. Its schema is shown in Figure 4.14

An initial design for this operation is shown in Figure 4.15. The objects involved are loading_bay, delivery_manifest, an allocation_list, and the collection of stores. In addition to these, two monitors are introduced: loading_bay_monitor to deal with output to the clerk and storage_monitor to interface with the storage system. The clerk agent is responsible for requesting this operation. The loading_bay is an appropriate candidate to take responsibility for this request and hence is assigned to be the controller.

This completes the first pass at producing an object interaction graph for this operation. We now consider the space_for_drum method that requires further decomposition. The description of this method can be made precise by developing a schema as shown in Figure 4.16.

It is now possible to construct an object interaction graph for the space_for_drum method. A drum, d, a store, and a collection of drums in the store are identified as the potential objects involved. It is already known that the store is responsible for this method, and it becomes the controller. All that remains to be done is to decide how to satisfy the schema specification and to document the design on an object interaction graph. One possible design is shown in Figure 4.17. This example checks first to see if the store has room for any more drums. Then the contents of the drum are determined. Depending on the type of chemical, a check is made to see if any conflicting (unsafe) chemicals are already in the store. To do this we need to know how many drums of each chemical type are stored.

Operation:	end_check_in
Description:	Informs system that all the actual drums have been checked in and are to be allocated to storage buildings.

Reads:	delivery_manifest, loading_bay
Changes:	store buildings in depot.
Sends:	clerk: {discrepancy_in_delivery, drums_to_be_returned}, drum_storage: {delivery_allocation}
Assumes:	The depot is safe.
Result:	If there is a discrepancy between delivery_manifest and loading_bay then discrepancy_in_delivery(excess, deficit: discrepancy_manifest) has been sent to clerk. If there is capacity then all the drums in Initial loading_bay have been allocated to store buildings in depot; otherwise as many as is possible of the drums have been allocated and drums_to_be_returned(return_list) has been sent to clerk. The delivery_allocation(delivery_allocation_list) has been sent to drum storage. The depot is safe.

Figure 4.14   Schema for end_check_in System Operation

4-2.4 Checking of Models

Object interaction graphs are developed for each schema in the operation model. There are two basic checks that need to be carried out once the developer is satisfied with the initial designs.

  1. *Consistency with the system specification.* Check that each of the classes in the system object model is represented in at least one object interaction graph. A class not represented is irrelevant to the defined system behavior, and should not be considered part of the system object model unless it exists for other reasons, such as reuse (see chapter 9).

  Note that new classes may be introduced during design, for example, to deal with output events to agents of the system. These classes will not be shown on the system object model developed during analysis.

2. *Verification of functional effect.* Check that the functional effect of each object interaction graph satisfies the specification of its system operation given in the operation model. Check that every clause in the schema **Results** is satisfied.

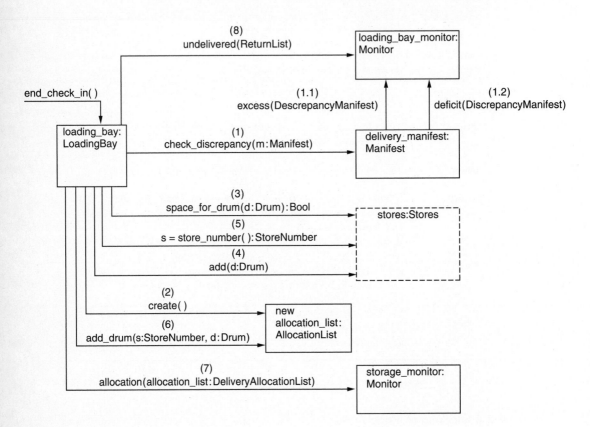

Description:
operation LoadingBay: end_check_in ( )

Check the loading bay manifest against the delivery manifest for discrepancies.	(1)
Create a new allocation list for the delivery.	(2)
For every drum in the loading bay try to find a store that has space for it.	(3)
Then add the drum to the store.	(4)
Add details of the allocation to the allocation list.	(5) (6)
Remove the drum from the loading bay. // internal method	
Notify the storage monitor of the allocation list.	(7)
Notify the loading bay monitor of any undelivered drums.	(8)

method Manifest:check_discrepancy (m:Manifest)

Compare the number of drums on the manifest with m.	
Notify the loading bay monitor of excess drums in the manifest.	(1.1)
Notify the loading bay monitor of deficit drums in the manifest.	(1.2)

Figure 4.15   Design for end_check_in

Operation:	space_for_drum
Description:	Find out if the store can accommodate a new drum

Reads:	*supplied* d : Drum, drums in store, max capacity of store
Changes:	
Sends:	
Assumes:	
Result:	Return true if the addition of d does not exceed the maximum capacity of the store and it is safe to store chemicals of the type in d. Return false otherwise.

Figure 4.16 Schema for space_for_drum

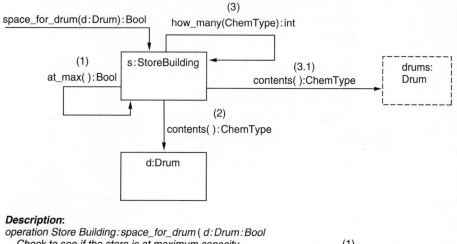

Description:
operation Store Building:space_for_drum (d:Drum:Bool
    Check to see if the store is at maximum capacity.   (1)
    If not then
      Find out the chemical type of the drum.   (2)
      Check if it is safe to add chemicals of this type to the store.
      (find out how many drums of each chemical type are stored)   (3)
      // type 1 not to be stored with type 2
      If safe return true otherwise return false
    Else
      Return false

method Store Building: how_many (ChemType) :int
    Find out how many drums in the store contain the ChemType.   (3.1)

Figure 4.17 Method Decomposition for space_for_drum

4-3 VISIBILITY GRAPHS

During the first stage of design, when developing object interaction graphs, the assumption is that all objects are mutually visible and can send messages to each other. The second stage in the design process is to decide how the communication paths in the system are realized. Objects must have access to other objects to allow the communication required by the object interaction graphs. The identification and addressing of objects is called *referencing*; an object must have a *reference* to another object to communicate with it. Another way of looking at this is to say that a server object must be *visible* to a client for the client to send a message the server.

The purpose of a *visibility graph* is to define the reference structure of classes in the system. The task is to identify for each class.

- Objects the class instances need to reference
- Appropriate kinds of reference to those objects

In this section, we list the kinds of reference that are possible and discuss how to design the reference structure to meet the requirements of the object interaction graphs. We first introduce the notation's syntax and then explain the different kinds of visibility relationships to objects. The process for developing visibility graphs is then introduced and, finally, rules for checking the models are given.

4-3.1 Notation

A visibility graph is a diagram whose components are *client boxes*, *server boxes*, and *visibility arrows*. Visibility arrows connect client boxes to server boxes.

Client Boxes and Server Boxes.

Visibility references for a class arise from the need of objects of this class to send messages to collaborating objects. A client box represents the class requiring the access, and server boxes represent the objects being accessed. A client box is a rectangle containing the name of the class. A server box is a rectangle containing the name of the object and its class. There are four types of server box: the rectangle of a server box can have a *single* or *double* border, and the border can have a *solid* or *dashed* outline. The explanation for these different types of server box is given in section 4-3.2.

Visibility Arrows.

The basic connection to a server object is the *visibility arrow*. This is a directed arrow from the client class, the class that needs the reference, to the server object. The arrow means that the client has access to instances of the server via an access path. The arrow may be a *permanent arrow*, which has a solid line, or a *dynamic arrow*, which has a dashed line. The explanation for these different types of visibility arrow is given in the next section.

4-3.2 Visibility Relationships

There are several design decisions that must be made when considering the reference structure of classes. These are organized into the following categories:

- Reference lifetime
- Server visibility
- Server binding
- Reference mutability

Each of these will be discussed in turn.

Reference Lifetime.

When a client only needs to message a server in the context of a single method invocation, access can be given through a parameter or by a local variable of the method. In this situation a *dynamic reference* is specified on the visibility graph and is denoted by a directed dashed arrow from the client class to the server object.

For example, a directory may need to know the source directory of libraries in the context of processing its files. The library directory is a parameter for the **pro-cessfiles** operation (e.g., **processfiles(library:Directory)**), yielding the visibility graph in Figure 4.18. The **Directory** class has a dynamic reference to the library directory.

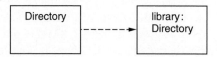

Figure 4.18   Dynamic Visibility Reference

Conversely, when reference to the server object persists between method calls, a *permanent reference* is required. Figure 4.19 shows a permanent reference from a **Directory** class to its collection of files. (The dashed outline to the server box indicates that a collection of server objects is being referenced.) This reference becomes a class feature (i.e., a class attribute), and objects of the **Directory** class will always have a permanent reference to a **files** collection.

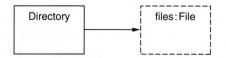

Figure 4.19   Permanent Visibility Reference

Permanent references are used when an object needs the same reference in many contexts. A directory is a typical example in which an operation to manipulate a file collection is designed as a directory operation. This means that all operations on the **files** collection are through the directory, so a permanent reference to the collection is a suitable design choice.

Server Visibility.

A server object that is sent a message from a client may be *exclusively* used by that client or it may be *shared* by several clients. For example, a file that is exclusively referenced by a directory is denoted as shown in Figure 4.20. The server object box has a double border.

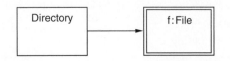

Figure 4.20   Exclusive Visibility Reference to Object

When the visibility of a server is shared, the server box has a single border. For example, if a file may be shared across several directories (i.e., the file is not exclusively used by one directory), then the server box just has a single border.

An exclusive visibility reference guarantees that at the time of any method invocation, only one client will have a reference to the server. However, there may be different clients at different times, but on any invocation there is only one client.

Server Binding.

The lifetime of an object begins when it is created and ends when it is deleted. There are typically many relationships between the lifetimes of objects in a system such that if one object is deleted then a related object should also be deleted, that is, it makes no sense for the objects to *live* independently of each other. When objects are related in this way we say that the lifetimes are *bound*.

When the lifetime of a server object is not bound to the lifetime of a client, the server box is shown outside the class box on a visibility graph, as shown in Figure 4.20. However, if the lifetimes are bound then the server box is shown inside the class box. If the client holds the only reference to the server, then the server object should be deleted when the the lifetime of the client comes to an end.

Figure 4.21 shows that instances of the class **View** have permanent references (indicated by the solid arrows) to four server objects: **d:DrawingArea**, **b:Border**, **s:ScrollBar**, and **t:TitleBar**. These objects are exclusively messaged from the client (indicated by the double borders around the server boxes), and the servers have their lifetimes bound to the lifetime of the client.

Reference Mutability.

The *mutability* of a reference indicates whether it can be reassigned after initialization. If a reference is not assignable after initialization, we say that it has *constant* mutability; that is, the reference is fixed when it is initialized. If the mutability is *variable*, then it may be reassigned. The mutability of a reference is shown by prefixing the server name with the keywords **constant** or **variable**, as appropriate. The default mutability is **variable**.

The example in Figure 4.22 shows two server objects: **father** and **mother**. The client class **Person** has permanent references to these servers, and the references are **constant**. Once initialized, the server objects cannot be changed. (Note that this does not imply that the attributes of the servers cannot be changed.)

4-3.3 Development of Visibility Graphs

We now describe how visibility graphs are used during design, using the ECO Storage Depot example for illustration.

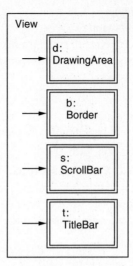

Figure 4.21   Lifetime of Client and Server Bound

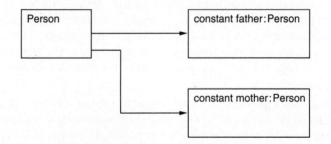

Figure 4.22   Constant Mutability of Reference

Recall that when developing object interaction graphs the assumption is that all objects are mutually visible; if a client sends a message to a server, we assume that the client has a reference to it. The task now is to determine how the required visibility references are provided and to check consistency by considering the visibility requirements of all object interaction graphs.

The visibility graphs are developed from the object interaction graphs in the following way:

1. All the object interaction graphs are inspected. For each arrow going from one object to another, the class of the sender requires a visibility reference to the receiver object.

2. Annotate the arrow with visibility information detailing where appropriate.

   - Reference lifetime.
   - Server visibility.

- Server binding.
- Reference mutability.

3. For each class C, consider all the annotated arrows from instances of C. Construct a visibility graph with C in the *client box* and with *visibility arrows* connected to the *server boxes*.

The labels on the arrows from the object interaction graphs (i.e., the method names) may be copied across to the visibility graphs where necessary. For example, there may be different visibility requirements for a particular server box with respect to different methods that it provides.

Example: ECO Visibility Graphs.

In practice it is necessary to complete all of the object interaction graphs before considering the reference structure of classes in the system. For the purposes of this example, however, we only consider three object interaction graphs from section 4-2.

- is_vulnerable (see Figure 4.10)
- depot_status (see Figure 4.12)
- end_check_in (see Figures 4.15 and 4.17)

The first step is to look at all the message arrows on the object interaction graphs. On is_vulnerable, for example, the **depot** is permitted to send the message is_vulnerable to store buildings in the collection **stores**. This implies that instances of the **Depot** class must have a visibility reference to the **stores** collection.

To decide this visibility reference the four classification categories need to be considered.

Reference lifetime. Does this reference to a collection of stores have to exist just for the purposes of a single method invocation, or is it required in several different contexts? For this example we reason that a depot is made up of a collection of buildings, and it seems probable that instances of the **Depot** class need to reference the buildings in the depot in several different contexts. Consequently, we decide to have a permanent reference.

Server visibility. For the collection of stores we need to consider if it is going to be referenced exclusively by an instance of the **Depot** class, or is it going to be shared by several objects?

For the object interaction graphs being considered the **stores** collection is sent messages from both the **depot** and the **loading bay**. So we provide shared visibility to the **stores** collection.

Server binding. Does the collection of stores have the same lifetime as the depot, or is the lifetime of this collection independent of the depot? We have already established that the **stores** collection is sent messages from both the depot and the loading bay. This indicates that other clients are interested in the server in addition to the depot. However, the depot does have an important role in this problem in the sense that a depot is made up of its collection of buildings and the loading bay (as shown on the system object model). So we bind the lifetime of the server collection to the **Depot** class. The same will be done for the loading bay.

Reference mutability.   Finally, is the reference to the server constant or can it change over time? For the purposes of the example we will allow the reference to be variable, the default.

This design process has to be carried out for all of the message arrows on the object interaction graphs. Once this has been done the visibility graphs for each of the classes can be constructed. We can now take a look at examples that result from considering just the object interaction graphs from the is_vulnerable, depot_status, and end_check_in operations.

Figure 4.23 shows a visibility graph for the **Depot** class. Instances of this class have three permanent visibility references. The first is to a shared collection of store buildings, called **stores**; the second to a depot monitor, which is exclusively referenced from the depot; and the third to a loading bay, which is also exclusively referenced. These are all bound references, so the lifetimes of the **stores** collection, the **depot_monitor** and the **loading_bay**, are bound to the lifetime of an instance of the **Depot** class.

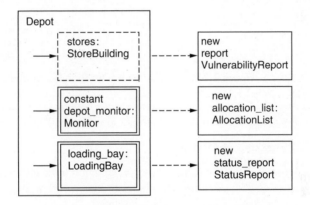

Figure 4.23   Visibility Graph for the Depot class

There are also three dynamic references defined for the **Depot** class. These are all examples of **new** objects that are created during the execution of methods at the interface of the class. A vulnerability report is created by the is_vulnerable method, and the allocation list and status report are created by depot_status.

The preceding process for designing the reference structure is carried out for all classes identified in the system. Two more examples of visibility graphs for the ECO depot are shown in Figure 4.24. The **StoreBuilding** and **LoadingBay** classes provide examples of various kinds of visibility relationships. In the examples, we have only shown the references needed to implement the is_vulnerable, depot_status, and end_check_in operations.

In summary, message passing between two objects implies that a reference is needed. The client class can have either a permanent or dynamic reference to a server object, the server may be shared or exclusively used by the client, the lifetime of the server may be bound to the lifetime of the client, or it may have an unbound

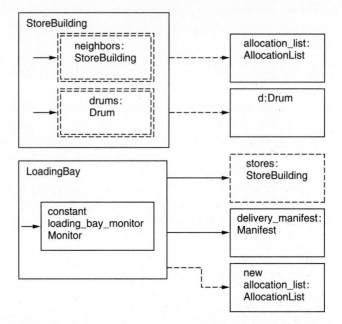

Figure 4.24   Visibility Graph for StoreBuilding and LoadingBay

lifetime, and the mutability of the reference may be constant or variable. These design decisions are recorded in the visibility graph for each class.

4-3.4 Checking of Models

The references in visibility graphs are structural links required to implement the message passing defined during the object interaction graph stage. Three important checks need to be made when they are completed.

1. *Consistency with analysis models.* The relationships identified during analysis define invariants that must be maintained between classes. A check has to be made that the object-oriented structures defined in the visibility graphs maintain these relationships. For each relationship on the system object model, we expect that there is a path of visibility between the corresponding classes at design.

   In the ECO Storage Depot example, the neighbors relationship from analysis is *implemented* by the exclusive reference to a collection of store buildings called neighbors. The visibility graph structure allows this relationship to be updated and maintained.

2. *Mutual consistency.* Check that exclusive server objects are not referenced by more than one client.

3. *Completeness.* Check to see that all message passing defined in the object interaction graphs is realized in the visibility graphs.

4-4 CLASS DESCRIPTIONS

After developing visibility graphs for all the classes, the next step is to collate information from the system object model, object interaction graphs, and visibility graphs in *class descriptions*, one for each class. At this stage, the methods, some data attributes, and object-valued attributes for each class are established.

When these initial descriptions have been produced, the inheritance structures required in the system are designed. Inheritance graphs will be discussed in section 4-5. The final step of design is to update the information in the class descriptions to reflect the new inheritance structures. Each class then has a description of its internal structure: its data and object-valued attributes, its methods (the messages it responds to as defined in the object interaction graphs), and its position in the inheritance graph. Class descriptions provide the foundation for implementation.

In this section the notation's syntax is introduced and then the role of class descriptions in the design process is explained.

4-4.1 Notation

A class description is a description of a set of objects that has the same attributes and methods, some of which may be inherited from superclasses. The description consists of the following information: class name, immediate superclass(es), attributes of the class, and the methods provided by the class. The notation used to document these is summarized in Figure 4.25. A full definition of the syntax is given in appendix C.

class *<ClassName>* [isa *<SuperClassNames>*]

    // for each attribute

    [attribute] *[Mutability]<a_name>*:*[Sharing][Binding]<Type>*
      ⋮
    //for each method

    [method] *<m_name>* *<arglist>* [:*<Type>*]
      ⋮
endclass

Figure 4.25 Class Description Syntax

A class description begins with the keyword **class** followed by the name of the class. The names of any superclasses that the class inherits from are then enumerated, preceded by the keyword **isa**.

Each attribute is optionally introduced by the keyword **attribute**. This is followed by the name of the attribute and then the type. Visibility information for object attributes is documented by appropriate keywords.

- *Mutability.* Details of the mutability of the attribute are given as **constant** and **variable** as appropriate. Mutability defaults to variable when not indicated in the class description.

- *Sharing.* Sharing information can be indicated as **shared** or **exclusive**. The default is shared.

- *Binding.* From the visibility graph, the lifetime of an object attribute will be either **bound** or **unbound**. The default is **unbound**.

Each method is optionally introduced by keyword **method** followed by the name of the method and its signature, i.e., the argument list and the type of any returned value. Descriptions of the method bodies are given in the data dictionary.

An example of a class description for the **View** class is shown in Figure 4.26. This class has four object attributes that are **bound** to the lifetime of a **view**. The **view** will also have **exclusive** access to the server objects. By default, the attributes are **variable**. (The attribute information has been derived from the visibility graph shown in Figure 4.21.) The **View** class provides the methods **dimensions** and **resize_view**. The complete method signatures are given; parameters are named and typed. (This information is derived from the object interaction graph shown in Figure 4.7.)

```
class View
    attribute d:exclusive bound DrawingArea // used exclusively by view
    attribute b:exclusive bound Border
    attribute s:exclusive bound ScrollBar
    attribute t:exclusive bound TitleBar

    method dimensions(height:int, width:int)
    method resize_view(scale:int)
endclass
```

Figure 4.26   Class Description: View Class

4-4.2 Development of Class Descriptions

Class descriptions are the specifications from which coding begins. They specify the internal state and external interface of a class. They are used in two stages of the design process. First, they are used to collate the method and object reference information from the object interaction graphs and visibility graphs. Data attributes are also obtained from the system object model and data dictionary. This information is derived rather then created. Second, when inheritance graphs have been developed, the class descriptions are updated to reflect the inheritance structures introduced.

At the end of design, there are four types of information collated in class descriptions: methods and parameters, data attributes, object attributes, and inheritance dependencies. The process for building class descriptions considers each of these in turn.

1. Methods are derived from the object interaction graphs. All object interaction graphs in which objects of the class participate should be considered together. The messages sent to the objects (i.e., the incoming arrows) are collected together to form the interface of the class. The message label on the object interaction graph provides the method name and the type of any parameters required. Additional parameters for methods are derived from the visibility graphs; dynamic references between objects occur in the context of a method call and are reflected in the parameters for the method.

2. Sources for data attributes are the system object model and the data dictionary. The system object model defines classes and their attributes. The attributes defined for a class during analysis can be implemented by data attributes of the corresponding class during design. The method descriptions in the data dictionary may also yield data attributes.

3. Object attributes are extracted from the visibility graph for the class. All permanent references are implemented by object attributes, and the class description specifies what kind of visibility reference has been designed, that is, constant/variable, bound/unbound, shared/exclusive.

4. The final aspect of class descriptions is the inheritance information. The inheritance dependencies are documented after the inheritance graphs are defined. For each class, it is easy to collate its immediate superclasses from its inheritance graph.

The sources of information for class descriptions are summarized in Figure 4.27.

Example: ECO Class Descriptions.

In section 4-3 a visibility graph for the **Depot** class was constructed (see Figure 4.23). This was designed considering two of the relevant object interaction graphs; **is_vulnerable** (see Figure 4.10) and **depot_status** (see Figure 4.12). We now continue the ECO depot example by developing the **Depot** class description.

First, we look for incoming arrows on the object interaction graphs to identify methods of the class. The **Depot** class receives **is_vulnerable** and **depot_status**. There are no data attributes on the system object model for the **Depot** class, so next we look on the visibility graph for the object attributes. There are three: a collection of **stores**, a **depot_monitor**, and a **loading_bay**. All of these have permanent visibility references that are bound to **Depot**. The **depot_monitor** and **loading_bay** attributes are exclusively referenced by the instance of the **Depot** class, but the **stores** collection is shared. At the moment we have no information about inheritance structures, and so this is all we know about **Depot**. This information is recorded in the class description in Figure 4.28.

The same process is followed to produce the class descriptions for **StoreBuilding** and **LoadingBay**, which are shown in Figures 4.29 and 4.30, respectively. The **StoreBuilding** has a data attribute **max_capacity** that was defined on the system object model. The object attribute collections **drums** and **neighbors** were derived from the visibility graph, and the methods were derived from the object interaction graphs. The visibility graph for **StoreBuilding** has a dynamic visibility reference to a server object,

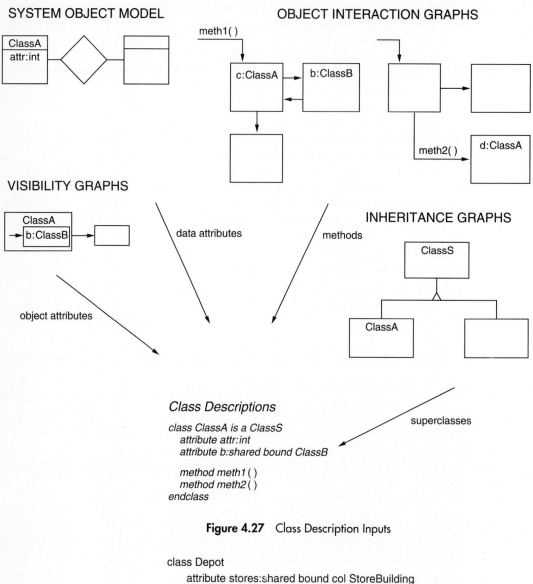

Figure 4.27 Class Description Inputs

```
class Depot
    attribute stores:shared bound col StoreBuilding
    attribute constant depot_monitor:exclusive bound Monitor
    attribute loading_bay:exclusive bound LoadingBay

    method is_vulnerable()
    method depot_status()
endclass
```

Figure 4.28 Depot Class Description

d, of class **Drum**. This is shown as a parameter to the methods **space_for_drum** and **add**. The description for **LoadingBay** has been similarly derived from the analysis and design models.

```
class StoreBuilding isa Building
    attribute max_capacity:int
    attribute neighbors:exclusive bound col StoreBuilding
    attribute drums:exclusive bound col Drum

    method is_vulnerable():Bool
    method space_for_drum(d:Drum):Bool
    method store_number():StoreNumber
    method contents():col Drum
    method add(d:Drum)
    method at_max():Bool
    method how_many(ChemType):int
endclass
```

Figure 4.29   StoreBuilding Class Description

```
class LoadingBay
    attribute stores:  shared col StoreBuilding
    attribute constant loading_bay_monitor:shared bound Monitor
    attribute delivery_manifest:  shared Manifest

    method end_check_in()
    method contents():col Drum
endclass
```

Figure 4.30   LoadingBay Class Description

To summarize, the class description notation is used to collate the class information from the other design notations. The method interface is derived from the object interaction graphs, object attributes are derived from visibility graphs, and data attributes are defined from the system object model and data dictionary. The inheritance relationships are derived from the inheritance graphs. Class descriptions provide the starting point for the class implementor.

4-4.3 Checking of Models

The information in class descriptions is derived and not newly generated. Provided the transcriptions are accurate, the descriptions will be consistent with the descriptions produced earlier in analysis and design. However, the following checks should be made:

1. *Data attributes.* Check that all data attributes from the system object model are recorded.

2. *Object attributes*. Check that all visibility references are recorded.

3. *Methods and parameters*. Check that all methods from object interaction graphs are recorded.

4. *Inheritance*. Check that all inherited superclasses are recorded.

4-5 INHERITANCE GRAPHS

An important consideration in object-oriented design is *inheritance*, a mechanism by which one class can be defined as a specialization of another. The initial steps of the design process have looked at the functional definition of operations in object interaction graphs and the consequences on the class reference structures given in visibility graphs. Here we build the inheritance structures, looking at the classes to identify commonalities and abstractions.

In this section the notation of the *inheritance graph* is introduced, and then its role in design is explained. Finally, rules are given to check the models produced.

4-5.1 Notation

The notation used for inheritance is the same as the object model notation used for generalization and specialization, described in section 2-2. A box represents a class, with the name of the class indicated in the upper section of the box. Attributes are named in the box below the line. For example, a **Shape** class is illustrated in Figure 4.31.

Figure 4.31   Shape Class Inheritance Graph

Subclasses are represented in the same style as specializations in the object model. Figure 4.32 shows the **Shape** class and two subclasses **Rectangle** and **Circle**.

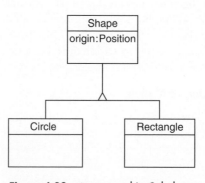

Figure 4.32   Shape and Its Subclasses

The *outline* subclass triangle indicates that no particular commitment is being made about the subclasses being disjoint or that they partition the superclass, that is, there may be other shape subclasses. A *solid* subclass triangle indicates that the subclasses are disjoint and that their union forms the superclass. This would imply that the superclass was *abstract* and had no direct instances.

4-5.2 Development of Inheritance Graphs

Before considering the process for building inheritance graphs, there is one distinction to be made between the generalization and specialization of analysis and the inheritance structures of design. During analysis, abstract *subtype* relationships between classes are identified. Specialization defines a semantic relationship between two classes: the general and specific ones. This semantic relationship is inherent in the domain of the system. Specialization and generalization are properties of the domain model and *not* of the system design or implementation.

At design, however, the inheritance relationship is a property of the system and *not* necessarily of the domain. One benefit of the object-oriented approach is that the semantic relationships of the domain can be directly modeled by the software structures. Hence, inheritance can be seen as a design construct for specialization. The analyst states the existence of such relationships and places no requirements on the design that the relationships are directly implemented. Inheritance relationships at design are prescriptive, whereas at analysis they are descriptive.

The purpose of this stage in design is to develop the inheritance structures for the system. In previous stages, we have defined algorithms for the functionality of operations and the reference structures needed for their implementation. We have also extracted this information into preliminary class descriptions defining the outline interface and references for each class identified in the object interaction graph.

We now look at the relationships between the classes and identify common abstractions. Inheritance graphs are built for all of the classes, with new classes being introduced when we organize the class structure into abstract layers. The inputs to this stage are the system object model, the object interaction graphs, the visibility graphs, and the class descriptions. The process for building inheritance graphs considers each of these in turn.

1. *System object model—generalizations.* The system object model generalization and specialization structures provide the obvious starting point for considering inheritance structures. A specialized analysis class is a subclass, and a generalized analysis class is a superclass. This is a direct implementation of the subtype inheritance of analysis. The aim in design is to preserve this subtyping structure. The subclasses and superclasses are semantically related by subtype inheritance. Inheritance structures may also be introduced for efficiency or code reuse reasons, but care must be taken that the newly introduced inheritance does not interfere with the initial subtyping semantic structures.

2. *Object interaction graphs and class descriptions—common functionality.* The next input descriptions to consider are the object interaction graphs and class descriptions. Each object interaction graph defines the functionality of an operation and drives the definition of the external interface of the object class involved

in the computation. These class interface specifications are documented in the class description for each class.

In building inheritance graphs, each class description is cross-checked to discover common functionality. This functionality can be extracted to build a new abstract class. More will be said about abstract classes in the design principles presented in section 4-6.

3. *Visibility graphs—common structure.* Visibility graphs are again considered at this stage of design. Each visibility graph is cross-checked against others to extract common structure. If two classes have a common reference structure then it may be possible to define an abstract class that defines the common references.

Finally, given a stable inheritance graph structure, the designer should update the class descriptions to reflect the new abstract classes and inheritance structures.

Example: ECO Inheritance Graphs.

The ECO depot system provides obvious candidates for inheritance structures. We start by looking at the generalization and specialization structures in the system object model. The generalization **Report**, for example, has two specializations: **Status Report** and **Vulnerable Report**. The generalization **Building** also has two specializations: **Admin/Lab Building** and **StoreBuilding**. The inheritance graphs for these classes are shown in Figure 4.33. Note that the only types of building are admin/lab buildings and store buildings. Consequently, the subclasses partition the superclass, as indicated by the *solid* inheritance triangle. However, there may be many types of report, and so no commitment has been made in this respect for the **Report** superclass.

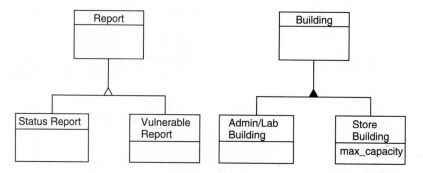

Figure 4.33   Report and Building Inheritance Graphs

Having identified these classes as candidates for inheritance we look for any common data attributes, object attributes, and methods that can be defined for the superclass. Attributes like **max_capacity**, however, and the related method **at_max** for the **StoreBuilding** subclass are not required in the superclass **Building**.

With the requirements given for the ECO system it may not be necessary to maintain the distinction between admin/lab buildings and store buildings. So far the functionality defined for the system has made no use of information about admin/lab buildings. Only collections of **StoreBuilding** have been defined on the object interaction graphs. In the full analysis there may of course be other reasons for keeping this distinction. For example, if the definition of depot vulnerability included admin/lab buildings, it would be necessary to define the **is_vulnerable** method for both kinds of building. This same method would then apply to two classes, perhaps taking on different implementations (thus making it *polymorphic*). However, if there were no examples of object interaction graphs making use of instances of admin/lab buildings, then a case could be made for removing this inheritance structure.

We look next at the object interaction graphs for common functionality. For example, both **LoadingBay** and **StoreBuilding** require a **contents** method in their interface. They both store collections of drums. We might, therefore, consider a loading bay to be a special kind of store building. Further evidence would be required, however, before a new inheritance structure was introduced. For example, does a loading bay have a maximum capacity, or can it be vulnerable? Another approach would be to consider **LoadingBay** and **StoreBuilding** as subclasses of a new **DrumRepository** superclass. Only if we convince ourselves that a new subclass is *semantically* related should it be included in the inheritance structures. The visibility graphs play a similar role to the object interaction graphs in providing evidence to justify new inheritance structures.

This stage in the design process will also cause us to iterate development of the other design models. For example, the **depot_monitor** has a method **notify_status** for the **depot_status** system operation and a method **notify_vulnerable** for the **is_vulnerable** operation. One has a **StatusReport** as a parameter and the other a **VulnerabilityReport**. Therefore, it may be possible to simplify the design to remove any unnecessary duplication in functionality and have just one **notify** method. Further work would then be required in the earlier stages of design before we could continue with the inheritance graphs.

These examples demonstrate some of the considerations made when designing inheritance structures.

4-5.3 Checking of Models

An important aspect of design is that we can trace design decisions through the models produced. To do this, each of the notations must be coherent. The inheritance graphs have to be checked with the following models:

1. *System object model.* Check that the subtype relationships are preserved. Remember that the purpose of the generalization and specialization relationship at analysis is to state the subtyping property between two classes. The system object model defines the abstract property; mechanisms, such as inheritance, to satisfy that property are introduced during design. One of the benefits of object-oriented software is that such properties can be directly described in the data structures.

2. *Object interaction graphs.* Check that all the classes are represented in an inheritance graph. A naive assumption is that each class in the object interaction graph is in the inheritance graph. This is generally the case, but we also need to

consider that the class structure may be reorganized because of the introduction of new abstract classes.

Every concept introduced at this stage must be related to the concepts in the object interaction graphs. A design reviewer should be able to trace the design decisions made.

Note that unchanged object interaction graphs will be compatible with new abstract classes; the classes in the object interaction graphs are represented by subclasses of the newly introduced abstract classes in the inheritance graphs. Object interaction graphs that are updated by replacing classes by their new abstract class are also valid if the messaging for the components of that class is part of the abstract class definition.

Of course, an important step in design for reuse is in making the object interaction graphs as generic as possible and maximally replacing classes with their abstract superclasses. See chapter 9 for further discussion of design for reuse.

3. *Visibility graphs.* Check that all the classes are represented in an inheritance graph. Abstract classes can be defined for common structure between classes in the visibility graphs.

4. *Class descriptions.* Check that the new class descriptions capture all the common methods of the preliminary ones and respect the inheritance graphs.

4-6 PRINCIPLES OF GOOD DESIGN

This section covers several aspects of good object-oriented design. In particular, attention is given to how the outputs from design can be reviewed. Each design model is considered in turn.

4-6.1 Object Interaction Graphs

Minimize Object Interactions.

One obvious property for object interaction graphs is to keep them simple. They should have a minimal number of objects and a minimal number of references. Minimizing the number of objects limits the dispersion of an operation's implementation across the object collection. Minimizing the number of references makes designs more efficient; implementations of operations will involve minimal method calling and function lookup. The fewer the number of references, the shorter the access paths needed to implement an algorithm.

The design should ensure that mutual message passing between objects is at a minimum. Mutual message passing requires copies of object references across object collections, known as *aliasing*. If this is the key to an algorithm, as in some user interface protocols, the cycle length should be reduced to localize potential aliasing. Localised aliasing in small structures can be managed once documented [55].

Cleanly Separate Functionality.

Each object interaction graph characterizes how objects communicate to realize an aspect of functionality. As functionality is distributed across the objects, there are two potential design approaches that would lead to a poor design.

1. The same functionality could be spread across a collection of objects. Functionality in a well-designed object interaction graph is tied to one class or the rooted inheritance graph for the class. Spreading functionality across a collection of objects makes change-control difficult. A change in one function may require changes to the other, but the reference is lost in the object-oriented structure.

2. Disassociated pieces of functionality are designed for the same object. This can happen when objects of the same class are involved in the algorithms for different system operations. Designing unrelated functionality in the same class loses the "real-world modeling" benefit of the object-oriented approach for that class.

Each individual object should serve a particular purpose. Object interaction graphs should be reviewed to check that the same functionality is not implemented by unrelated classes and that each class is coherent with strongly associated functionality.

Develop Modular Systems.

Object interaction graphs should be used to design modular systems. A good design principle is ensure systems are partitioned into modular subsystems. Closely coupled objects can be grouped in subsystems. The control structure of a subsystem can be designed in a layered fashion. An object can serve two main roles.

- As a controller or interface object that transfers subsystem calls to auxiliary objects
- As an auxiliary object invoked by only the controller objects

Designs that localize control in one controller object are too centralized, hierarchical, and overly dependent on one object. Designs with many interface objects and no auxiliary objects expose too much of the subsystem representation at the method interface. The ideal is somewhere between the two. A design should have interface objects for each related set of operations at the subsystem interface.

4-6.2 Visibility Graphs

Minimize Data and Functional Dependencies.

The visibility graph shows the structural references between classes. The aim here should be to reduce the data and functional dependencies across object collections.

A guide to help achieve this is given by the *Law of Demeter* for message passing [72], [74]. This states that for each object, **o**, and each of its methods, **m**, the objects that can be messaged are the

- Object itself, that is, **o**
- Object-valued attributes of **o**
- Arguments of **m**

An object observing this law only messages the objects that are immediately referenced.

The law is generalized for classes, allowing for class-based encapsulation. An object of a class observing this (weaker) law can message any object of its attribute classes or parameter classes without needing an immediate reference.

Following the Law of Demeter improves the modularity of a system. An object is dependent only on its immediate structure and makes no assumptions about the structure beyond the immediate references. Applying this law, one can achieve "loosely coupled" systems and localization of information.

A stricter approach is advocated by Johnson [60]. His recommendation is that an object should message only its object-valued attributes and not itself. This is to maintain a hierarchical control structure. The object acts as controller and its component objects respond to it. In this way the control and data structure reflect each other.

4-6.3 Inheritance Graphs

Restrict Inheritance-Based Reuse.

The organization of object-oriented classes into class hierarchies is an aid to reuse. Classes can be tailored and specialized to produce new classes. However, reuse by inheritance is not always the best option. Classes can be extended through inheritance *or* composition. Deciding when to build new classes by inheritance and when to build using composition is an aspect of object-oriented design.

Inheritance should be used when the complete interface of the old class applies to the new class. Inheritance should not be used when a high proportion of code needs to be rewritten or when some of the methods of the old class are irrelevant.

Building by composition allows the designer more control of the new class interface. The designer can decide which aspects of the old class are relevant and can be reused, and which parts can be effectively discarded. Researchers and practitioners now argue in favor of component-based rather than inheritance-based reuse [77].

Develop Shallow Inheritance Graphs.

Classes in a system should be organized as a "forest" of inheritance graphs, each covering a particular category of related classes. Classes should be organized into shallow hierarchies of about four to five levels. A subclass is dependent on its superclasses, and it is difficult to follow control flow with deep inheritance structures [83]. At the implementation stage, compile times for deep inheritance structures can be very long because of such subclass/superclass dependencies.

Root in an Abstract Class.

Each inheritance graph should be rooted in an abstract class that serves only as a definition of an interface [70]. The abstract class should define a minimal attribute set (preferably empty) so that potential subclasses are not restricted in their representation. This makes the state space as wide as possible giving maximal freedom for representing subclasses.

Grade Levels of Inheritance.

Each inheritance graph should be *graded*. This means that the siblings at each level should differ in the same respects. For example, a **Shape** abstract class can have immediate subclasses **Ellipse** and **Rectangle** that differ in how they are drawn. Ellipses are drawn by arcs and rectangles by straight lines. These can be further specialized to **Circle** and **Square**, the regular variants.

Preserve Subtype Inheritance.

Inheritance should be used for subtyping. The emphasis in design is on behavioral subtyping. Subclasses should be designed that *respect* the general properties of the superclass.

Formal measures can be taken to preserve behavior from superclass to subclass, although these are not always needed [7], [70]. However, it is worthwhile reviewing the inheritance graphs and checking that subclasses satisfy higher-level abstractions. The places where subtyping is violated should be documented. Note that it is difficult to restrict designs to behavioral subtyping as inheritance is a code reuse mechanism and not a subtyping facility [32].

4-6.4 Class Descriptions

One Class; One Abstraction.

The class is the unit of modularity in object-oriented systems. Ensure that classes are cohesive units representing complete abstractions. The data and procedural abstraction should be maintained in the class code.

It has already been mentioned that we want to check against one class having two different types of functionality. One way of measuring the cohesion of classes is to consider pairs of methods at the class interface and the data attributes involved in their definition. Two methods without common data attributes serve separate functions and may indicate that the class is not cohesive. The class may be representing two abstractions that should be separated.

Encapsulate Representation.

A good encapsulation principle is to keep the representation hidden and reduce the interface's dependence on the representation. This then permits easy replacement of representations to implement the same interface. This is useful in design and especially for reuse.

Each method should serve a well-understood and -accepted purpose. The composition of functions should be left to the client and not the server. A class provides the primitive building blocks (i.e., methods), and users of the class group the primitives into useful compositions. For example, a **pop** method of a **Stack** class should remove the top of the stack, and a **top** method should select the top of the stack. Combining these two separate functions into one method would restrict the usefulness and flexibility of the stack interface. The **Stack** interface should include the two primitives **pop** and **top**. For efficiency purposes, the class may provide the combination, but this is only valid when the primitives are also part of the provided interface. Methods should be orthogonal, that is, there should be no overlap of functionality across methods.

The interface should be complete. Each class has an abstract state space that defines the semantic state of the class. The actual concrete representation of that state is encapsulated. The complete *abstract* state space of a class should be *reachable* from the class interface. This may involve extra steps in design but is especially important.

Documentation of methods should be separated into *selector* methods, *write* methods, *control* methods (those that pass control through the class interface to components), and *utility* methods that provide auxiliary functions.

4-7 SUMMARY

This chapter has presented the design phase of the Fusion method.

- During design, software structures are introduced to satisfy the abstract definitions produced from analysis.

- The functional implementation of each system operation is designed by considering run-time object interactions that realize the abstract definition of behavior in the operation model. Object interaction graphs document this dynamic behavior and identify the required method interface of objects.

- Visibility reference structures are designed to allow the communication required by the object interaction graphs.

- Inheritance structures are introduced to preserve the subtype inheritance from analysis and to provide abstract class definitions of commonalities and abstractions from subclasses.

- Class descriptions document the method interface, attribute structure, and inheritance relationships for every class identified in design. They provide a blueprint for implementation.

- Checks at each stage of design are made to maintain completeness and consistency of the models produced.

CHAPTER

5

Implementation

5-1 INTRODUCTION

The final stage of Fusion is mapping the design into an effective implementation. This transition is relatively straightforward, as most complex design decisions have already been made. The implementation should be *correct*; the implementation should behave in the way described by the design and thus satisfy the requirements. (Of course, errors may be introduced during any stage of development; no method can eliminate human fallibility.) The implementation should also be *economical*; it should not make excessive demands on resources, such as time and storage. The output of the implementation stage is a piece of software that satisfies the functional and nonfunctional requirements.

Because Fusion is not directed at any particular programming languages, we discuss implementation techniques in a general way, with particular emphasis on C++ and Eiffel. We do *not* attempt to provide a complete survey of techniques for any of these languages; readers are referred to texts such as [33] and [88].

5-1.1 Implementation Process

The basis of the implementation phase is the class descriptions, object interaction graphs, and data dictionary produced by the design phase, plus the life cycle generated by the analysis phase. The implementation process can be divided into three parts, each with its own sub-structure: *coding*, *performance*, and *review*.

Although we present these parts as proceeding in a particular fixed order, this is only a convenient idealization. In practice, different parts of the design can be implemented in parallel and be at different stages of their realization. In particular, some aspects of performance must be considered before coding begins; for example, it is important to have decided on storage management issues before starting on the class descriptions, and the design itself must have been done with performance in mind. Other performance issues do not appear until code is actually running. Reviewing can start before all the code is completed.

5-1.2 Coding

This part of the implementation phase, described fully in sections 5-3 to 5-5 and 5-10, translates the output of design into code in the implementation language. There are four elements of the translation: the life cycle, the class descriptions, the method bodies, and the data dictionary. In addition, real programs must be robust against errors. Section 5-6 discusses error detection and recovery in the light of the contractual model of programming.

Life Cycle.

The *life cycle* is translated into a *state machine*, which can then be implemented in the programming language. The translation process is straightforward, with interleaving presenting the most difficulty. Although translation of the life cycle can start as soon as analysis is complete, we delay discussion of it until section 5-10, as it is the least object-oriented part of the implementation process. Once the life cycle is implemented, it can serve as the framework on which the rest of the system is assembled.

Class Descriptions.

The Fusion class descriptions must be translated into the class notations of the implementation language, as described in section 5-3. Attributes become slots of their classes. Class-valued attributes are implemented by pointers for **unbound** attributes and may be implemented as embedded subobjects for **bound** attributes. Attributes marked **constant** in the class description can be made unassignable in the implementation class. Method declarations in a class description become the appropriate implementation-language feature: member functions in C++, routines in Eiffel, and generic functions in CLOS.

Once the attribute and method declarations have been translated, a "class stub" is constructed for the class, allowing its methods and attributes to be referred to by method bodies. The class stub includes the inheritance information from the Fusion class description, taking special care to account for the proper sharing of common parent classes. In C++ this stub is just the class declaration that would appear in a header file. In Smalltalk or CLOS, it is a partial implementation of the class, and in Eiffel it is a class definition with the method bodies implemented as exception-raising code.

Method Bodies.

The object interaction graphs and their associated text define the bodies of methods and system operations. The principal implementation decision is the handling of the iterations derived from messaging collections. Section 5-4 discusses these issues.

Data Dictionary.

Any functions, types, or predicates found in the data dictionary and used by methods must be implemented. Some non-class types will be supplied by the implementation language (e.g., integers, characters, and booleans). Others will have to be constructed, perhaps in terms of classes. Assertions in the data dictionary can affect *any* method in the system. Section 5-5 explains what must be done.

5-1.3 Order of Implementation

Fusion does not dictate a particular order of implementation; it is not necessary to first implement the life cycle, then all the class descriptions, then all the method bodies, and so forth. However, it is convenient to be *event driven*. Use the life cycle to order events. Choose system operations corresponding to early events, preferring the simpler operations first. Implement the classes required by those system operations, giving them the minimum functionality required for the system operations to work.

Then extend the implementation to cover later events. This will force the extension of partially implemented classes to meet their full specification. Eventually, all the system operations will be implemented, and the remaining functionality—typically generality for later extension—can be implemented.

5-1.4 Performance

Performance cannot be obtained by an independent "tuning" step in the implementation phase; it must be considered all the way through implementation, and designs must be evaluated against performance criteria. When a system is wasteful of any resource, it must be *profiled* to find out where the resource is being consumed. Once the "hot-spots," whether of space, time, or other resource, have been found, that code must be improved. Section 5-7 discusses general performance issues, and section 5-8 addresses store management.

5-1.5 Review

Once code has been produced, it should be reviewed. *Inspections* require that code be read and understood by people other than its author. *Testing* checks the actual behavior of the system, or part of the system, against predictions made from the requirements and specification. The goal of both is to detect errors before they escape into production code.

Code should be inspected as it is produced. This allows the inspection group to enforce (or develop) standards from the beginning of the implementation phase, and ensures that problem code does not lie hidden until it is too late. Similarly, testing should start early. Section 5-9 discusses reviews and testing in object-oriented code.

We do not discuss issues of maintainability, not because they are unimportant, but because it depends as much on local programming standards as it does on the details of object-orientation. However, chapter 9 contains material on the related issue of reuse.

5-2 OBJECT IDENTITY

Recall that an important property of objects is their *identity*—objects are distinguishable even if their attributes have the same value. This notion continues to be important in implementation.

When objects are represented as regions of store, one way to give them identity is by using their *storage address*. This is convenient—it is readily accessible, takes up no additional room in the object, and is easily tested. In Eiffel, objects are naturally handled by references, which correspond to addresses; the infix operator "=" compares *references*, which is to say identities, whereas the method **Equal** is used for comparing the *contents* of objects. In C++, pointer equality can be used as an identity test, while structural equality is handled by overloading "=" on class objects. Smalltalk and CLOS, in common with Eiffel, represent all objects via references, and provide tests for reference equality, for example, CLOS using Lisp's **EQ**.

Sometimes this approach breaks down. If the underlying object store does not have a notion of identity (e.g., when storing object representations in a relational database), then each object must be equipped with an explicit identity attribute, different for each object. This can be done by, for example, incrementing a counter on each object allocation and storing the counter in a reserved element of the object. A similar problem arises when an application is distributed across multiple address spaces (e.g., different computers); in this case, the use of object identity and object references has to be considered very carefully.

5-3 TRANSLATION OF CLASS DESCRIPTIONS

The class descriptions generated during the design phase provide most of the class specification: the attributes, method signatures, and position in inheritance hierarchy. Most object-oriented languages provide at least this much information in their own class notations, and some (such as C++) provide much more.

During translation, some Fusion identifiers may have to be renamed to avoid clashes with reserved words of the implementation language or implementation restrictions such as identifier length. These renamings should be noted in the data dictionary as part of the entry's description.

5-3.1 Attribute Declaration

The **attributes** of the class descriptions will usually be slots of the named class; that is, in C++ they will be class members, in Eiffel nonfunction features, and in Smalltalk they will be instance variables. (We use the term *slot* as an implementation-neutral way to refer to places in an object where a value can be stored.)

However, it is permissible, and may be necessary, to implement an attribute as a method. There are several reasons for doing this.

- The attribute may be a simple function of other variables. Rather than holding its value, it may be more effective to recompute it on demand; this can save a slot in every instance.

- There may be reason to expect the representation of the class to change, and permitting access to the slots may make this more difficult. This applies particularly if the language makes syntactic distinctions between slot access and zero-argument method invocation, as C++ does.

- Making access to a slot go via a method makes it easier to add and remove tracing code, or to monitor updates to slots in the event of errors being discovered in the code. The method can simply be recompiled and relinked into the application.

In C++, the wisest course is to make all member variables **private** or **protected**, and to provide access and update methods for slots that are part of the interface. Direct access to the slots can be provided if the type being implemented is normally identified with its representation (such as pairs, or points in the plane in window systems). Our examples provide direct access to keep them uncluttered.

Attribute Scope.

The attributes and methods of classes that appear in a Fusion class description are present because they express essential features of the design. Thus all methods and attributes of a server are in scope to any of its clients: In C++ terms all members are **public**, and in Eiffel all features are **exported**. However, an attribute that is referenced *only* by the methods of its class can be made **private** to that class, although this may make later extensions difficult.

Attributes and methods that may be introduced for implementation reasons, such as efficiency or to exploit some existing class library, should not be accessible outside the class. They should be made **private** in C++ and not be **exported** in Eiffel.

5-3.2 Attribute Types

Attribute types can be divided into three kinds: *object-valued* attributes, whose type is a class; *collection* attributes, whose type is **col** T for some type T; and the remaining *plain* attributes, whose types are neither classes nor collections.

Object-Valued Attributes.

An object-valued attribute should be implemented using a *pointer*. In Eiffel, Smalltalk, and the Lisp-based languages, this is the underlying implementation technique. In C++, a pointer or reference type is required, except when the attribute is **bound**, as in section 5-3.3. See 5.8 for some other implications of the use of pointers.

Collection Attributes.

A collection should be implemented as a suitable type from the implementation language's repertoire, considering all the operations that will be performed on it. Candidates include sets, bags, lists, vectors, and hash tables. Smalltalk has a rich collection of these as built-in classes, and various C++ libraries do too. A collection of objects should be implemented as a collection of *pointers* to objects.

Plain Attributes.

Attributes of nonclass types should be implemented in whatever way the programming language permits. See section 5-5.3 for suggestions on the implementation of non-Fusion types.

5-3.3 Attribute Qualifiers

Any attribute can have a mutability, but only object-valued attributes can have sharing or binding qualifiers. Mutability may be expressible directly in the programming language, but the other two qualifiers are not; usually they remain as constraints on the programmer or suggest alternative implementation strategies.

Mutability.

The mutability of an attribute controls whether or not it may be updated after initialization. C++'s **const** attribute has approximately the same meaning, and so **constant** attributes should be marked **const** in C++. Other implementation languages do not support the notion, allowing all fields to be mutable. In this case, the immutability of the attribute is an obligation on the programmer to assign to the slot only in initialization.

Note that an object will be represented as a pointer in C++ (except as discussed later) and that the **const** applies to the *pointer*, not to the thing pointed to.

Binding and Sharing.

The binding of an object-valued attribute allows the implementer tighter control over the lifetime of the server object. An **unbound** object must be implemented by some form of pointer, as discussed earlier. However, an object referred to by **bound** attribute can disposed of when the client object vanishes. A **constant bound** attribute can be implemented by *embedding* the server in the client—in C++ terms, by using a class type rather than a pointer-to-class type—so long as the class of that object is known exactly. If it might belong to some derived class not known at compile time, it cannot be embedded.

Any other references to a server object referred to by a **bound** attribute become illegal once the client has disposed of it.

The sharing of an object-valued attribute expresses how many additional references to the server object are permitted.

An object referred to by a **shared** attribute may be referred to in many other places. It can be freely passed as a parameter, returned as a result, or assigned into other variables. In C++, a **shared bound** attribute implemented by embedding must be converted to a reference before being passed as an object.

An **exclusive** attribute provides the only reference to its server. It should not be passed as a parameter or returned as a result. It can be assigned into another variable only if the **exclusive** attribute is made to refer to some other object before any other method is invoked.

Example: Depot **Attributes.**

Consider the class **Depot** whose description is presented in the previous chapter and reproduced in Figure 5.1.

```
class Depot
    attribute stores:shared bound col Storebuilding
    attribute constant depot_monitor:exclusive bound Monitor
    attribute loading_bay:exclusive bound LoadingBay

    method is_vulnerable( )
    method depot_status( )
endclass
```

Figure 5.1   Class Depot

We will ignore, for the moment, the method part of **Depot**, and concentrate on the attributes, assuming them to be implemented as slots in the class structure. In C++, this could appear as in Figure 5.2. **stores** is made part of the public part of the interface. The other attributes are used only in methods of **Depot**, so they are made **protected** (visible only to derived classes). Because loading_bay and depot_monitor are both **bound**, they are implemented by embedding, not by reference.

```
class Depot
    {
public:
    Set <Store &> stores;
protected:
    LoadingBay loading_bay;
    Monitor depot_monitor;
    };
```

Figure 5.2   Class Depot Represented in C++

There is no need for any special structure on the collection of stores, so we pick **Set**. (Although Fusion does not deal with general parameterized types, its collections *are* such types and can be implemented with any suitable C++ template class.) This decision is not immutable—if **Set** has overhead not shared by (for example) **List**, then **List** could be used. We assume the availability of a class library including at least sets and lists.

The elements of the set are given as *references* to **Store**s, as required by 5.3.2; the collection refers to **Store** objects kept elsewhere.

A full C++ class description requires constructors, destructors, and probably an overloading on assignment as well. The default constructor—which will run the default constructors for the components—is adequate for this example. If the component **Store** objects are not owned by the **Depot**, the default destructor will be adequate too. Given that we are unlikely to want to copy **Depot** objects in this application, defining a dummy **operator=** and making it **private** is the best approach.

The Eiffel implementation of the **Depot** attributes is shown in Figure 5.3. Again, **stores** is exported from the class. We assume the existence of a library of collection types and pick **Set** for the same reason as before. The elements of the set are automatically references—this is the default Eiffel behavior.

```
class Depot export
    stores
feature
    stores: Set [Store];
    depot_monitor: Monitor;
    loading_bay: LoadingBay;

    Create is
        do
        depot_monitor.Create;
        loading_bay.Create;
        stores.Create;
        end
end - - class Depot
```

Figure 5.3   Class Depot Represented in Eiffel

When a **Depot** object is constructed, by invoking **create**, it also creates its loading bay, store set, and monitor sub-objects. We assume that new **Set**s are empty.

5-3.4 Method Declaration

The **method**s of a Fusion class description are implemented by appropriate code in the corresponding programming-language class: they will be member functions in C++, routines in Eiffel, and methods in Smalltalk. In CLOS they become generic functions.

In Fusion, *all* methods are redefinable in descendant classes. This is the norm in Eiffel and Smalltalk, but not in C++, where redefinable member functions must be declared as **virtual** in the base class.

Virtual Methods in C++.

One weakness of C++ is that decisions about access control and virtuality must be made during development of the base class, thus requiring the developer to make assumptions about possible future uses of the class. In particular, as the use of **virtual** can reduce performance (section 5-7.3), there is a temptation to restrict its use to those classes intended to be used polymorphically.

However, Carroll [20] has demonstrated that the use of **virtual** may be required to permit even nonpolymorphic derivation. For similar reasons, use of the more restricting access control qualifiers should be very well justified to minimize the necessity of having to modify a base class to permit derivation.

Method Arguments.

Objects are passed to methods by reference, so that the server is referring to the same object as its client. In Eiffel, Smalltalk, and CLOS, this is the default. In C++, a reference type should be used. Sometimes, the use of references will result in a performance penalty (see section 5-7.2 for more details).

Collections will usually be passed by reference and other argument types by value, again subject to performance considerations.

Example: Depot **Methods.**

Using the same class description as before (this time omitting the attribute translations), we have Figures 5.4 and 5.5.

```
class Depot
    {
public:
        virtual void depot_status( );
        virtual void is_vulnerable( );
    };
```

Figure 5.4   Class Depot with C++ Member Functions

```
class Depot export
        depot_status, is_vulnerable
feature
        depot_status is do ... end
        is_vulnerable is do ... end
end - - class Depot
```

Figure 5.5   Class Depot with Eiffel Routines

Anticipating section 5-7 on performance slightly, in this application we happen to know that Depot is not subclassed. In this case, it is possible to make both C++ methods non-**virtual** without changing the meaning of the program. Even if Depot were to be part of an inheritance lattice, if all references to Depot-like objects were direct (i.e., not through pointers or references), it would still be permissible to make the methods non-**virtual**.

5-3.5 Inheritance

The **isa** clauses of class descriptions name the parents of the given class. The order in which the parents appear does not matter in Fusion. Note that Fusion's inheritance scheme *shares* common parent classes (see appendix C). This has language-specific consequences.

- In C++, class derivations which share base classes should make appropriate use of **virtual**. (Automatic use of **virtual** should be avoided because it introduces a performance penalty.)

- In Eiffel, repeated inheritance results in sharing by default. It is possible to arrange for individual *features*, as opposed to *classes*, to be duplicated rather than shared (using renaming), but such abilities are beyond the scope of this chapter.

- In single-inheritance languages, such as traditional Smalltalk, multiple inheritance has to be implemented by the programmer. The dynamic typing of Smalltalk makes this straightforward, as it is only necessary to provide code for the full set of methods and "forward" them to appropriate objects, but any such device must consider the sharing properties of Fusion inheritance.

5-4 METHOD BODIES

The object interaction graphs contain much of the information required for the implementation of the method bodies. Each system operation has been decomposed into the invocations it may make on the collaborating objects, sequencing is available on the diagrams, and the text (or pseudocode) annotations provide further information. Schemata for complex sub-methods may be provided. Most method bodies end up being relatively simple, but there are four issues that require further detail: *error handling*, *iteration*, *local variables*, and the special method **create**. Error handling is dealt with in section 5-6.

5-4.1 Iteration

Iteration arises from invoking methods on collections. (Message invocations *from* collections reduce to invocations by some object *in* the collection, and hence need no special implementation work.) In the simplest case, that is, when no **Predicate** appears on the message on the object interaction graph, a method invoked on a collection is invoked on *all* the elements of that collection.

In languages that allow methods to be passed as arguments, collections may provide *mapping functions*, which apply some argument method to each element in the collection. Where such mapping functions are provided, and the collection type is appropriate, use them. It is likely to be more efficient than code you write yourself. (The implementer can use fast hidden access methods to retrieve the next element to be messaged, because the context is known.)

In the next simplest case, the method is invoked on a subset of the objects in the collection, namely those satisfying the selection predicate. It is less common for a collection class to supply a mapping function with a filter (i.e., a predicate to select elements), and so it will be necessary to write some explicit iterations.

It is tempting to write the following abstract loop:

```
for element in collection do
        if predicate( element ) then element.method( args ) endif
endfor
```

This is *incorrect* when execution of the method on one element might change whether or not another element would satisfy **predicate**. Recall that the elements to be messaged are decided (by using the predicate) *before* any invocations occur.

The correct approach is to gather all the selected elements into a separate collection first and then iterate over all the elements of that collection. Because this temporary collection is only there as a "loading bay" for the elements, it can be any convenient collection type—it does *not* need to be the same kind of collection as the original. This is, of course, less efficient than testing the predicate on the fly. If the overhead is intolerable, and yet correctness would be compromised, this area of the design would have to be reviewed.

The most complex case is that where the invocation has both a selection condition **Select** and a stopping condition **Stop**. In this case, either of the **Stop** condition and the method send might interfere with **Select**; and yet part of the point of the **Stop** condition might be to eliminate the necessity for building a complete sub-collection! In these circumstances, the designers of the object interaction graph must make their intentions clear in the description associated with the diagram.

5-4.2 Local Variables

The body of a method may require an object-valued local variable. When this refers to an existing object, the normal implementation technique of references may be used. However, a local variable may refer to a **new** object. In this case, there are two possibilities.

The object may outlive the invocation of the method. In this case, it must be given full rights: in C++, it will be allocated by **new**, or possibly out of some implementation-specific pool of objects. In Eiffel and Smalltalk, this is the norm. This corresponds to **unbound** for class attributes.

The object may be needed only for the duration of the method. In C++ and later versions of Eiffel, it may be implemented by value rather than using a reference. This reduces storage management overhead and corresponds to **bound** for class attributes.

5-4.3 Special Method create

Recall that the method **create** on an object interaction graph is special; it marks the point at which a **new** object is initialized. In C++, **create** corresponds to a *constructor* method (i.e., a method whose name is the same as that of its class). The body of such a constructor must implement the specification of **create**. It is not possible to inspect a C++ object between the moment its store is allocated (implied by **new** on the object interaction graph) and when its constructor has been applied.

Similarly, in Eiffel the Fusion **create** corresponds to the Eiffel special feature with the same name; again, it is not possible in Eiffel to make a new object without applying **create** to it. (In fact, Eiffel's **create** corresponds to a Fusion **new** immediately followed by an invocation of Fusions **create**.)

In Smalltalk it *is* possible to create instances of a class without having them "properly" initialized. Code written to implement Fusion methods should never need to do this, except in the very process of **creat**ion.

5-4.4 Process of Putting It Together

We are now in a position to give examples of code developed from object interaction graphs. Continuing with the ECO example, we shall show C++ code for the is_vulnerable operation and Eiffel code for **depot_status**.

Example: is_vulnerable.

Consider Figure 5.6, which reproduces the object interaction graph for is_vulnerable. A possible encoding of this in C++ appears in Figure 5.7.

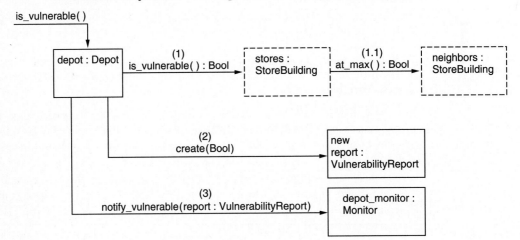

Description:
operation Depot : is_vulnerable( )
  Find out if there is a store in the depot that is vulnerable.   (1)
    If there is, then create a 'true' vulnerability report.   (2)
    Else create a 'false' vulnerability report.
  Notify the manager about the vulnerability report.   (3)

method StoreBuilding : is_vulnerable( ) : Bool
  If the store is at maximum capacity then
    Find out if a neighboring store building is at maximum capacity. (1.1)
    If it is then return true else return false.
  Else return false

method StoreBuilding : at_max( ) : Bool
  If store is at maximum capacity then return true.
  Else return false.

Figure 5.6 Graph for is_vulnerable

```
void Depot::is_vulnerable( )
    {
    Bool vulnerable = FALSE;
    for (Index i = stores.start( ); i.more( ); i.next( ))                    // (1)
        if (i.element( ).at_max( ))
            for (Index j = i.neighbors.start( ); j.more( ); j.next( ))       // (1.1)
                if (j.element.at_max( )) vulnerable = TRUE;                  // (1.1)
    depot_monitor.notify_vulnerable( VulReport( vulnerable ) );             // (2, 3)
    }
```

Figure 5.7   is_vulnerable in C++

Let us discuss the assumptions that have been made here. We have not (explicitly) decided on a type for the **stores** of the depot (or for the **neighbors** of the stores), but we have assumed that there is a way of iterating over the elements of that type.

- **stores.start** must deliver an **Index** object, representing an iteration in progress and initialized to refer to the first element of the collection ("first" from the viewpoint of the iteration).

- **Index::more** must deliver **TRUE** if there are more uninspected elements in the collection, and **FALSE** if no more remain to be inspected.

- **Index::next** must advance the index to the next object in the collection.

- **Index::element** must supply a reference to the current element of the collection.

The reader eager for optimizations will note that, if **at_max** has no side effects, it would be possible to message the **depot_monitor** as soon as any store was found that was itself **at_max** and with an **at_max** neighbor, and then immediately return from **is_vulnerable**. Of course, such an optimization would be rendered ineffective if vulnerability reports were to be made more detailed, for example, by saying *which* stores were themselves at risk.

VulReport converts the boolean **vulnerable** into a vulnerability report suitable for handing on to the depot monitor—that is, it handles the **new** and **create** of the **VulnerabilityReport** object.

Example: depot_status.

Consider the object interaction graph for **depot_status** (Figure 5.8, reproduced from chapter 3). This could be implemented within the Eiffel class **Depot** by the code of Figure 5.9. Notice how the multiple invocations on the arrows with the sequencer **(2)** have been interleaved in the loop, as suggested by the annotation of the diagram.

We make various assumptions about the behavior of the undefined entities of the code. An **AllocationList** maintains some map of stores to drums, initialized to empty on creation. Creating a **Report** requires an allocation list and a collection of drums, such as that returned by asking **loading_bay** its **status**. For iterating over the various stores, **Set**s can supply **SetWalker**s, which can supply successive elements of the set on demand, similarly to Index earlier. In a full development, of course, these would not be assumptions, but part of the documented behavior of the classes.

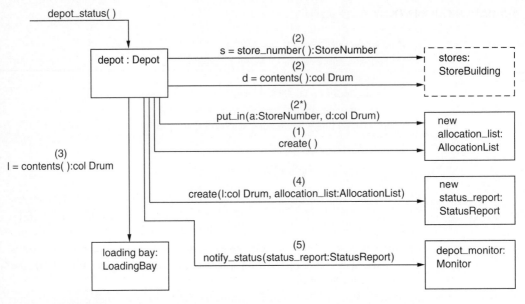

Description:
operation Depot : depot_status( )

Create a new allocation list.	(1)
For all s in the stores collection put details of the store contents into the allocation list.	(2)
Retrieve details of the contents of the loading bay.	(3)
Create a new status report initialized with the loading bay contents and the allocation list.	(4)
Notify the depot monitor of the status report.	(5)

Figure 5.8 Graph for depot_status

```
depot_status is
    local
        s: SetWalker [Store];      - - will iterate over stores
        alloc: AllocationList;     - - short for allocation_list
        report: StatusReport;      - - short for status_report
    do
        alloc.Create;              - - (1)
        s.Create; – part of (2)
        from                       - - from ... end is rest of (2), (2*)
            s := stores.start
        until
            s. finished
        loop
            alloc.put_in( s.this.store_number, s.this.contents );
            s.next
        end
        - - (3), (4), and (5), sequenced by feature call
        monitor.notify_status( report.Create( alloc, loading_bay.contents ) )
    end
```

Figure 5.9 depot_status in Eiffel

5-5 DATA DICTIONARY

The data dictionary contains supporting definitions used in the description of the system being implemented. Some of these things—classes, attributes, and methods, for example—are handled by the rest of the design and implementation process. In this section, we deal with those remaining: predicates, functions, assertions, types, and events.

Note that only those dictionary entries that are used by methods need be implemented. Entries whose purpose is to make the analysis clear, but that have been "designed away," can be ignored.

5-5.1 Functions and Predicates

It is convenient to regard predicates just as special cases of functions with Boolean results, so we shall use the term "function" to refer to both in this section. Functions in the data dictionary are used to capture behavior shared by schemata. Any that are used by method bodies have to be implemented. Two issues arise: the expressiveness of the language in which they are written, and whether or not the implementation language supports nonmethod functions.

Expressiveness.

Fusion does not prescribe the language in which to write function bodies: this is left to the users of the method. These bodies must be translated into the implementation language. If the language used in the data dictionary is at a much higher level than the implementation language, then this is nontrivial.

Only Methods Allowed.

Some languages (Eiffel, Smalltalk) have no notion of functions that are not methods; others (C++, CLOS) do. When a function must be translated into a language of the first kind, a class for the resulting method must be chosen.

Sometimes one of the arguments of the function provides an obvious "home class"; in this case, the techniques of chapter 4 can be used to decompose the body. Otherwise, one of the arguments has to be picked arbitrarily or another class introduced to hold the method. Such classes should be designed as carefully as those that arise naturally during analysis.

5-5.2 Assertions

Assertions arise when the analysis stage of Fusion needs to state global properties of the system. They have effects on different scales: they may apply to single objects, to several related objects, to all objects of some class, or all objects in the system.

All code must respect every assertion. The power this gives to assertions during analysis is reflected in the heavy responsibility of the implementer to respect them. The execution of a method must maintain an assertion, and (in robust code) when an assertion becomes **false** some kind of error should be raised.

The easiest assertions to handle are those that make statements about all objects of a single class. Because object orientation only permits modifications to be made to objects by the methods of a class, assertions can be violated only by such methods.

If the methods of a class are kept together (as is encouraged in C++ and required in Eiffel), it is straightforward to check that the assertion is maintained.

Surprisingly, it is more difficult to provide code for assertions about a *single* object. This is because the only place available to check or maintain such assertions is in methods belonging to the class of that object, which are thereby cluttered by checks to see if they are being applied to *that* object rather than some more mundane sibling.

Finally, assertions that relate objects of different classes must be maintained by code that appears, in principle, in *all* methods of *all* of those classes. In practice, of course, the checks or maintenance can be confined to those methods that change attributes and relationships mentioned in the assertion.

5-5.3 Types

The data dictionary is not restricted in the kinds of types it can describe. These have to be mapped into the implementation language. Data dictionary types will usually fall into one of the following categories:

- *Enumerations.* These are named, distinct, simple values; see appendix C for details. They can be implemented directly in languages that support them, such as C++, or as named (usually integer) constants in other languages.
- *Records or vectors.* The implementation language may support these directly, or it may be necessary to implement them as classes. C++ **struct**s serve as records (and are, in fact, degenerate classes), and arrays and pointers implement tuples. Eiffel provides vector classes. Smalltalk uses classes for records and has special support for vectors.
- *Collections* (*lists, sets, sequences*). These may be supported directly by the language and its libraries. If not, they must be implemented as part of this development stage, using language support for parameterized types. Even when the provided implementation is richer than required, it is worth using:
  - The more a type is used, the more likely it is that errors in it will be detected and removed, and the more incentive for the supplier to make it efficient.
  - Effort spent on implementing a new type is effort not available elsewhere.
- *Other parameterised types.* Eiffel and C++ both support parameterization of types, C++ with *templates*, and Eiffel with *generic classes*. Smalltalk and CLOS support parameterized types by virtue of dynamic typing, at the cost of losing compile-time type checking.
- *Functional types.* It is sometimes convenient to treat functions (or methods) as data in the analysis stage. This presents no problems when implementing in C++ or CLOS, both of which allow functions to be treated as data. It is not directly possible in Eiffel; however, a function like object (sometimes called a "functionoid") can be implemented as an instance of a class with one method. The method performs the required action and is invoked in the usual way. C++ even allows the usual function-call notation to be overloaded on such objects.

5-5.4 Events

There are two kinds of events: input events and output events. Input events arrive from the environment, possibly carrying extra information, and they need to be represented in the program. Output events are generated by the program as a result of system operations.

One simple choice is to represent input events as a range of integers starting at zero (or one); this is especially convenient for the state machines used in the life cycle. (e.g., see Figure 5.23). However, if input events carry data, this is inadequate. In this case, events can be represented as classes, each different class being used to carry the data appropriate to its event, and all such class inheriting from one **Event** class. It is convenient if **Event** then carries the event number.

Output events, if they need to be manipulated, can be treated similarly.

5-6 ERROR HANDLING

Exactly what counts as an error varies among languages, programmers, and designers. In Fusion, we define an error as

The violation of a precondition.

Following Meyer [80] we adopt the *contractual* model of programming, where each method promises to achieve its postcondition if it is invoked with its precondition **true**. In turn, each method is obliged to invoke any further methods with *their* preconditions **true**. If the precondition of every system operation is **true** whenever that operation could be invoked (i.e., when it is permitted by the life cycle), then the execution of the system will achieve the desired results.

If the system has been built correctly, then no method will ever be called with its precondition **false**, and error conditions will never arise. But people are fallible, and it is wise for our systems to be robust against both internal and external failure. How should we cope with this in our implementations? There are two aspects to consider: the *detection* of errors and *recovery* from errors.

5-6.1 Error Detection

A naive approach to error detection is to start the body of each method with code to test the precondition. This approach has three disadvantages.

1. It may be difficult or impossible to express the precondition in the programming language. For example, the precondition may assert that a solution to some equation exists without specifying what it is. Or it might state some global property of the system, not all of which is visible to the executing method. Programming languages are, for good reasons, weak at expressing the full range of mathematical possibilities. (When preconditions are expressed only in natural language, it is even more difficult translate them into code.)

2. The performance overhead of testing the precondition may be prohibitive. For example, suppose that a graph-theoretic algorithm works only on acyclic graphs. The test for acyclicity is nontrivial, and the cost of executing it may be far greater

than the cost of the algorithm itself. (The graph may have been required to be acyclic precisely to avoid such overheads in the algorithm.)

3. Some conditions belong to the system, or perhaps to a class rather than to a single precondition. (Another way to look at it is that they are found in *every* precondition *and* every postcondition.) For example, a graph may be required to remain acyclic.

The advantages of the approach—that errors are detected as soon as practicable, and that as a consequence more informative messages can be generated—mean that it should be considered despite the disadvantages. Typically such checks are conditionally compiled, so that "production" versions of the code can run at full speed while still being built from the same source as the checked version. (This has, however, been likened to requiring sailors to wear life jackets while practicing on land but discarding them once at sea.)

Eiffel encourages preconditions and postconditions to be attached to any routine, using them to define the semantics of methods. It also allows *invariants* to be attached to classes. It is possible to compile a system with varying amounts of condition checking enabled; this addresses disadvantage 2. Class invariants are convenient places to handle global assertions, weakening disadvantage 3. And, by permitting conditions to contain a mixture of executed code and commentary, it attempts to cope with problem 1.

C++ has no such machinery, instead supplying a macro **assert** to check that a condition is **true**. (**assert** is based on the ability to abort an executing program; there is nothing particularly special about it otherwise.) The programmer has the responsibility of placing these assertions appropriately, and enabling or disabling them as performance and robustness dictate. It is wise for a project to have a set of rules governing the definition and use of a collection of such assertion-checking macros.

5-6.2 Error Recovery

It is one thing to detect an error and another to know how to respond once an error has been detected. One rule of thumb is

> *Do not test for an error whose presence you cannot handle.*

Fusion permits *anything* to happen when a precondition is violated. This grants implementers the freedom to do whatever they like—including doing nothing—and one option is to abort the program. This is definitely not robust behavior. But if a precondition is violated, then the program is already broken, so how can it be expected to recover?

One approach is to raise an *exception*. Exceptions generally cause control to be passed in some nonstandard way to an *exception handler*, which can execute code in an attempt to fix the error. The contractual model of programming gives rules for using exception handling in constructs for those languages that have them.

Code should raise exceptions on discovering errors. Our definition of error means that the method detecting the error cannot satisfy its contract because its invoker has defaulted on its part of the bargain. Raising the exception notifies the caller that the method has failed. *Handling* the exception means that the handler should either fix the error—that is, satisfy its own contractual obligations in some other way—or, in turn, admit that it cannot do so.

Exceptions in Eiffel.

Eiffel provides exactly such an exception-handling mechanism: if an exception occurs in a method, *rescue* code is executed, which may try and fix the problem and retry execution of the entire method. If the rescue code does not retry the method, the exception is passed up to the next invoker, and so on, until either a handler can successfully fix the problem or the program dies (which is, in fact, a degenerate case, the "fix" being to abandon the program).

This implies that some method has instead of the "natural" interface suggested by

assumes: Precondition

result: Postcondition

the more forgiving interface

assumes: **true**

result: (Precondition **and** Postcondition)
   or ((**not** Precondition) **and** OtherPostcondition)

where **OtherPostcondition** describes what the state looks like when **Precondition** was **false**.

Eiffel programmers should use its exception-handling abilities to make their programs more robust. See [80] for further instructive discussion on this point.

Exceptions in C++.

The Annotated Reference Manual [40] introduced an exception-handling mechanism into C++. This mechanism is not yet standard in C++ compilers, and its implementations may be deficient. If an Eiffel-style exception handling method is desired, it can be imitated using C++ exceptions as shown in Figure 5.10.

```
try
    {
    }
catch (...)
    {
    // attempt to patch up state
    // Either: satisfy postcondition or: raise exception again
    }
```

Figure 5.10   Error Handling in C++

Some aspects of the Eiffel **retry** can be obtained by labeling the **try** statement and recovering with a **goto** the label. Eiffel allows the **retry** to be executed within a method invocation, but the C++ **goto** cannot cross function boundaries. C++ provides additional information about the exception, which may help in deciding the recovery action. Note that the exception-handling strategy should be determined for an entire application (program, library, etc.) rather than being an ad hoc scattering of techniques.

5-7 PERFORMANCE

The performance of a system cannot always be decoupled from its correctness. For example, many real-time systems *must* be fast enough to handle incoming data; otherwise they will be wrong and possibly dangerous. Interactive systems must be responsive to the user; if they are too slow, they can be uncomfortable, or impossible, to use.

Systems must be built within the bounds of predetermined constraints on space and time. Inefficient coding will result in unsatisfactory systems. There is usually a trade-off between space and time requirements. Efficient performance may require extra space; effective use of memory may require additional table lookups affecting performance. As usual, each system should be judged separately. Effective solutions in one domain may not apply to other domains.

The most important rules of performance improvement are the following:

- Performance cannot be obtained as an afterthought.
- Optimizing rarely executed code is ineffective.

The first rule says that performance must be considered throughout the analysis, design, and implementation process. It is not necessary to be obsessive about it; it *is* necessary to be convinced that performance leaks are not an intrinsic part of the design. A system that runs ten times too slowly is unlikely to meet its performance requirements by tuning its individual parts.

The second rule is obvious and yet often ignored. For object-oriented code, even more than traditional code, it is difficult for the programmer to have a good feel for where its resources, such as time or space, are going. This leads to the imperative:

- Profile your system in as many ways as you can.

If your implementation language has performance monitoring tools, use them. If it has not, develop them, or institute a programming style that makes it easy to get performance numbers. Monitor both time and space. If there are other important resources—such as disc blocks, windows, network connections, open files, and window display regions—monitor those. Use the information to decide where to concentrate your efforts.

There are several techniques that can be used, individually and in combination, for controlling performance trade-offs. We shall discuss three aspects, with particular application to C++.

- Inline methods
- Values *versus* references
- Dynamic method binding

5-7.1 Inline Methods

An inline method is a method whose body, with appropriate parameter substitutions, can be inserted at each point where it is invoked. Such inlined calls are (typically) faster, because the overhead of the normal method call is avoided, but more significantly because the method body is available for optimization by the compiler. This technique is available in C++, although in principle it could be used in any language with a sufficiently sophisticated compiler. Judicious use of macros, preprocessors, or simple cut-and-paste editing can have similar benefits, albeit in a rather more haphazard way.

Carefully applied, inlining can introduce significant improvements in performance. The existence of inlining makes it reasonable to use very small methods, for clarity, and for the code to run as fast as if written with larger methods. Should *all* methods be declared inline? No, for the following reasons:

- It is usually pointless to inline large functions; the overhead of calling them is insignificant. (If the inlining can make large optimizations available it can still be worth it.)
- Excessive use of inlined functions can lead to "code bloat," which can *reduce* performance in paging environments or when the processor cache is small.
- Use of inline member functions in a class means that a change to the implementation of the function will require that all the code that uses that function be recompiled. If the function were not inlined, then only relinking would be necessary. This can increase development time.
- Inlined functions can increase compilation time and space requirements.

The decision as to what functions to inline should be made in the light of the performance measurements made on the system. As a general rule, simple access methods can usually be made inline with little danger of bloating code.

5-7.2 References versus Values

In languages like C++, where objects may be embedded in other objects or allocated directly on the stack, the implementer has to decide whether objects should be passed to methods, or allocated as attributes, as the *object* or as a *reference* to that object.

Method Arguments.

Class-valued arguments to methods should be passed by reference, reflecting the importance of object identity. However, passing by reference introduces an extra level of indirection in accessing values, which can lead to complex structures and aliasing problems. These do not arise with passing objects by value, but copying objects can be space consuming. In C++, where even stack allocation of objects can invoke constructors and destructors, it can also be surprisingly time-consuming.

Only when the identity of a class-valued argument to a method is unimportant, and the overhead of constructing and destroying a new object is less than the cost of indirection, should class-valued arguments be passed by value. The issue does not arise in Eiffel or Smalltalk, where the option of pass-by-value is not available.

Class-Valued Attributes.

In C++, a subobject (a class-valued attribute) may be stored as a reference or by value. The option is not available in Smalltalk and has only been added to the later versions of Eiffel. There are three reasons why it is more efficient to contain subobjects physically rather than maintaining a reference to them.

First, accessing values can be done directly rather than through the reference. Indirection costs, sometimes heavily. Note, though, that once the reference has been loaded into a machine register, access to other components of the object may be just as cheap as if the object were embedded. Once again, measurement is the key.

Second, there is no extra freestore allocation and deallocation, and the synchronization of subobject and object lifetimes is guaranteed.

Third, because the C++ compiler knows that the static and dynamic type of the subobject coincide, virtual functions can be statically bound, removing levels of indirection in function call. This can be even more effective if the virtual method is inlined.

When the attribute is **bound**, the implementer is free to embed the subobject. When it is **unbound**, however, this freedom is unavailable. If performance requires the use of embedded objects, the design will have to be revisited.

Cline [24] recommends that references are used for application domain objects. An application domain object may be referenced in many contexts, and therefore its identity is more important than its value. Because application domain objects will be accessed less frequently, the performance costs associated with resolving references are less important. In contrast, lower-level objects are smaller and are typically accessed more frequently. They may have been introduced as part of the design, and their identity may be unimportant. For them, embedding is the better choice.

5-7.3 Impact of Dynamic Binding

Dynamic binding is the process whereby the actual method code for a method invocation is selected. It is required when a method accepts arguments of any subtype of its argument type, and the compiler cannot determine at compile time what the actual type of an argument is. This is the norm in Smalltalk (where there are no static types) and Eiffel (when objects are usually handed around by reference, and a reference to an object of class **C** may refer to any object of any subtype of **C**). In C++, it is required when invoking a virtual method on an object accessed though a pointer or C++ reference.

Clearly, dynamic method binding is slower than static binding. But, in general, the often-cited performance hit resulting from dispatching dynamically bound messages is not an issue with C++. Gorlen [49] has measured the effects of dynamic dispatch on a Sun-3/50 running SunOS 3.5 and release 2.0 of the AT&T C++ translator. Figure 5.11 summarizes the results and reports a factor of 2.9 increase in overhead for a virtual call. Reed [90] reports similar results but points out that a fair comparison should also consider the functionality that virtual calls replace. Functionality equivalent to dynamic binding i.e., **shape**→**draw** in C++) is achieved in C using a union and switch statement as illustrated in Figure 5.12. For such constructs, dynamic binding through virtual functions can improve performance.

Member Function Type	Overhead(μ)s	Ratio of Overhead to Nonvirtual Member Function
Nonvirtual	3.6	1.0
Virtual	7.6	2.1
Virtual baseclass nonvirtual	4.1	1.2
Virtual baseclass virtual	10.3	2.9

Figure 5.11   Member Function Call Execution Overhead

```
switch (shape->type)
    {

    case circle: /* draw a circle */
        draw_circle(shape);
        break;

    case square: /* draw a square */
        draw_square(shape);
        break;

}
```

Figure 5.12   Polymorphism in C

In most cases, the flexibility that virtual functions give the programmer outweighs the effects on performance. Dynamic binding and virtual functions should be used when it is natural to regard a subclass instance as a superclass instance. For example, when drawing a collection of **Shapes**, the actual elements of the collection may be **Circles** or **Squares**, but each element can be regarded as a **Shape** to draw it.

A comparison of virtual functions with inlined functions is less favorable. Dynamic dispatching and the resultant dynamic table lookup can obstruct the optimizations of a compiler. For example, using a virtual function in an inner loop results in an order of magnitude or more decrease in speed as the compiler cannot vectorize and unravel the loop. This is because a virtual function call requires a table lookup, and only loops with simple machine instruction bodies can be optimized by vectorisation. Lea [69] proposes some changes to the type system of C++, which would give the developer the ability to indicate whether virtual functions should be statically or dynamically bound. This would enable a programmer to customize the binding of virtual function calls to methods.

5-8 OBJECT LIFETIME

An important issue alluded to, but avoided, in our discussions of correctness and performance is that of *object destruction*. When there is no further use for an object, any resources it uses can be reclaimed by the system; the most obvious such resource is the store occupied by the object, but other resources include file descriptors, window handles, and dictionary entries. Two issues arise. First, how can we tell if an object is no longer required? And second, how can we arrange for its resources to be reclaimed?

5-8.1 Lost Objects

Objects allocated as local variables on the language control stack, such as local variables in C++, have their store reclaimed on exit from their scope. This process is automatic, and unavoidable, and in C++ the problem for local objects is not so much to ensure that they are properly disposed of as to ensure that no references to such objects remain. A reference to a destroyed object is said to be a *dangling* reference. Using such a reference is an error, but C++ systems are not obliged to notice it, and inadvertent use of a dangling reference will make the system become unpredictable.

The C++ programmer must thus ensure that references to local objects do not persist beyond the lifetime of the object itself. Interfaces that accept pointers or references to objects—indeed, to any C++ type except functions, which cannot be reclaimed—should document how long they expect that reference to be valid for. Where the stack-based lifetime for an object is inadequate, consideration should be given to allocating the object on the *heap*, using **new**.

Objects allocated in the heap (normal for Eiffel, Smalltalk, and CLOS, and those using **new** in C++) are harder to handle. It is no longer easy to determine when an object becomes useless, for so long as any reference to it remains, it may be accessed. There are three broad strategies that can be used.

The first strategy is *garbage collection*. When a request for store cannot be satisfied (and perhaps at other convenient moments, such as when waiting for the next input event, or when no response to external events is needed for a known time) the store of the program is examined, looking from some well-defined starting places (such as global variables and stack frames) to find all objects still in use. The remaining store, being inaccessible, can be recycled. Clearly this requires that descriptions of store layouts be accessible at run time, and that pointers cannot be "concealed" from the garbage collector. Because of this, garbage collection is usually supplied as part of a language, where it frees programmers from many of the burdens of store management.

The second strategy is *reference counting*. In this technique, the system keeps track of the number of references to a particular object. When another reference to an object is made, such as it being passed by reference to a method, or being reference assigned to a variable, the count is incremented. When a reference goes away (e.g., a reference variable goes off scope, or a containing object is destroyed), the count is decremented. When the number of references goes down to zero, the object is lost, and its memory is reclaimed. Naive reference counting algorithms do not work for cyclic structures (such as doubly linked lists) because such a structure may not be externally referenced, but each element can be "kept alive" by other elements in the list. A common source of errors in the InterViews [76] tool kit has been attributed to reference counting problems.

The third strategy is less general. Where some set of objects have a lifetime bounded in some way, they may be allocated out of a *pool* of objects; when their lifetime ends, the entire pool is reclaimed in one go. This works best for structures where many objects are allocated and processed, none being lost, until a moment when they may *all* be lost. For example, this can be used for allocating parse trees in a compiler; the tree can be constructed for a top-level unit (perhaps a procedure), transformed (doing scope and type analysis), and then discarded once code generation is complete.

There are two other approaches, neither of which is particularly deserving of the name "strategy." One is to trust that there is enough store available to hold all the objects a program will create, and do no explicit de-allocation. This works only for small programs on large enough machines. The other is to trust in the programmers intuition about the right points to destroy objects. Neither approach is recommended for production software.

Eiffel and the Lisp-based object-oriented languages have garbage collection provided as part of the run-time system, and so the programmer is left only with the task of avoiding the generation of unnecessary objects. Because it is part of the underlying system, it can be made general and reasonably efficient. However, the design aims and implementation strategies of C++ act against providing garbage collection in a safe, secure form (see later). They do, however, permit the programmer to provide reference counting in a reasonably convenient fashion, and we shall discuss this in more detail.

5-8.2 C++ and Garbage Collection

There are no commercially available garbage collectors for C++, although there are several research prototypes available. This means that relying on garbage collection to reclaim objects will reduce program portability (unless you are prepared to port the garbage collector too). To enjoy the benefits of automatic garbage collection for C++, stringent programming practices must be adopted, for the following reason.

The types of objects in C++ are, in general, not available at run time. Thus it is not possible to tell, given a pointer to a piece of store, what kind of object that object represents. Even supposing that the compiler collaborated with the garbage collector—perhaps by leaving store maps in the program—the types of objects in C++ can be obscured by casting. For example, a pointer referencing an object may be cast to an integer. The garbage collector will not be able to check that such an object is still alive as its references masquerade as integers or other types. Hence, a "live" object may be collected, violating the safety requirements of storage management.

One solution is to prohibit such programming practices. Another is to mark such objects as *uncollectable*, but this then has consequences for the space requirements of such programs. More detail on different garbage collection algorithms and their use in C++ development can be found in [33].

5-8.3 Reference Counting in C++

Readers who are not experienced in C++ may wish to skip this section.

It is much easier to do reference counting than garbage collection in C++. (The reader is again referred to [33].) The simplest (not necessarily the best) technique is as follows.

Suppose that some class **X**, whose objects are likely to be allocated on the heap, is to be controlled by reference counting. We invent a class **X_rep** to describe the objects, and give it an additional member, its **count**, initialized to **1** when an instance is created.

The class **X** has a body consisting only of a *pointer* to an **X_rep** object. Whenever such an **X** object is constructed, it must refer to an **X_rep**, and increments its count. When an **X** object is destroyed, the **X_rep** object's count is decremented; if this count goes to zero, no references to the **X_rep** object remain, and it can be deleted.

Of course, more has to be done with such objects than simply creating and destroying them; all the interesting methods belong to **X_rep** objects, not **X** objects. So the class **X** must have a method for each method of **X_rep** which just "forwards" the method to its embedded object. Careful choices for the constructors of **X** allow **X**'s to be made with new **X_rep**'s inside them.

Here is an example, using strings. Figure 5.13 shows the C++ class description that could be used for manipulating strings; Figure 5.14 shows the underlying representation of strings. Note that both of these descriptions are incomplete—they are intended to give the flavor of the technique rather than being definitive.

```
class String
    {
public:
    int length( ) { return actual->length; }
    String( const char *chars )
        { actual = new StringBase( chars ); }
    ~String( )
        { if (- -actual->count == 0) delete actual; }
    String &operator=( const String &string )
        {
        string.actual->count++;
        if (- -actual->count = = 0) delete actual;
        actual = string.actual;
        return *this;
        }
private:
    StringBase *actual;
        };
```

Figure 5.13 Class String

In **String**, there is just one way of making a new object, by providing a (C-style) string. A **StringBase** is allocated on the heap, and the slot **actual** points to it. When

```
class StringBase
    {
    friend String;
private:
    int length;
    int count;
    char *chars;
    void init( const char *given_chars )
        {
        length = strlen( given_chars );
        chars = new char [length + 1];
        strcpy( chars, given_chars );
        }
    StringBase( const char *given_chars )
        {
        this->init( given_chars );
        count = 1;
        }
    StringBase &operator=( const StringBase &base )
        {
        if (chars != base.chars)
            {
            delete [ ] chars;
            this->init( base.chars );
            }
        return *this;
        }
    ~StringBase( ) { delete [ ] chars; }
    };
```

Figure 5.14 Class StringBase

the **String** is destroyed, the count of its **StringBase** is decremented and the **StringBase** destroyed if there are no more references.

Copying one **String** into another increments the count of the "new" string, decrements the count of the "old" string (the order is *important*—consider the case in which both **String**s point to the same **StringBase**), and then assigns the new pointer into the **actual** slot.

Note that the **length** operation on **String**s just fetches the **length** member from the associated **StringBase**.

StringBase objects can be constructed from strings, when they allocate space for a copy of the string and point to the copy, setting the length at the same time. Destroying the **StringBase** just needs to delete the underlying string. Precautions have to be taken in assignment to ensure that assigning a **StringBase** to itself does not involve unwarrented destruction of its contents.

5-9 REVIEWS

Just as our acknowledgment of human fallibility leads us to protect our code with error-handlers, we must protect the development process with checks. In the absence of completely automatic tools, we must take other measures to catch mistakes before they escape into production code.

This section considers the applicability of traditional verification techniques to object-oriented software development. Ghezzi et al. [46] discuss three basic approaches to verification: analysis, testing, and symbolic execution. Inspections are one of the primary analysis techniques for verifying software. Differences in the structure of function-oriented and object-oriented software, however, limit the efficiency of traditional inspection procedures. We discuss inspection techniques appropriate for object-oriented software. Standard techniques for testing software are also reexamined in the light of some fundamental distinguishing features of object-oriented software: additional levels of abstraction, object state, and inheritance.

5-9.1 Inspections

Inspections are a cost-effective technique for the detection of defects in software [5] [94]. Preparing for and participating in inspections requires that software be read and paraphrased by engineers other than the original developer.

The central problem in dealing with unfamiliar code is developing *program understanding*. This problem is also experienced by those involved in maintaining [106] and reusing (chapter 9) software, where practical realities often dictate that the only way to develop an understanding of a module is by static and dynamic analysis of code.

CASE tools can assist with this process by providing various static views of the code such as cross-references, "flattened" hierarchies, and graphical displays of the various relationships common in object-oriented software (e.g., inheritance, uses and used by, has method, calls method, etc.). However, static analysis of the flow of control is significantly complicated by the following:

- The absence of a direct mapping between functional requirements and high-level functions. High-level system operations are achieved through the interaction of numerous objects of different classes [83]. This information is not easily extracted from the code because object-oriented languages emphasize the inheritance relationship rather than the control relationship. Object interaction graphs, however, express exactly the required information.

- The smaller size of data structures, access functions used to implement classes, and classes as a whole compared with typical module sizes in function-oriented systems.

- The dispersal of method specifications and implementations among the classes in an inheritance graph and across graphs.

- Dynamic binding can make it difficult to determine which code is actually executed for a method invocation [101].

Having access to documentation of the mapping between system operations and object interactions as discussed in section 4-2 helps in understanding the intended interactions between objects. Tools that provide dynamic visualizations of object interaction can help with the first two constraints [65]. Problems resulting from the use of inheritance can be minimized by controlling the depth of inheritance hierarchies (see section 4-6).

Inspections of object-oriented code should, in addition to tracing the flow of control, focus on detecting the typical flaws present in object-oriented systems. For example, Cline [25] recommends not inspecting a single class at once or attempting to follow the flow of control through method calls but instead walking an inheritance hierarchy to confirm that all subclasses implementing a specific method conform to the method specification. The availability of formal documentation of the semantics of class interfaces, as discussed in chapter 9, would help this process.

5-9.2 Testing

Testing is a complementary technique to inspections for exposing defects in software. Two testing approaches are well established in the software engineering community: specification-based (black-box) testing and program-based (glass-, or white-box) testing.

The goal of black-box testing is to demonstrate that the software is deficient with respect to its external specification. The goal of white-box testing is to identify superfluous or "dangerous" code present in the implementation (e.g., infinite loops). Myers [82] summarizes numerous techniques for both approaches that differ in the degree of coverage provided and efficiency in exposing different types of defects. Naturally these techniques were developed with function-oriented models in mind.

This section discusses three differences between function-oriented and object-oriented systems that affect the extent to which traditional approaches to testing must be modified for the latter: additional levels of abstraction, object state, and inheritance.

Note that precondition/postconditions and assertions are useful testing tools in themselves. Their performance overheads are more acceptable during testing, and, because the idea of testing is to *detect* errors rather than handle their consequences, simply aborting when they are violated is sufficient.

Levels of Abstraction.

Smith [98] enumerates the different levels of object-oriented systems that must be tested.

- *Function*. Traditional unit in function-oriented systems
- *Class*. Maintenance of intraobject invariants and correct outputs in the interaction of procedures and object state
- *Cluster*. Maintenance of interobject invariants and correct outputs in the interaction of groups of collaborating objects
- *System*. Response of the system to external inputs

For testing the first and last levels, standard techniques for specification and program testing of function-oriented systems can be employed. For example, Fiedler

[44] employed complexity metrics to drive the development of test cases for testing the member functions of C++ classes.

For testing classes, many of the traditional approaches to specification testing have been found lacking [98]. This is because these approaches derive from a function-oriented model of computation, where an input is specified and the output result is compared against an expected value; consequently they neglect to account for the prominent role of object state.

Classes are also less amenable to standard program testing techniques such as decision coverage. If the order of member function invocation is viewed as a "path," then the number of branches grows exponentially with the number of member functions even for very small numbers of consecutive function invocations.

Note that the finer granularity (and by implication larger numbers) of modules in object-oriented systems increases the number of class and cluster test cases that must be generated. Indeed, Smith [98] has suggested that the essential problem in testing classes is a search for the the right combinations of method invocations to yield the largest number of errors.

Existing techniques for generating *integration* test cases, such as data flow techniques, are applicable to the task of generating test sets for class and cluster testing [51] [52] .

In the absence of such a formal approach, a minimum checklist of test cases for classes should include the following:

- Check state observation and manipulation (i.e., read and write methods, or attribute access).

- Apply algebraic properties such as associativity and identity preservation to member function invocation (e.g., for two strings s_1 and s_2, $s_1 > s_2$ should yield the same result as $s_2 < s_1$).

- In C++, check that destructors are consistent with the corresponding constructors. In Eiffel, make sure that the default values for features are correct. (Incorrect values will often be caught by class invariant checks, of course.)

- Check the proper use of initialization, so that all objects at least start off in a sensible state.

- In C++, check that casting is being used in safe ways, and that potentially type-unsafe cases (e.g., casting toward the leaves of the inheritance lattice) is justified, (e.g., by a global convention about type tagging.)

- Try to trigger exception handling capabilities via extreme boundary value inputs.

The object interaction graphs for methods of the class can often give a convenient hint as to which external operations will invoke methods, and thus suggest tests which might provoke errors in those methods.

Example: Doubly-Linked List.

Suppose that (after a process of refinement) we have the doubly-linked list classes shown in Figure 5.15.

```
class DLink
      attribute length: Integer              // Current length
      method insert( Item x )                // Put an item at the front
      method remove( DLinkElement )          // Remove an item from the end
      method wipe( )                         // Remove all items
      attribute first: DLinkElement          // Head of chain
      attribute last: DLinkElement           // Last element of chain
endclass


class DLinkElement
      attribute next: DLinkElement           // Forward link
      attribute prev: DLinkElement           // Backward link
      attribute this: Item                   // Item in list
endclass
```

Figure 5.15   Class Description: Doubly-Linked List Class

A **DLink** gives access to a series of **DLinkElement**s, which are linked into two chains. The **length** attribute of a **DLink** is a cache of the value obtained by walking round the chains until the same element is met again. Examples of applicable tests include the following:

1. **length** = 0 after **wipe** is called.
2. **length** should have been in/de-cremented after an **insert/remove**.
3. The **length** should remain constant after an **insert** followed by a **remove**. (Not necessarily after a **remove** followed by an **insert**, as the **remove** might have been applied to an empty list—presumably outside its precondition.)
4. The order of elements in the **next** and **prev** chains is unchanged after a **insert** or **remove**, apart from at the point of addition/deletion.

Object State.

Once an adequate set of test cases has been chosen, Cline [25] proposes focusing on checking the intraobject invariants or *coherence* of an object's state at the entrance to and exit from each member function (including constructors and destructors). The argument for this approach is that an object's attributes often have constraints which result in the *bitwise* state space of the attribute being much larger than the *legal* state space. An example would be an integer valued **month** attribute which has 2^{32}—1 possible bitwise values but whose legal values are $1 \leq$ **month** ≤ 12. Secondly because an object's state is usually "larger" (i.e., has more bits) than a return variable, a logical error in a member function is more likely to show up as a random perturbation of an object's state than in a return variable.

Coherence checking detects when an object's attributes violate legal values and is an effective technique for detecting a large percentage of a class's logical errors. Cline points out, however, that universal application of coherence checking can lead to severe performance degradation and therefore should be done selectively using conditional compilation techniques. For the doubly linked list example, the following constraints should hold:

1. Verify that **length** is correct.
2. If **length = 0**, the **first** and **last** pointers should refer to nothing (void references in Eiffel, **NULL** in C++).
3. If **L** is a **DLinkElement** of some nonempty **DLink**, **L.prev.next** and **L.next.prev** should both be **L**.

Impact of Inheritance.

An efficient testing strategy (whatever the color of its box) demonstrates the greatest degree of coverage with the least effort, that is, the smallest number of test cases. A common misconception about object-oriented software is that "proven" (i.e., tested and reused) classes can be reused as superclasses with minimal retesting. The implication of this is that inheritance in some sense improves the efficiency of whatever strategy is employed in testing.

However, the fact that integration testing approaches are applicable to testing classes suggests that the motivations for integration testing (i.e., testing a module in context), also indicate a requirement to retest a superclass's methods in the context of a subclass. Perry [88] presents a more formal argument for this point. The only case where the retesting of inherited methods is unnecessary is when the subclass is a pure extension of a superclass, and there are no interactions in either direction between the new features and any inherited features.

5-10 IMPLEMENTION OF LIFE CYCLE

Somewhere the implementation must convert environment events into system operations, respecting the system life cycles. How this is done will depend on the programming environment; it will be different for command-line interfaces, graphical interfaces, remote servers, and library services, to name but four. *How* external activities are recognized as events is not discussed here.

(It is only system operations triggered by *events* that are controlled by the life cycle. The method that implements a system operation may be invoked by other system operations, directly or indirectly, as part of their implementation.)

When the system recognizes a particular event, it must check to see if that event is admissible.

Several cases arise. The simplest is when no explicit life cycle has been provided; every event is acceptable at all times. All that need be done is to invoke the appropriate system operation when its associated event arrives.

The next simplest case is when the life cycle is provided, but it contains no interleaving. This is catered for using *state machines*; the discussion in sections 5-10.1 to 5-10.4 explains state machines, how to convert regular expressions into them, and how to execute such a state machine.

The most complex case is when the life cycle involves interleaving. Section 5-10.6 discusses how to handle this.

5-10.1 Life Cycles with No Interleaving

The implementation of life cycles occurs in two stages. First, the regular expression of the life cycle is translated into a (nondeterministic) state machine. (See [6], [42], or [95], for more details.) Then this machine must itself be implemented. Because output events are *generated* by system operations, they are irrelevant to this translation.

A state machine is some collection of *states* and labeled *transitions* between them. Here, the labels are the (names of) events that the environment can present to the system, and the states are a way of encoding which events are currently permitted. The machines we deal with are *nondeterministic*; when they have a choice of transitions, they make *all* of them at once. It is as though the machine is in several states at the same time. (An alternative view is that the machine magically chooses the "right" transition to make to allow future events to be accepted. This view is, however, unhelpful to implementers.)

State machines can be displayed as tables or as bubble diagrams. For each state, the tables give the resulting new state for each possible input event. Bubble diagrams show the same information, with states being represented as named bubbles and transitions as labeled arrows; one of the states is marked as the *start state* of the machine. The tables are more compact, but can be more difficult to follow; the diagrams are easier to follow in simple cases, but can become rather complicated.

We shall show the development of state machines using bubble diagrams, but express the final results as tables, as these are more suitable for implementation purposes.

Example: ECO Life Cycle (Simplified).

Consider part of the life cycle of the ECO example, shown in Figure 5.16. (We ignore the interleaving and the outer level to make the example simpler.) To translate this into a state machine, we begin with two states—a *start state* we call Initial, and an *end state* we call Final. (The machine will start executing in Initial, and accept events from the outside world, changing state at each event. If it arrives in Final, with no other states being active, then it can accept no more events; the system has stopped.)

---

lifecycle DeliveryAndCollection: (load_bay_empty. (Delivery | Collection))*

Delivery   = enter_manifest. check_in_drum*. end_check_in
Collection = initiate_collection

Figure 5.16   DeliveryAndCollection Life Cycle

We note first that **DeliveryAndCollection** is a zero-or-more repetition. This means that one way to end up in the **Final** state is to do nothing—the machine needs no events to do this. To represent this, we have an *empty* transition, ε, from **Initial** to **Final**. (One-or-more repetitions do not generate ε-transitions, but are otherwise translated the same way.) Further, when the body of the repetition is translated, it must end up at **Final** and also back at **Initial** (for the next possible repetition); we show this with the notation RE[Initial] on the diagram. This gives us figure 5.17.

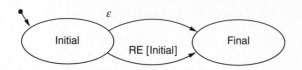

Figure 5.17 Initial Bubble Diagram for DeliveryAndCollection

To find other transitions, we look within the repetition. It is a sequence, which means a new state must be introduced. We call it **State1**. The first operand of the sequence has to get us from **Initial** to **State1**, and the second has to get us from **State1** to **Final**.

The regular expression **load_bay_empty** will accept the event with that name, so we can add that to the state machine, giving us Figure 5.18.

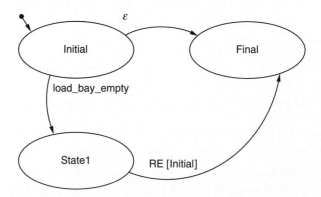

Figure 5.18 DeliveryAndCollection, Repetition Expanded

The second operand of the sequence is the alternation **Delivery | Collection**. This gives two routes from **State1** to **Final**, one through **Delivery** and the other through **Collection**. Both of these supply us with transitions. A local name is just shorthand for the regular expression it names, so **Collection** is easily dealt with; it just introduces a new transition named **initiate_collection**. Figure 5.19 shows the resulting bubble diagram.

Finally we consider **Delivery**, which is a sequence with three elements. It introduces *two* new states. **enter_manifest** makes a transition into the first new state, **State2**, and **end_check_in** makes a transition from the second, **State3**, to both **Final** and **Initial**. The repetition of **check_in_drum** gives an empty transition from **State2** to **State3** (for the empty case of the repetition), and transitions for **check_in_drum** to **State3** and back to **State2**. The final result is shown in Figure 5.20.

The same state machine is described by Figure 5.21. Translations for the remaining regular expressions—bracketed, optional, and empty—should now be obvious; for details, see the algorithm described in appendix D.

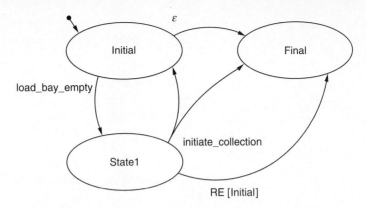

Figure 5.19   Delivery and Collection, Alternation Expanded

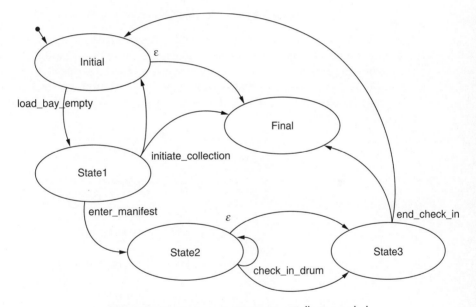

Figure 5.20   DeliveryAndCollection, Fully Expanded

5-10.2 Removing Empty Transitions

Once the state machine has been generated, all the ε-transitions can be eliminated, using the following rule:

> If S_1 has a transition by event E to S_2, and S_2 has an ε-transition to S_3, then S_1 also has an E-transition to S_3.

State	Event	Next State(s)
Initial		
	ε	Final
	load_bay_empty	State1
State1		
	enter_manifest	State2
	initiate_collection	Initial Final
State2		
	ε	State3
	check_in_drum	State2 State3
State3		
	end_check_in	Initial Final
Final		

Figure 5.21   DeliveryAndCollection State Machine

Repeated application of this rule until no new transitions are added to any state results in a revised state machine from which the ε-transitions can be dropped. This simplifies the implementation of the state machine. If we apply this rule to Figure 5.21, we see that transitions into **State2** should also go to **State3**, and that any transition to **Initial** should also go to **Final**. Applying this, and removing the ε-transitions, gives Figure 5.22.

State	Event	Next state(s)
Initial		
	load_bay_empty	State1
State1		
	enter_manifest	State2 State3
	initiate_collection	Initial Final
State2		
	check_in_drum	State2 State3
State3		
	end_check_in	Initial Final
Final		

Figure 5.22 ε-Free DeliveryAndCollection Machine

Note that while the original machine started in one state—**Initial**—the revised machine may start in several states, because of ε-transitions from **Initial**.

5-10.3 Execution of Machine

Having derived the state machine from the regular expression, we turn to implementing state machines. There are various ways of implementing the state machine. We shall discuss one and hint at some simplifications; further alternatives and more detail are given in the references.

We model the nondeterministic state machine by keeping track of *sets* of states; all of these states are active (i.e., the machine being modeled is in all of these states) at once. Suppose some set S of states is active and an event V arrives. If V is not the label of any transition of any of the states S, then it must be rejected. Otherwise, it is accepted (and the associated system operation executed), and the new set of active states is the set of all those states for which V-transitions exist in S. (Note that, had the ε-transitions not been eliminated, they would have to be followed at this point to complete the set of active states.)

To begin with, the active state is the set {Initial}, plus any states originally reachable from Initial by ε-transitions; in our example, this means that it also includes Final.

A convenient implementation labels states with a range of integers $0 .. N$ and uses bit operations on integers $0 .. 2^N$ to implement sets. This is particularly simple when N is no more than the word size of the underlying machine or when the implementation language provides bitsets of arbitrary size. Be careful in such languages, however, as bitset values may be dynamically allocated on each operation—the algorithm we discuss needs no more than two set values at any time.

The interpreter can be table driven, or it may be specific to the particular state machine. The former has the advantage of only needing the code to be written once, and the corresponding disadvantage that it may be too slow. Note that, if the table can be automatically generated, so can the specific code—it is better to use tools for the job rather than repeated hand-coding.

5-10.4 ECO State Machine Interpreter

The C++ code of Figure 5.23 is a state machine interpreter for Figure 5.22. It is table driven, and so suitable for a wide range of state machines when its State and Event types are generalized. We assume the existence of a Bool type with suitable values for FALSE and TRUE.

The macro bit simply serves to convert a bit index into the corresponding bit pattern; bit2 is just a shorthand for two bits together. The State and Event typedefs introduce constants naming the states of the machine and events from the environment. The order of the names in the enumerations is important, because table will be indexed by State and Event values, and it is initialized so that table[s][e] gives all the states that can be reached if e arrives when in state s. LAST_EVENT and LAST_STATE make looping and array declaration simpler.

The variable states holds the set of currently active states, initialized with the starting set of states, that is, Initial and Final.

The function handle_event is to be called when event e arrives. It delivers TRUE if the event is accepted, FALSE if it is rejected. (A realistic program would have to arrange that the type Event was available to callers of handle_event.) To decide whether e is accepted, handle_event iterates over all the active states, accumulating all the possible next states in next. If next is zero, that is, represents the empty set, then the event is rejected. Otherwise, the event is accepted, and next becomes the value of states.

```
#define bit(n)          (1 << (n))
#define bit2(n, m)    (bit( n ) | bit( m ))

typedef enum
    { Initial, State1, State2, State3, Final, LAST_STATE }
    State;

typedef enum
    {
    load_bay_empty,
    enter_manifest,
    initialise_collection,
    check_in_drum,
    end_check_in,
    LAST_EVENT
    } Event;

static int table[LAST_STATE][LAST_EVENT] =
    {
    // LBE EM IC CID ECI
    { bit( State1 ), 0, 0, 0, 0 } ,   // Initial
    { 0, bit2( State2, State3 ), bit2( Initial, Final ), 0, 0 }, // State1
    { 0, 0, 0, bit2( State2, State3 ), 0 }, // State2
    { 0, 0, 0, 0, bit2( Initial, Final ) }, // State3
    { 0, 0, 0, 0, 0 } // Final
    };

static int states = bit2( Initial, Final );

Bool handle_event( Event e )
    {
    int next = 0;
    int i;
    for (i = 0; i < LAST_STATE; i++)
        if ((bit( i ) & states) != 0)
            next |= table[i][e];
    return next = = 0 ? FALSE : (states = next, TRUE);
    }
```

Figure 5.23 ECO State Machine Interpreter

5-10.5 Opportunities for Optimization

The code exemplified by **handle_event** may not be fast enough in some applications; for example, the iteration over states may be too costly, especially if only a few states out of a great many are active at a time. We shall briefly discuss three ways in which the interpreter can be made faster. (The micro-optimization of exchanging the order of indices for **table**, so that **table[e]** would be invariant during the loop, is unlikely to be useful in real cases.)

Specialization.

One technique is to *specialize* the interpreter, rather than relying on tables to describe the machine. Consider inverting **table**, that is, indexing first by **Event** and then by **State**, so that each row maps a **State** to a set of **States**, and their union is the new set of **States**. This form of table can be open coded with explicit tests for particular states. For example, consider receiving **enter_manifest**; it is legal only in **State1**, and makes **State2** and **State3** active. The body of **handle_event** would then be a switch on the event, and the code for **enter_manifest** would be

```
case enter_manifest:
    if ((states & bit( State1 )) == 0) return FALSE;
    else return states = bit2( State2, State3 ), TRUE;
```

In the ECO example, we are in the happy position of each event being acceptable in exactly one state, so this kind of explicit code is compact and fast. This will not always be true.

Choiceless Machines.

A particular degenerate case is the *choiceless machine*, where all transitions out of every state have different labels. In this case the machinery of sets of states can be dispensed with, and the state machine replaced by a simple array lookup, switch, or if statements.

Sets as States.

In fact, it is always possible, and sometimes convenient, to turn a nondeterministic machine into a choiceless one. The key insight is to regard each possible *set* of states as a new *single* state. A choice of states to move to in the old machine becomes a single state in the new, representing *all* the old states. The "possible" sets of states are those reachable through transitions of the old machine, so an N-state machine may end up with rather less than 2^N states after transformation.

We illustrate this by considering the ECO state machine, where the new machine has *fewer* states than the original; be warned that this is atypical. We note that **Initial** is always accompanied by **Final**, and **State2** by **State3**; **State1** is still required, but **Final**, **State2**, and **State3** are never required other than in the stated combinations. This gives the choiceless machine of Figure 5.24.

To compute the states of a choiceless machine, start with the single state corresponding to the set of all active states at the start of the original machines execution (in the ECO example, {**Initial**, **Final**}). This gives a set of "unconsidered" new states. While there are unconsidered states, pick one, say **S**. For each possible input event **E**, find the set of possible (old) states that could become active by **E**-transitions from the (old) states comprising **S**. If such a set has not appeared before, make a new state **S'** for it, and add it to the unconsidered set; otherwise it already corresponds to a state **S'**. Give **S** an **E**-transition to **S'**.

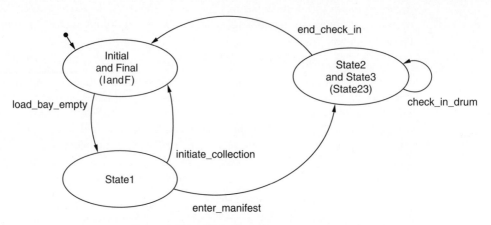

Figure 5.24   Choiceless DeliveryAndCollection

When there are no more states to consider, we have constructed the new choiceless machine. The new state corresponding to the empty set should never be entered: it corresponds to a rejected transition. Assuming a suitably set-up **table**, **handle_event** reduces to

```
void handle_event( Event e )
    {
    State next = table[states][e];
    return next == NO_STATES ? FALSE : (states = next, TRUE);
    }
```

where **NO_STATES** is whatever value (preferably zero) that corresponds to the empty set of original states.

5-10.6 Life Cycles with Interleaving

Interleaving in life cycles leads to multiple "parallel" state machines. There are two ways to implement such parallel machines; we can combine them into a single "product" machine, or we can keep them apart and simulate the parallelism.

Product Machines.

Consider the full ECO life cycle of chapter 3, reproduced in Figure 5.25. A state machine for the **Status** component is shown in Figure 5.26. (For pedagogical reasons, we have deliberately not simplified this down into the obvious one-state machine.)

A state machine for the entire life cycle can be formed by constructing a *product machine*. The states of this machine are all the pairs of states of its components. A state (X,Y) has an E_1-transition to (X',Y) if X has an E_1-transition to X', and an E_2 transition to (X,Y') if Y has a E_2 transition to Y'. (All ε-transitions should have been eliminated from the component machines before taking the product.) This product generalizes naturally to more than two machines.

Taking the product of Figures 5.24 and 5.26, and representing the composite names with a "." separator, gives the six-state machine of Figure 5.27, which can be implemented in the usual way.

lifecycle ECO StorageDepot: (Delivery|Collection)*‖(Status)*

Delivery =   load_bay_empty.
              enter_manifest.
              (check_in_drum.#drum_identifier)*.
              end_check_in.
                  [#discrepancy_in_delivery.
                  #delivery_allocation.
                  [#drums_to_be_returned]

Collection=   load_bay_empty.
              collect.
                  #fulfilled_part_of_order.
                  #drums_to_be_retrieved

Status=   (depot_status?.#status_report |
              is_vulnerable?.#vulnerability report)*

Figure 5.25 Full ECO Life Cycle

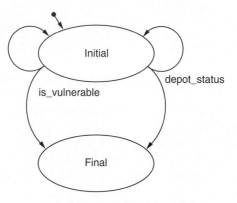

Figure 5.26 Status Machine

Other Implementations.

Suppose that a life cycle interleaves six machines, each with ten states. Then the product machine has a million states, which makes for rather large tables. Can we do better than this?

When the interleaved expressions have no input events in common, they cannot interfere with each other, and we can return to our intuitions about "running the machines in parallel." (See appendix C for what constitutes "interference.") When translating regular expressions to state machines, we add an additional case to those of section 5-10.1: to translate the expression $E_1 \| \ldots \| E_n$, starting from some state **A** and ending up at **Z**, we translate each of the E_i independently, giving n new machines. We then connect **A** to the initial state of each new machine by an *activate* transition, and the final state of each new machine to **Z** by an *exit* transition. We say that A is the *activation state* for the E_i, and that **Z** is the *exit state*.

State	Event	New State(s)
landF.Initial	is_vulnerable	landF.Initial landF.Final
	depot_status	landF.Initial landF.Final
	load_bay_empty	State1.Initial
landF.Final	load_bay_empty	State1.Final
State1.Initial	is_vulnerable	State1.Initial State1.Final
	depot_status	State1.Initial State1.Final
	initiate_collection	landF.Initial
	enter_manifest	State23.Initial
State1.Final	initiate_collection	landF.Final
	enter_manifest	State23.Final
State23.Initial	is_vulnerable	State23.Initial State23.Final
	depot_status	State23.Initial State23.Final
	check_in_drum	State23.Initial
	end_check_in	landF.Initial
State23.Final	check_in_drum	State23.Final
	end_check_in	landF.Final

Figure 5.27 Product Machine

Both activate and exit transitions are forms of ε-transition, in that they consume no input events.

Initially, only one machine—corresponding to the outermost regular expression—is running; the others are inactive. Whenever a state machine moves into an activation state, the corresponding machines are made active and can consume events. When a machine can make an exit transition, the corresponding exit state is made active in its owning machine; if a machine ends up in (only) its **Final** state, it can be de-activated. The "product machine" is implemented as an implicit product in the actual machine rather than having the actual machine emulate the abstract product.

In the case of the **ECOStorageDepot**, the two interleaved expressions indeed have no input events in common. Further, there is no event-handling before or after the interleaving. Rather than having a product machine, we can simply implement a machine for **DeliveryAndCollection**, another for **Status**, and dispatch incoming events to an appropriate copy of **handle_event**.

5-11 SUMMARY

In this chapter we have seen how to convert the output of the design stage into code. We have covered the issues of

- Translating class descriptions into programming language classes, and translating the method descriptions of object interaction graphs into the corresponding code.
- Handling run-time errors, using the contractual model of programming for guidance.
- Understanding performance issues, with particular mention of the problems of storage management in C++.
- Reviewing and testing object-oriented code.
- Converting the life cycle to a state machine and learning how to execute this machine.

CHAPTER 6

Case Study

6-1 INTRODUCTION

In this chapter we take a requirements statement and show how to apply the steps of the Fusion method. Each of the steps in the method is illustrated in the example. Note that the development of some of the models involves a significant amount of iteration; those presented here are the final outcome of this iterative process.

The chapter is divided into four main sections. The first section sets out the requirements statement which was devised by Chris Wallace of the University of the West of England for a meeting of the British Computer Society in May 1992. The second section describes the analysis phase for the example and the resulting models. The third section describes the development of the design from the outputs of the analysis phase. The fourth section implements some of the outputs of the design process, using C++ as the implementation language.

6-2 REQUIREMENTS

A computer-based system is required to control the dispensing of petrol, to handle customer payment, and to monitor tank levels.

Before a customer can use the self-service pumps, the pump must be enabled by the attendant. When a pump is enabled, the pump motor is started, if it is not already on, with the pump clutch free. When the trigger in the gun is depressed, closing a microswitch, the clutch is engaged and petrol pumped. When it is released, the clutch is freed. There is also a microswitch on the holster in which the gun is kept that prevents petrol being pumped until the gun is taken out. Once the gun is replaced in the holster, the delivery is deemed to be completed and the pump disabled. Further depressions of the trigger in the gun cannot dispense more petrol. After a short standby period, the pump motor will be turned off unless the pump is reenabled.

A metering device in the petrol line sends a pulse to the system for each 1/100 liter dispensed. Displays on the pump show the amount dispensed and the cost.

There are two kinds of pump. The normal kind allows the user to dispense petrol ad lib. The sophisticated pumps, imported from New Zealand, allow the customer to preset either an amount or a volume of petrol. Petrol will then be pumped up to a maximum of the required quantity.

Transactions are stored until the customer pays. Payment may be either in cash, by credit card, or on account. A customer may request a receipt and will get a token for every 5 pounds spent. Customers sometimes abscond without paying and the operator must annotate the transaction with any available information (e.g., the vehicle's registration). At the end of the day, transactions are archived and may be used for ad hoc inquiries on sales.

At present, two grades of petrol are dispensed from five pumps on the forecourt. Each pump takes its supply from one of two tanks, one tank for each grade. The tank level must not drop below 4% of the tanks capacity. If this happens, the pumps serviced by that tank cannot be enabled to dispense petrol.

6-3 ANALYSIS

In this section we begin with the analysis phase of the development. The purpose of this phase is to build a more precise description than the requirements statement of what the system is supposed to do. We build the object model and use scenarios to help determine the system interface (and hence the system portion of the object model) and construct the life-cycle model. Then the schemata comprising the operation model are developed.

6-3.1 Object Model for Problem Domain

A customer uses a pump to deliver petrol and then pays for a delivery (or absconds!). Associated with each customer is the registration number of his or her car. Each pump has a display. A display shows a delivery comprising the cost, volume, and grade of the petrol delivered.

From this part of the requirements we get the following classes and relationships:

Classes: These are Customer, Pump, Delivery, Payment, Display.

Relationships: A customer uses a pump, a customer pays for a delivery with a payment, a display shows a delivery.

With this information we can now draw an initial object model for this part of the requirements. To model the fact that there are five pumps the Pump class has a pump_id attribute. The fact that each pump has a display is modeled by an aggregation relationship. The **Display** class is thus shown nested inside the **Pump** class. Once we have this initial model we can refine it by adding attributes, cardinalities, and any role names. The final model for this part of the requirements is shown in Figure 6.1.

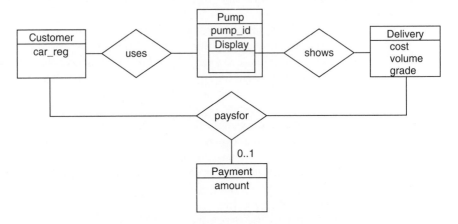

Figure 6.1   Object Model for a Petrol Sale

The next part of the model we develop is centered on the transaction. First we aggregate the previous fragment of the model into a **Sale** class. The details of each sale are recorded in a transaction. If the customer absconds the attendant annotates the transaction. The transactions are stored in a daily record, which in turn is stored in the archive for later retrieval.

At this point we could leave this part of the object model, because it shows all the relationships pertaining to a transaction. However, there are some more details concerning payments and pumps that we will add here since they are small enough not to merit a separate diagram.

Each payment can earn tokens. The attendant can also request a receipt for a customer. Finally a pump is supplied by a storage tank. Each storage tank has a capacity, a current level, and an identifying number.

From this part of the requirements we get the following classes and relationships:

Classes: These are Transaction, Sale, Attendant, DailyRecord, Archive, Token, Receipt, StorageTank.

Relationships: A sale **is recorded** in a transaction, an attendant **annotates** a transaction, transactions are **stored in** a daily record, daily records are **stored in** an archive, each payment **earns** tokens, an attendant **requests** a receipt for a payment, a pump **is supplied by** a storage tank.

This information allows us to draw the fragment of the object model that is centered on the transaction. This is shown in Figure 6.2. We have left the detail in the **Sale** class, because there are some relationships that cross the aggregation boundary.

The next part of the object model we develop concentrates on the pump. A pump has a complex structure and is modeled by an aggregation; it is composed of a gun, holster, motor, clutch, petrol line, and display. The petrol line contains a meter which sends pulses to the display. A pump may be in one of several states. This is modeled by introducing an attribute, **status**, which can be either *enabled*, *disabled*, or *out of service*. The attendant can change a pump from being disabled to enabled. A pump is disabled by replacing its gun in its holster.

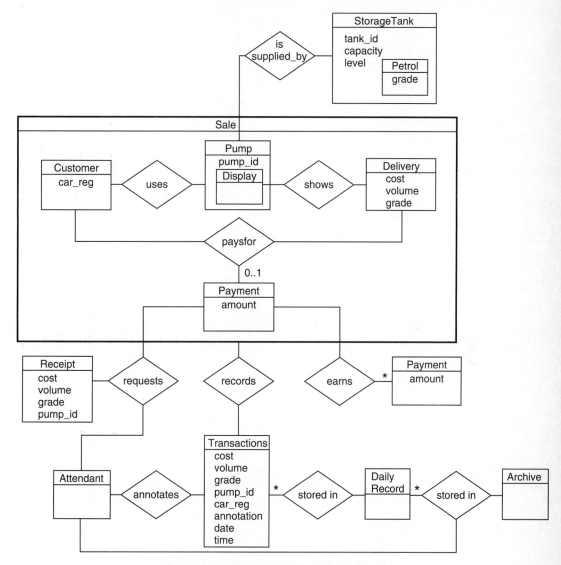

Figure 6.2 Object Model for Sale and Transaction

The requirements state that the pump motor is turned off after a short standby period. To model this we introduce a timer. It is started by replacing the gun in the holster, and it turns the motor off after the appropriate standby period. The **start** relationship is thus a ternary relationship between timer, gun, and holster. This

makes the diagram a little difficult to understand, so we have chosen to introduce the
GunHolsterAssembly aggregation to make the relationship binary.

The clutch and motor are controlled by the **GunHolsterAssembly**, and they
pump the petrol down the petrol line. The **controls** and **pumps** relationships are thus
also ternary, and once again we introduce an aggregate class, **ClutchMotorAssembly**,
to simplify the diagram.

From this part of the requirements we get the following classes and relationships:

Classes: Gun, Holster, Motor, Clutch, Petrol Line, Meter, Timer, GunHolsterAssembly, Clutch-
MotorAssembly.

Relationships: a petrol line **contains** a meter, a meter **pulses** the display, an attendant **enables**
a pump, a pump is **disabled** by the gun holster assembly, the gun holster assembly **starts**
the timer, the time **turns off** the motor, the gun holster assembly **controls** the clutch motor
assembly, the clutch motor assembly **pumps** petrol down the petrol line.

This information allows us to draw the fragment of the object model which is
centered on the pump. This is shown in Figure 6.3.

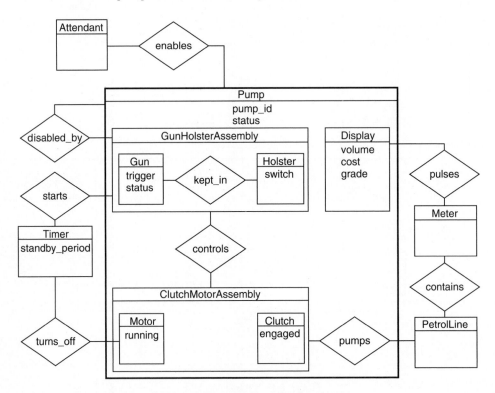

Figure 6.3 Object Model for Pump

The preceding object model fragments have concentrated on identifying the
classes and relationships for major components of the system. We have captured

most of the static information about the system that is present in the requirements. At this point it is appropriate to look at our models and the requirements to see if there are any useful generalizations we can make.

Looking through the models reveals that there are no opportunities for generalization, because none of the classes have large shared sets of attributes or participate in the same relationships. The classes' daily record and archive both participate in a **stored in** relationship, but the other participants are different classes that have no generalization, and thus the two **stored in** relationships are in fact different.

However, the requirements statement contains two examples of generalization. Payments can be made either in cash, by credit card, or on account. These payment methods require different information in each case, and so these are candidates for payment specializations. Also there are two kinds of pump: the simple one that we have already described in our models, and the sophisticated version from New Zealand, which allows the customer to preset the volume or amount. This can also be modeled by an inheritance relationship. We will make no decision about whether the subclasses are a disjoint union or not, so we leave the triangles empty. These inheritance relationships are shown in Figure 6.4.

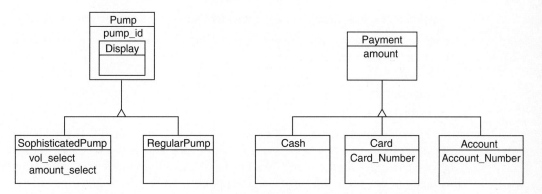

Figure 6.4 Inheritance Relationships

Figures 6.2 to 6.4 constitute the complete object model for the system and its environment. During the construction of these models each class, relationship and attribute were entered into the data dictionary. Figure 6.5 shows some example entries from the data dictionary for the object model. We have disambiguated attribute names by prepending their owning class names.

6-3.2 Determination of System Interface

The object model developed up to this point covers the system and its environment. The next step in Fusion involves determining the boundary between the system and its environment. Once we have done this we can identify those classes and relationships that form part of the system and the information that the system should record.

In this phase of the analysis we use scenarios to help identify the system boundary. These allow us to trace through the likely use of the system in terms of its inter-

Name	Kind	Description
Customer	Class	A customer who buys petrol.
Delivery	Class	The details for one delivery of petrol.
Transaction	Class	A permanent record of each petrol sale.
Token	Class	A token is issued for each 5 pounds of petrol purchased.
shows	Relationship	The display shows the details of the delivery.
pays_for	Relationship	A customer pays for a delivery of petrol with some form of payment.
requests	Relationship	The attendant requests a receipt for a particular payment.
is_supplied_by	Relationship	A pump is supplied with petrol by a tank.
Pump.pump_id	Attribute	Each pump is identified by a number.
Customer.car_reg	Attribute	The registration number of a customer's car.
Display.grade	Attribute	The grade of petrol in a particular tank.
StorageTank.capacity	Attribute	The amount of petrol a tank will hold when it is full.

Figure 6.5   Example Data Dictionary Entries for Classes, Relationships, and Attributes

actions with the external environment. We develop scenarios for the following three uses of the system:

- Delivery of petrol
- Payment for delivery
- Display of delivery

First we consider the use of the system for the delivery of petrol. The following interactions happen during the delivery of petrol. The attendant enables the pump. The customer operates the pump by removing the gun from the holster, depressing the trigger in the pump gun (allowing the petrol to flow), releasing the trigger and replacing the gun. This can be shown as the timeline diagram in Figure 6.6.

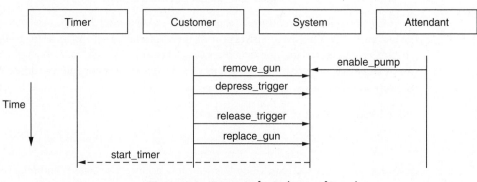

Figure 6.6   Scenario for Delivery of Petrol

This scenario clearly reveals that customer and attendant are active agents that lie outside the system. They interact with the system to achieve the delivery. The scenario also identifies a number of system operations: enable_pump, remove_gun, depress_trigger, release_trigger, and replace_gun.

The next use of the system we will consider is the customer making a payment. The attendant enters the payment details and, if the customer wants a receipt, requests one. The timeline diagrams cannot show conditionals so this scenario will need two diagrams to describe it completely. For the sake of brevity we show only the diagram including the requesting and issuing of a receipt. The system also issues tokens to the customer. The timeline diagram for this scenario is shown in Figure 6.7.

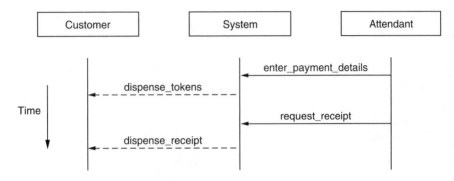

Figure 6.7 Scenario for Payment

This scenario identifies two more system operations: enter_payment_details and request_receipt. It also identifies some events which are sent to the environment by the system. These are dispense_receipt and dispense_tokens.

The final use we consider is the display of the delivery. This scenario involves the meter in the petrol line and the customer. The customer depresses the trigger and this starts the meter pulsing. In response the system updates the display with the amount of petrol dispensed. This repeats until the customer releases the trigger. The timeline diagram for this scenario is shown in Figure 6.8.

This scenario identifies the meter as a part of the environment as well. In addition it identifies a new system operation, pulse, and a new event, display_amount.

The use of just these few scenarios has already identified several classes that are outside the system, and several system operations and events that define the interactions between the system and its environment. The agents, system operations, and events are added to the data dictionary. Figure 6.9 shows some of the entries derived from the preceding scenarios. Note that the entries for the events and system operations are not complete, because they do not have any arguments. These are filled in later after the operation model schemata have been developed.

6-3.3 Life-Cycle Model

At this point in the development we can do either of two things. We can use the scenarios to develop the life-cycle model, or we can use the output of the scenarios to build the system object model and the operation model. We have chosen to develop the life cycle first.

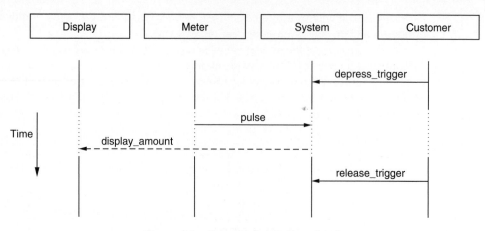

Figure 6.8 Scenario for Display of Delivery

Name	Kind	Description
customer	Agent	Delivers petrol using the gun and makes payment
timer	Agent	Turns off the pump motor a certain time after the pump has been disabled
tank	Agent	Indicates that the petrol level in the tank has dropped below 4%
enable_pump	System operation	Enables the pump to start pumping petrol unless the pump is out of service
remove_gun	System operation	Enables the gun to start pumping petrol when the trigger is depressed
depress_trigger	System operation	Engages the clutch of the pump that starts pumping petrol if the pump is enabled
start_timer	Event	Starts the timer for turning off the pump motor
dispense_receipt	Event	Receipt listing the details of the customer transaction
display_amount	Event	Details of the current delivery are shown on the display

Figure 6.9 Example Data Dictionary Entries for Agents, System Operations, and Events

The life cycle of the system is essentially a sequence of delivery followed by payment. It is also possible that the pumps are taken out of service if the tank levels fall too low. At the end of the day the transactions are archived. This is captured by the following regular expression:

lifecycle PetrolStation: ((Delivery . Payment)* | PumpsOutOfService)* . archive

Delivery, **Payment** and **PumpsOutOfService** expand to regular expressions describing the sequence of system operations and events that achieve them. **archive** is a system operation.

The **Delivery** regular expression describes the interactions between the agents and the system to achieve a delivery of petrol. Most of this has been extracted from the scenario for delivery and display of delivery shown previously. The interactions between the system and the pump motor and timer are also shown.

The regular expression also includes some extra interactions generated by the sophisticated pumps. Thus the line labeled **(a)** permits an optional preset of amount or volume, and the line labeled **(b)** allows the delivery to be terminated not only by a **release_trigger** event but also by a **cut_off_supply** generated when the required amount or volume has been delivered.

```
Delivery = enable_pump .
           [start_pump_motor] .
           [(preset_volume | preset_amount)] . // (a)
           remove_gun_from_holster .
           depress_trigger .
           ( pulse. #display_amount )* .
           (release_trigger | cut_off_supply) . // (b)
           replace_gun .
           #start_timer .
           [turn_off_motor]
```

The **Payment** regular expression can be conveniently split into two cases: one for the normal payment by a customer and the other dealing with the sequence of events when a customer absconds.

In the normal case the payment details are entered, and the tokens for the payment are dispensed. A receipt may be optionally requested. If this is done then the receipt is dispensed. The case in which the customer absconds consists simply of the system operation **enter_annotation**.

```
Payment = NormalPayment | CustomerAbsconds

NormalPayment = enter_payment_details . #dispense_tokens .
                [request_receipt . #dispense_receipt]

CustomerAbsconds = enter_annotation
```

Finally, the **PumpsOutOfService** regular expression describes the sequence of events leading to a pump being taken out of service. This happens when the tank level indicator signals that the level is too low, and the system responds by sending the event to take the pumps out of service.

```
PumpsOutOfService = tank_level_low .
                         #take_pumps_out_of_service
```

6-3.4 System Object Model

Consideration of the system interface allows us to draw the boundary between the system and the environment on the object model to produce the system object model. We consider each of the main object model fragments from section 6-3.1 separately.

First consider the object model for sale and transaction (which appeared in Figure 6.2). During the identification of the system interface we decided that customer, attendant, and storage tank are outside the system. (The storage tank is outside the system because it is an agent that invokes the system operation **tank_level_low**.) The system object model in Figure 6.10 shows the customer, attendant, and storage tank outside the system boundary.

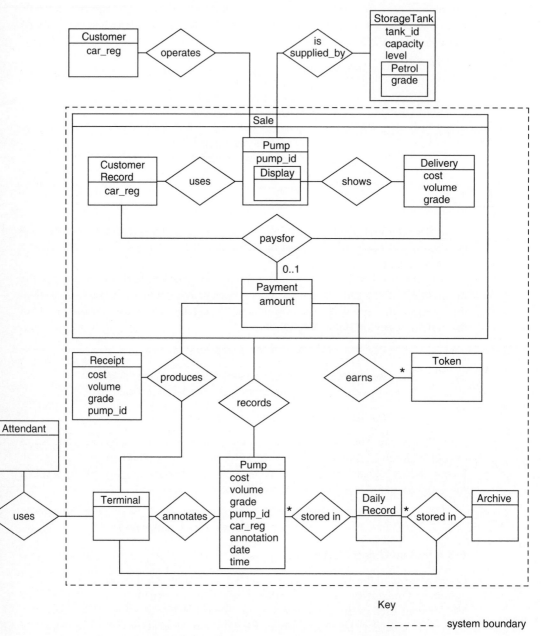

Figure 6.10   System Object Model for Sale and Transaction

However, the system still has to model the customer as part of a sale. To avoid a name clash the customer component of a sale has been renamed **CustomerRecord**. A new class, **Terminal**, and a new relationship, **uses**, are introduced to deal with the attendant being outside the system. The **Terminal** class serves as a point of communication for the attendant.

Next consider the object model for the pump (which appeared in Figure 6.3). Once again the scenarios identified the meter and the timer as outside the system, and thus part of the environment. We have already decided that the attendant is outside the system. Consideration of other scenarios revealed, not surprisingly, that the petrol line was a part of the environment.

The updated diagram is shown in Figure 6.11.

6-3.5 Operation Model

In this section we develop the schemata that make up the operation model. We develop the schemata for the operations from the scenario for the delivery of petrol. These are

- enable_pump
- remove_gun
- depress_trigger
- release_trigger
- replace_gun

Schemata are best developed by considering the desired effect of an operation first (i.e., the **Result** clause). An initial look at the requirements reveals the following effects for the **enable_pump** operation:

The display of the pump is initialized.

The motor is running.

The clutch is free.

However, this is not sufficient. The object model introduced an attribute of pump called status. The **enable_pump** operation must set this attribute appropriately. Also the pump cannot be enabled if it has been taken out of service because the supplying tank level is too low. Thus the **Result** clause needs to be modified to consider these two situations.

Once we have completed the **Result** clause, we can fill in the **Sends** clause. The result of **enable_pump** does not send any events to the environment, and so the **Sends** clause is empty.

The next step in developing the schema is to write the **Assumes** clause. One possibility for the **Assumes** clause for **enable_pump** is to state that the operation can only be invoked if the pump is *not* already enabled. The disadvantage of doing this is it would unnecessarily complicate the task of the agent invoking the operation, since it would be required to check whether the pump was enabled or not before invoking **enable_pump**. In this case we decide to leave the **Assumes** clause empty, indicating that the operation can be invoked in all circumstances.

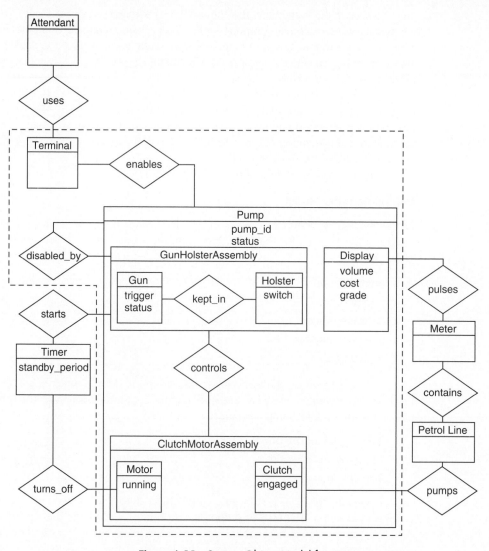

Figure 6.11   System Object Model for Pump

This decision means we need to consider the case when the pump is already enabled in the **Result** clause. This is fairly straightforward, because if we invoke the **enable_pump** operation when the pump is already enabled we need do nothing (although it is important to state this in the **Result** clause, otherwise the designer would be entitled to think that the behavior was undefined).

All that is left to do to complete the schema is to fill in the **Reads** and changes clauses with the objects and attributes from the **Assumes** and **Result** clauses. The complete schema for **enable_pump** is shown in Figure 6.12.

The result of removing the gun from the holster is fairly simple: the gun is no longer in the holster, the holster switch is released, and the gun is enabled ready to

Operation:	enable_pump	
Description:	Enables the pump ready to dispense petrol.	

Reads:	**supplied** n	*//number of the pump to be enabled*
Changes:	Pump **with** pump.pump_id = n, motor, clutch, display	
Sends:		
Assumes:		
Result:	If **pump** is enabled or out of service then no effect otherwise	
	Status of **pump** is enabled.	
	Its **display** has been initialized.	
	Its **motor** is running, and its **clutch** is free.	

Figure 6.12 Schema for enable_pump

pump petrol. The operation does not send any events to the environment and so the **Sends** clause is empty.

The operation does not make sense if the gun is not in the holster before the operation is invoked. Thus we need to state this in the **Assumes** clause. The way the system can detect whether the gun is actually in the holster is by the state of the holster switch. If the switch is depressed, then the gun is in the holster. If the switch is released, then the gun is *not* in the holster. Thus the **Assumes** clause for remove_gun states that the operation assumes that the switch is depressed. If this is not the case, then it doesn't make sense to invoke the operation, and the behavior of the operation if it is invoked in these circumstances is undefined.

Figure 6.13 shows the complete schema for this operation.

The schemata for **depress_trigger** and **release_trigger** are fairly straightforward and are shown in Figures 6.14 and 6.15.

The schema for **replace_gun** is more interesting. The result of replacing the gun in the holster is that the holster switch is depressed, and the gun is disabled (i.e., the converse of the **remove_gun** operation). However, the requirements also state that replacing the gun in the holster signals the end of a delivery. If the pump was initially enabled then it must now be disabled to prevent further delivery of petrol. The system must also create a new transaction to record the sale. Finally, the system must also send the start event to the timer to start the countdown of the standby period for the pump motor.

The **Result** clause for this operation involves sending an event to the environment (i.e., the start event to the timer). This event is recorded in the **Sends** clause.

It does not make sense for the operation to be invoked when the gun is already in the holster. Thus the operation has an **Assumes** clause which states that the holster

Operation: remove_gun

Description: Enables the gun so it can pump petrol.

Reads:

Changes: **supplied** holster.switch, **supplied** gun.status

Sends:

Assumes: Holster switch is depressed.   *//Gun in holster*

Result: Holster switch is released.
                 The gun is enabled.

Figure 6.13   Schema for remove_gun

Operation: depress_trigger

Description: Starts the delivery of petrol by engaging the pump clutch.

Reads: **supplied** gun.status, **supplied** pump.status

Changes: **supplied** clutch.status, **supplied** gun.trigger

Sends:

Assumes:

Result: The gun trigger switch is closed.
                 If initially the pump was enabled and the gun was enabled, then
                 the clutch is engaged; otherwise, no effect.

Figure 6.14   Schema for depress_trigger

switch must be released before the operation can be invoked (i.e., the gun is not in
the holster).

Now we have completed the **Result**, **Sends** and **Assumes** clause we can extract
the information to go into the **Reads** and **Changes** clauses. The complete schema
for replace_gun is shown in Figure 6.16.

The process of building the operation model schemata has identified the arguments associated with system operations and events. For completeness these ar-

Operation:	release_trigger
Description:	Stops the delivery of petrol.

Reads:	**supplied** gun.status, **supplied** pump.status
Changes:	**supplied** clutch.status, **supplied** gun.trigger
Sends:	
Assumes:	
Result:	The gun trigger switch is open. If initially the pump was enabled and the gun was enabled, then the clutch is free; otherwise no effect.

Figure 6.15   Schema for release_trigger

Operation:	replace_gun
Description:	Disables the gun and the pump so no more petrol can be dispensed. Creates a new transaction.

Reads:	Display
Changes:	**supplied** pump, **supplied** gun.status, **supplied** holster.switch, **supplied** timer, **supplied** terminal, **new** transaction
Sends:	Timer: {start message} Terminal: {transaction}
Assumes:	Holster switch is released. //Gun not in holster

Result:	Holster switch is depressed.
	Gun is disabled.
	If the pump was initially enabled then
	    The pump status is disabled.
	    A transaction has been created with the values of the pump display and sent to the terminal.
	    A start message has been sent to the timer for the pump.
	Otherwise there is no effect.

Figure 6.16   Schema for replace_gun

guments should be added to the data dictionary entries for the system operations and events. Figure 6.17 shows the modified entries for the system operations **enable_pump, remove_gun** and **depress_trigger,** and the event **start_timer.**

Name	Kind	Arguments	Description
enable_pump	System operation	pump pump_id	Enables the pump to start pumping petrol unless the pump is out of service
remove_gun	System operation	holster.switch gun.status	Enables the gun to start pumping petrol when the trigger is depressed
depress_trigger	System operation	gun.status pump.status clutch.status gun.trigger	Engages the clutch of the pump that starts pumping petrol if the pump is enabled
start_timer	Event	none	Starts the timer for turning off the pump motor

Figure 6.17   Updated Data Dictionary Entries for System Operations and Events

6-3.6 Checking of Analysis

At this stage the analysis models are checked for completeness and consistency.

- Completeness against the requirements.

  Checks are made that

  – All possible scenarios are covered by the life cycle.
  – All operations are defined by a schema.
  – All static information is captured by the system object model.
  – Technical definitions and invariant constraints are in the data dictionary.

- Simple consistency.

  These checks deal with areas of overlap between the models of analysis.

  – All classes, relationships, and attributes on the object model appear in the system object model.
  – The boundary of the system object model is consistent with the interface model.
  – All system operations in the life-cycle model have a schema.
  – All identifiers in all models have entries in the data dictionary.

- Semantic consistency.

  We must ensure that the implications of the models are consistent.

  – Output events in the life-cycle model and operation model are consistent.
  – The operation model must preserve system object model invariant constraints.
  – Desk check scenarios using the schemas.

6-4 DESIGN

In this section we take the models we have built during analysis, and design a system that has the behavior described. Recall that four models are built during design: object interaction graphs that show how the objects cooperate to provide the system level functionality, visibility graphs that show how the objects reference each other, class descriptions that document each class, and inheritance graphs that show how the classes are related through inheritance.

6-4.1 Object Interaction Graphs

An object interaction graph is produced for each system operation. It shows what objects are involved in the computation and defines how they collaborate. We will develop an object interaction graph for each of the operations for which we built schemata in section 6-3.5.

The first step is to identify the objects (and possibly agents) that are involved in the realization of a system operation. For **enable_pump** the objects involved are a **Pump**, **Display**, **Motor**, and **Clutch**. Because the attendant invokes this operation, a **Terminal** must also be involved, because this is how the attendant interacts with the system.

In the second step the role of each object in implementing the operation is decided. One distinguished role is that of the *controller*. The controller receives the system operation message. In this example we will take the terminal as the controller because it is the part of the system with which the invoking agent (the attendant) interacts. This means that the other objects are the collaborators.

The third step is to decide how the functionality of the operation is distributed among the various objects involved. It would seem appropriate for the **Pump** to be responsible for starting the **Motor**, resetting the **Display**, and freeing the **Clutch**, because they are all components of the **Pump**. The **Terminal** then only needs to invoke **enable_pump** with the appropriate pump number.

In the final step, the distribution of functionality of the system operation is recorded in an object interaction graph. The object interaction graph for **enable_pump** is shown in Figure 6.18.

The next operation we consider is the **remove_gun** operation. The objects involved in this operation are the **Holster** and the **Gun**. Because the **Holster** switch determines whether the **Gun** is enabled or not, we will make the **Holster** the controller for this operation. This means the **Gun** is the collaborator. When **remove_gun** is invoked on the **Holster**, it enables the **Gun**. Figure 6.19 shows the object interaction graph for the **remove_gun** operation.

The operations **depress_trigger** and **release_trigger** involve the same group of objects, namely the **Pump**, **Clutch**, and **Gun**. In each operation the agent invoking the system operation does so using the **Gun**; thus this is the best choice for the controller. The **Clutch** and **Pump** are therefore collaborators.

Now we have to decide on the distribution of functionality. For the **Gun** to check the status of itself and the **Pump** it needs to send messages. Then the **Gun** needs to send the **Clutch** the **engage** or **free** message as appropriate.

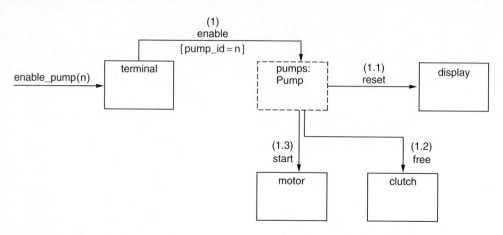

Description:
On receipt of the call to enable_pump(n) *the terminal invokes* enable_pump *with identifier* n. *If the pump is in service and not already enabled then its display is reset, its clutch is freed, and its motor is started.*

Figure 6.18   Object Interaction Graph for enable_pump

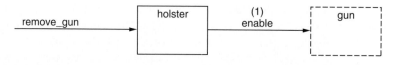

Description:
Removing the gun from the holster results in the gun being enabled.

Figure 6.19   Object Interaction Graph for remove_gun

Figures 6.20 and 6.21 show the object interaction graphs for **depress_trigger** and **release_trigger**, respectively.

The last operation we build an object interaction graph for is **replace_gun**. The objects involved in this operation are the **Display**, the **Pump**, the **Gun**, the **Holster**, a new **Transaction**, and the **Timer** agent. (The agent is involved in the object interaction graph because it is sent a message as part of the result of the operation.) **replace_gun** is invoked by the **Gun** being replaced in the **Holster** by the customer agent. Thus the **Gun** is a sensible choice for the controller. The remaining objects and the **Timer** agent are therefore collaborators.

Now we need to decide on the messaging required to implement the operation. The **Holster** can message the **Gun** directly to disable it, because they are both part of the **Pump**. The **Holster** then messages the **Pump** to notify it that the delivery is complete. The **Pump** then sends the **start** message to the **Timer**, disables itself, reads the display, and then creates a new **Transaction** and sends it to the **Terminal**. This messaging structure is shown in Figure 6.22.

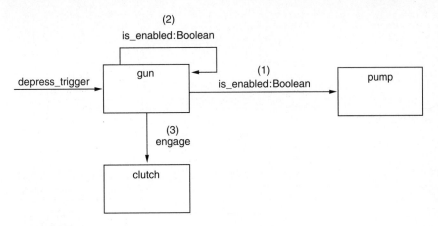

Description:
If the pump is enabled and the gun is enabled, then the clutch is engaged.

Figure 6.20   Object Interaction Graph for depress_trigger

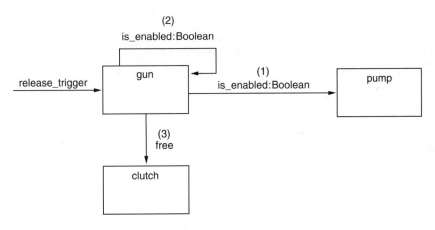

Description:
If the pump is enabled and the gun is enabled, then the clutch is freed.

Figure 6.21   Object Interaction Graph for release_trigger

Extension of Data Dictionary.

At this stage we can refine some of the data dictionary entries, particularly those referring to the attributes of **Gun**, **Holster**, and **Clutch**. We can give them types, and define data dictionary entries for those types. Figure 6.23 shows the entries.

All the types here are enumerations. The types **Volume**, **Cost**, and **Grade**, needed for **Display**s and **Transaction**s, can be put in the data dictionary, but their definitions are not supplied; without knowing what operations are needed on these types, they are incomplete.

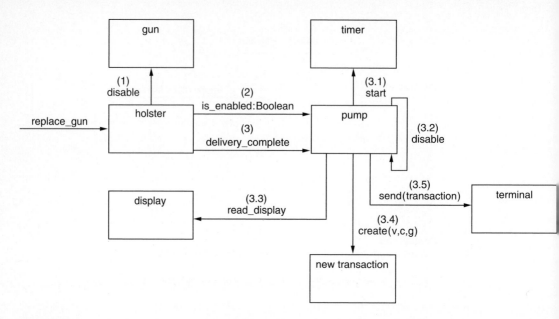

Description:

The holster disables the gun. If the pump was initially enabled, then it is sent delivery_complete. This results in the timer being started and the pump being disabled. The (final) value of the pump display is then read. A new transaction is created and initialized with the value, cost, and grade of the delivery. The transaction is then passed to the terminal for further processing, for example, by enter_payment_details.

Figure 6.22   Object Interaction Graph for replace_gun

Name	Kind	Type	Description
Gun.trigger	attribute	TriggerStatus	pressed or not
Gun.status	attribute	GunStatus	enabled or not
Holster.switch	attribute	SwitchStatus	pressed or not
Clutch.engaged	attribute	ClutchStatus	engaged or free
Pump.status	attribute	PumpStatus	see below
TriggerStatus	type	depressed | released	enumeration
GunStatus	type	enabled | disabled	enumeration
SwitchStatus	type	depressed | released	enumeration
ClutchStatus	type	engaged | free	enumeration
PumpStatus	type	enabled | disabled | out_of_service	enumeration

Figure 6.23   Data Dictionary Entries for Attributes and Types

Checking of models.

The object interaction graphs have to be checked for

- *Consistency with analysis models.* Each of the classes in the system object model should be represented in at least one object interaction graph.

- *Verification of functional effect.* A check is made to ensure that the functional effect of each object interaction graph satisfies the specification of its system operation given in the operation model.

6-4.2 Visibility Graphs

Once we have developed the object interaction graphs for all the system operations, we can construct a visibility graph for each class in the system. Visibility graphs define the scoping needed for object communication. To build a complete design we really need to consider all the object interaction graphs when building the visibility graphs. However, for the purposes of the case study we will only construct the visibility graphs needed to implement the object interaction graphs in section 6-4.1.

We will look at the development of the visibility graphs for the following classes:

- Pump
- Gun
- Terminal
- Holster

The first step in building the visibility graph for a class is to look at the object interaction graphs which involve it and extract the names of the classes of all the objects it messages. For **Pump** we get the following classes: **Display**, **Clutch**, **Motor**, **Terminal**, and **Transaction**. The object interaction graph for replace_gun also has a **Pump** sending a message to the timer agent, so this should be included in the visibility graph for **Pump**.

The next step is to consider the four visibility classification categories for each of these references. First we will consider the *lifetime* of the references. **Pump**s message a **Display** in two of our object interaction graphs. We can therefore assume this reference is useful in several contexts, so it should be permanent. Terminals, motors, clutches, transactions, and timers are only messaged in one context, so we could make all these references dynamic. However, each **Pump** has an associated (i.e., component) **Motor**, **Clutch**, and **Timer**, so we make these references permanent. This will allow us to nest **Motor** and **Clutch** inside **Pump** later on. Similarly, because there is only one **Terminal** in the system, it is simpler to make it a permanent reference. This leaves only **Transaction** as a dynamic reference.

Now we consider the *sharing* of the server objects. In our object interaction graphs, **Display**s are only messaged by **Pump**s. This is also the case for **Motor**s and **Timer**s. Thus each of these references can be **exclusive** to Pump. **Transaction** objects are messaged by both **Pump**s and the **Terminal**, so these references should be **shared**. Similarly, the **Terminal** may be messaged by any one of the five **Pump**s, and a **Clutch** may be messaged by a **Pump** or **Gun**, so their references are all **shared** as well.

The next step is to consider the *binding* of the server objects. The **Display**, **Clutch**, and **Motor** objects are components of the **Pump** and have lifetimes that are the same as the **Pump**. Thus we have chosen to make them **bound**, and they appear within the **Pump** client. The **Terminal** and **Transaction** objects have lifetimes that are separate from the pump. (For example the **Terminal** may be messaged by a different **Pump**; a **Transaction** can be archived.) The **Timer** is a part of the environment and so it also has a lifetime separate from the **Pump**. All these classes are **unbound**, and so appear outside the client.

Finally we consider the *mutability* of the server objects. The only reference that will change with time is the dynamic reference to **Transaction**. All the others can be marked **constant**. (Recall that it is the mutability of the *reference* we are considering, not that of the object referred to.)

Putting all this information together we get the visibility graph for the pump that is shown in Figure 6.24.

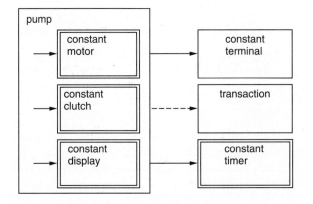

Figure 6.24   Visibility Graph for Pump

We consider the remaining classes. **Guns** messages **Pumps** and **Clutches**, **Holsters** messages **Guns** and **Pumps**, and the **Terminal** messages **Pumps** and **Transactions**. We proceed as for the **Pump**.

First, reference lifetime. **Guns** message **Pumps** and **Clutches** in more than one object interaction graph, so these should be permanent references. Similarly, **Holsters** message the gun in more than one object interaction graph, so that should also be a permanent reference. **Holsters** only message **Pumps** in one object interaction graph, so we could make this a dynamic reference. However, because each **Holster** is actually part of the **Pump** it messages, we make this a permanent reference also. The **Terminal** can send a message to any **Pump** on the forecourt, so we give it a permanent reference to the **pumps** collection. We do not know whether the **Terminal** messages any **Transactions**, but we do know the **Transaction** is passed to it as a parameter. It is thus a dynamic reference.

Next, reference sharing. Pumps are messaged by Guns, Holsters, and the Terminal, so this reference has to be **shared**. Clutches is messaged by Guns and Pumps, so this reference is also **shared**. However, Guns are only messaged by Holsters, so this reference can be **exclusive**. Finally, Transactions are messaged by the Terminal and by Pumps, so this reference is again **shared**.

Now we consider binding. Guns, Clutches, and Holsters are all parts of Pumps, so their lifetimes all coincide with that of the Pump. However, it is not really useful to further nest these classes inside each other. Transaction lifetime is probably independent of the Terminal because Transactions are archived.

Finally, mutability. Once again, all the permanent references can be marked **constant**, as they encode structural properties of the system. Figure 6.25 shows the resulting visibilities for Gun, Holster, and Terminal.

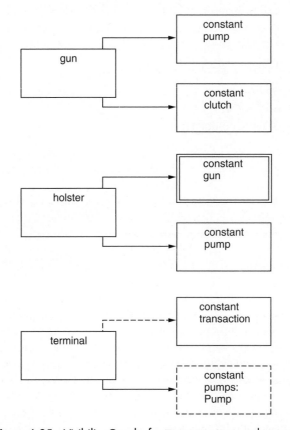

Figure 6.25   Visibility Graphs for Terminal, Gun, and Holster

Checking of Models.

The visibility graphs have to be checked for

- *Consistency with the analysis models.* For each relation on the system object model a check is made that there is a path of visibility for the corresponding classes on the visibility graphs.

- *Mutual consistency.* A check is made that exclusive target objects are not referenced by more than one class.

6-4.3 Class Descriptions

Now that we have completed the object interaction graphs and the visibility graphs we can construct the initial class descriptions. These collate the information from the previously developed analysis and design models. They are used along with the system object model to build the inheritance structures, which in turn allows us to complete the class descriptions.

The first step is to collect together the methods and parameters for **Pump**. The first place to look for these is in the object interaction graphs which involve **Pump**, i.e., those that send it a message. This yields the following methods:

- enable( ): Boolean
- disable( )
- is_enabled( )
- delivery_complete( )

When we look at the visibility graph for **Pump** we see there is one dynamic reference. This is to the newly created transaction, and so it is not a parameter for any of the methods of the pump class.

The next step is to look at the object model and object interaction graphs involving **Pump** again, to extract any value attributes. From the object model we get the attributes: **pump_id** and **status**. We need to define the values that the status attribute can take. This will be an enumeration consisting of the values **enabled, disabled,** and **out_of_service**. The object interaction graphs involving **Pump** reveal no extra value attributes.

Now we consult the visibility graph for the pump class to add any object-valued attributes. Any object to which **Pump** has a permanent reference will become an object-valued attribute in the class description. The visibility graph for **Pump** reveals the following object valued attributes: **terminal, motor, clutch, display,** and **timer**. Note that **transaction** will become a local variable in the **delivery_complete** operation, because **Pump** only accesses it during the execution of this method; hence it is a dynamic reference in the visibility graph. Also, because **timer** is an agent in the environment, it does not make sense to bind it to the pump class, so it too is a reference even though it is not shared.

With this information we can now complete the initial **Pump** class description. This is shown in Figure 6.26.

The rest of the class descriptions can be done in a similar fashion. The most interesting of the remaining classes are **Gun** and **Holster**. **Gun** has the following methods: **depress_trigger, release_trigger, enable, disable,** and **is_enabled,** which delivers a **Boolean** result. It has two value attributes, namely the status of the gun (either enabled or disabled) and the status of the trigger (either depressed or released). Consulting the visibility graph for **Gun** reveals two object-valued attributes: permanent **constant shared** references to a **Clutch** and a **Pump**. The class description for **Gun** is shown in Figure 6.27.

Holster has two methods: remove_gun and replace_gun. It has only one value attribute, namely **status**. It has two object-valued attributes: an **exclusive** permanent reference to **Gun** and a **shared** permanent reference to **Pump**. Both are **constant**. The resulting class description is shown in Figure 6.28.

```
class Pump
    attribute pump_id: integer
    attribute status:  PumpStatus
    attribute constant terminal:    Terminal
    attribute constant clutch:  Clutch
    attribute constant motor:  exclusive bound Motor
    attribute constant display:  exclusive bound Display
    attribute constant timer:  Timer // Timer is an agent
    method enable( )
    method disable( )
    method is_enabled( ):  Boolean
    method delivery_complete( )
endclass
```

Figure 6.26 Class Description for Pump

```
class Gun
    attribute constant clutch:  Clutch
    attribute constant pump:  Pump
    attribute trigger:  TriggerStatus
    attribute status:  GunStatus
    method depress_trigger( )
    method release_trigger( )
    method enable( )
    method disable( )
    method is_enabled( ):  Boolean
endclass
```

Figure 6.27 Class Description for Gun

```
class Holster
    attribute switch:  SwitchStatus
    attribute constant gun:  exclusive Gun
    attribute constant pump:  Pump
    method remove_gun( )
    method replace_gun( )
endclass
```

Figure 6.28 Class Description for Holster

The class descriptions derived for the other classes are shown in Figure 6.29. Those methods with arguments (**enable_pump**, **send**, and **create**) have them shown. The types **Volume**, **Cost**, and **Grade** should appear in the data dictionary.

Checking of Models.

The class descriptions have to be checked to ensure that

- All methods and parameters have been recorded.
- Data attributes from the system object model are recorded.
- Object attributes from the visibility graphs are recorded.
- Inheritance superclasses are recorded (checked after next stage).

```
class Terminal
    attribute constant pumps:  col Pump
    method enable_pump( pump_id )
    method send( t: Transaction )
endclass

class Transaction
    method create( v:  Volume, c: Cost, g: Grade )
endclass

class Motor
    attribute running:  Boolean
    method start( )
    method stop( )
endclass

class Clutch
    attribute status:  ClutchStatus
    method engage( )
    method free( )
endclass
```

Figure 6.29   Class Descriptions for Other Classes

6-4.4 Inheritance Graphs and Updating Class Descriptions

The final step in the Fusion design process is to build the inheritance graph for the classes identified by the object model and object interaction graphs and documented in the class descriptions. The first step is to look at the object model for the generalization relationship. When we constructed the initial object models we found two uses of the generalization relationship: **Pump** has two specializations, **SophisticatedPump** and **RegularPump**; and **Payment** has three specializations, namely, **CashPayment**, **CreditCardPayment**, and **AccountPayment**.

While developing the example further we have explored the design of only one class, **Pump**. During the development we have not considered its two subclasses at all. We see that **RegularPump** has no functionality beyond **Pump** and can therefore be dispensed with. The resulting part of the inheritance graph dealing with **Pump**, and its subclasses is shown in Figure 6.30

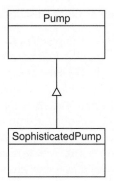

Figure 6.30   Inheritance Graph for Pump and SophisticatedPump

We can now build a class description for **SophisticatedPump** based on the **Pump** class we already have, because they are related by generalization. If we look at the object model we see that the sophisticated pump has two extra value attributes, **vol_select** and **amount_select**. If we consider the life-cycle model we see that there are two system operations that involve sophisticated pumps: **preset_volume** and **preset_amount**. It is reasonable to suppose that the controller for these operations will be the sophisticated pump, so the operations should be methods in its interface. The sophisticated pump will not require any visibilities beyond those for **Pump**. Figure 6.31 gives the class description for **SophisticatedPump**.

```
class Sophisticated Pump isa Pump
     attribute vol_select : Volume
     attribute amount_select : Amount
     method preset_amount( a: Amount )
     method preset_volume( v: Volume )
endclass
```

Figure 6.31   Class Description for SophisticatedPump

An inspection of the object interaction graphs and visibility graphs reveals no new opportunities for introducing abstractions. Thus we will not introduce any new superclasses, and so there are no changes to the existing class descriptions and other design models. This step concludes the design phase of Fusion.

6-5 IMPLEMENTATION

In this section we take the models developed previously in analysis and design and show the implementation of some of them in C++. There are two relatively independent activities involved here: implementing the life cycle, and implementing the classes and method bodies. This section develops implementations for the pump and gun, along with their associated methods. As the PetrolStation life cycle involves no interleaving, it yields readily to the method described in section 5-10, and we do not explore it here.

6-5.1 Implementation of Class Descriptions

In this section we look at implementing the class descriptions for Pump and Gun. The information we need for this task has already been collected up into the class descriptions, so this task is essentially one of translating them into the implementation language.

First consider Pump. The first step is to translate the attributes from the class description into C++ declarations. Pump has two value attributes, pump_id and status, and four object-valued attributes, terminal, motor, display, and timer. We will define the pump_id to be a C++ **int**, with a comment that it should be in the range 0 to 4. The status will be defined as a C++ enumeration type.

The object-valued attributes are more interesting. They are all **constant**. The motor and display attributes are **exclusive bound** and can therefore be object-valued attributes in C++ (i.e., not pointers; their representation is embedded in Pump instances). The Clutch is also **bound**, so it too is embedded, despite being **shared**. In contrast, attributes terminal and timer are **shared** and not **bound**; they become C++ references.

We make all these attributes **protected** rather than **private**, because we know that there is a derivation of Pump, namely, SophisticatedPump.

The reference members must be initialized when a Pump is created. We do this by declaring a constructor for Pump, which takes references to the appropriate objects as parameters.

The next step is to develop the declarations for the methods of Pump. There are four: enable, disable, is_enabled, and delivery_complete. Because we know that Pump is a superclass we will make all the methods virtual, that is, redefinable. The methods have no parameters, and only is_enabled has a return value (of type Boolean). The usual representation of Boolean values in C++ is **int**.

Figure 6.32 shows the resulting C++ class definition.

The reader may be surprised that Pump does not have Gun and Holster components, despite their appearing on the object model in section 6-3.1. This illustrates that aggregation on the object model is a matter of descriptive convenience rather than physical containment. Only the structure necessary to implement the references on the visibility graph appears in the class description, and hence the C++, for Pump.

Now we will develop the implementation of Gun's class description. Gun has two value attributes, trigger and status. Both can take on one of two values so we will implement them as **int**s with restricted value either 0 or 1. Gun has two object-valued attributes, both **constant**: clutch, an **exclusive** reference to a Clutch, and Pump, a **shared** reference to a Pump. We make clutch an embedded object, and pump a reference, initialized in the Gun constructor. This time the attributes are declared **private**, because we do not expect any derivations from Gun.

```
typedef enum pstatus { ENABLED, DISABLED, OUT_OF_SERVICE } PumpStatus;

class Pump {
    protected:
        int pump_id; // Value between 0 and 4
        PumpStatus status;
        Terminal &terminal;
        Clutch clutch;
        Motor motor;
        Display display;
        Timer &timer;
    public:
        Pump( Terminal &term, Timer &tim ) // Constructor
          : terminal(term), timer(tim) {} // initializes references
        virtual void enable( );
        virtual void disable( );
        virtual int is_enabled( );
        virtual void delivery_complete( );
};
```

Figure 6.32   C++ Class Definition for Pump

Gun has five methods, which we will implement using nonvirtual C++ member functions because we do not expect **Gun** to have any derivations. Once again these methods have no parameters and only **is_enabled** has a return value. This is modeled as before using C++ **int**.

The full class definition for **Gun** is shown in Figure 6.33.

```
class Gun {
    private:
        int trigger; // 0 = released, 1 = depressed
        int status; // 0 = disabled, 1 = enabled
        Clutch clutch;
        const Pump &pump;
    public:
        Gun( Pump &p ) : pump(p) {}
        void depress_trigger( );
        void release_trigger( );
        void enable( );
        void disable( );
        int is_enabled( );
};
```

Figure 6.33   C++ Class Definition for Gun

The remaining classes can be implemented in C++ in the same manner.

6-5.2 Implementation of Method Bodies

In this section we look at implementing some of the method bodies. In the example we have identified several system operations and constructed object interaction graphs for them. Most of the object interaction graphs have turned out to very simple, and we will only consider the implementation of two of them here. These are **enable** and **delivery_complete**, both of which are operations on a **Pump**.

First consider the operation **enable**. The object interaction graph for this operation is shown in Figure 6.18. The **Display**, **Clutch** and **Motor** are all attributes of the **Pump**, so there are no parameters and no local variables. The code for **enable** is shown in Figure 6.34.

```
void Pump::enable( )
{
    display.reset( );
    clutch.free( );
    motor.start( );
}
```

Figure 6.34   C++ for enable on Pump

The next operation we will look at is **delivery_complete**. Again this operation has no parameters, because all the objects it messages are attributes of pump, with one exception, the **Transaction**. When the delivery is complete the pump creates a new **Transaction** and sends it to the **Terminal**. The **Transaction** is therefore only accessed by the **Pump** during the **delivery_complete** operation and is thus not an attribute, but a local variable. The transaction has a lifetime that is separate from the pump, so it must be allocated in the heap using **new**. The code for **delivery_complete** is shown in Figure 6.35.

```
void Pump::delivery_complete( )
{
    Volume vol;
    Cost cost;
    Grade grade;
    Transaction* transaction;

    timer.start( );
    disable( );
    display.read(vol, cost, grade);
    transaction = new Transaction (vol, cost, grade);
    terminal.send (transaction);
}
```

Figure 6.35   C++ for delivery_complete

6-6 SUMMARY

In this chapter we have taken a requirements statement for a petrol station forecourt system and developed some of the components to C++ code. Specifically we have covered the following:

- Developing the object model showing the structure of the classes in the problem domain.
- Producing the interface model, consisting of the life ycle, system object model and operation model to describe the required functionality of the system.
- Creating object interaction graphs for a selection of the system operations in the object model to show how the objects interact to achieve the system functionality. From the object interaction graphs we have produced the visibility graphs showing the links needed by the messaging structure.
- Combining the information from the object interaction graphs and visibility graphs with information from the system object model to produce class descriptions.
- Implementing the design in C++.

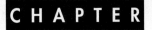

CHAPTER

7

Exercises

This chapter provides several exercises, of varying difficulty, for reinforcing Fusion model building skills. We do not provide any exercises that concentrate on individual models. The reason for this is that the Fusion method is foremost a process for building a set of closely coupled models of a system. Therefore, the exercises focus on developing the complete set of Fusion models.

The first two exercises directly follow from the examples developed in the exposition of Fusion (chapters 3 to 5) and the case study (chapter 6).

The next four exercises are led projects for which the development of simple models of each kind employed in the Fusion method is required. The first three of these are fairly lightweight; the last is more involved.

The final three exercises require the application of the entire Fusion method as summarized in appendix A. They are suitable for the workshop portion of a Fusion training course.

7-1 ECO DEPOT

1. Consider the addition of a new class of store building, a store that only stores chemicals of type3. Where is this class best placed in the inheritance graph for the ECO Depot? Justify your answer.

2. Develop an object interaction graph for the **collect** operation on the ECO depot.

3. Develop implementations for the **end_check_in** and **space_for_drum** methods for which object interaction graphs are provided in chapter 4. Compare one or more implementations, and discuss the advantages and disadvantages of particular implementation choices.

4. The ECO depot problem developed in chapters 3 to 5 is extended with the following new system operations:

- **stores_for_load**. Given a load L of two types of chemicals, type3 and one of type1 or type2, this operation calculates all the stores capable of storing part of this load. For each store it returns a (type × **capacity_left**) record.
- **calculate_invoice**. To discourage waste production, each source for the loads is charged an annual fee as a function of the percentage of the total store they use. Chemicals type1 and type2 are more expensive than type3. The rate of charging is as follows:

	type3	type1/type2
x > 50%	$1000	$2000
10% ≤ x ≤ 50%	$500	$1000
x < 10%	$100	$200

- **bonus/penalty**. Each source for the loads gets a bonus if the total amount of chemical loaded in one year is less than the total amount the previous year per chemical type. There is also a penalty system if the total amount deposited is greater than in the previous year. The calculation is done according to the following equations for each chemical type:

$$\text{bonus} = \text{number of kgs less} \times (10\% \text{ cost/kg})$$
$$\text{penalty} = \text{number of kgs more} \times (15\% \text{ cost/kg})$$

- **recover_from_leakage**. There is the possibility that a **Drum** leaks at a given store. There is emergency action for this when type1 or type2 chemicals leak. Each neighboring store of the store to which the drum belongs must be cleared of the noncompatible chemical.

    – Define an operation model for the **recover_from_leakage** operation. You may want to use an amended version of **stores_for_load** to find the possible stores to which the chemicals can be moved.
    – Redefine the **deliver_load** operation model and object interaction graph so that recovery from leakage is always possible. Consider two models.
      * Minimize neighbors with noncompatible chemicals.
      * Ensure that there is enough spare capacity to which the maximally moved load can be reallocated.

(a) For each new query, define an operation model for this functionality and update the object model as necessary.

(b) Design object interaction graphs for the new operations.

(c) Check that the classes participating in these new object interaction graphs have the required visibilities. If not, revise the relevant visibility graphs.

(d) Incorporate the new operations into the life-cycle model presented in section 3-6.1.

(e) Develop implementations for the new operations.

5. Use the ECO depot as an analogy for memory management. Consider how the object model in chapter 2 may have to be modified. Also consider how the object interaction graph for the **deliver_load** operation is to be modified for memory management.

6. What other analogies can be developed for the ECO depot example?

7-2 PETROL STATION

The requirements for the petrol station system, described in chapter 6, state that the system will control the dispensing of petrol, handle customer payment, and monitor tank levels. The chapter develops the interface model and classes responsible for controlling the dispensing of petrol. Consider now the petrol system's role in monitoring tank levels. Extend the system so that an alarm is raised to notify the attendant if any of the tanks drop below 10% of their capacity. If the alarm is not acted on, the tank level may go below 4% capacity, causing the pumps to be put out of service. When a tank has been refilled so that its level is above 4% capacity, the pumps should be brought back into service. Decide whether the tank levels should be monitored by the pumps (periodically or with every petrol sale) or whether the tanks should "inform" the pumps when they are refilled.

1. Update the system object model to reflect this new scenario.
2. Develop object interaction graphs for the new operations.
3. Revise the life-cycle model to account for the new operations/events.
4. Develop/revise visibility graphs for **Tank** and **Pump**.
5. Construct a class description for **Tank**.

7-3 PCB ASSEMBLY

The automated manufacture and assembly of everything from office tables to electronic devices is becoming increasingly commonplace. We describe here a system to control the assembly of printed circuit boards (PCB).

The PCB assembly line consists of two PCB racks, a conveyer, and several assembly stations. The assembly of PCBs is carried out at the assembly stations. The stations are located along the conveyer, which carries the boards from and to racks at either end, containing, respectively, empty and filled boards. The assembly line is started manually by an operator when the racks are attached to the conveyer. At each conveyer cycle, as many empty boards are loaded onto the conveyer from a rack as there are assembly stations, the empty boards are moved to position at the stations, the boards are filled with components, and, lastly, the filled boards are taken to and unloaded onto a rack. The number of conveyer cycles is equal to the capacity of a rack divided by the number of assembly stations.

An assembly station consists of a tray that contains the components to be mounted and a movable beam onto which are mounted "hands" that can rotate, pick up, place, and solder components. Once the board is in position at a station the mounting cycle begins. The beam moves from its quiescent position to the tray, and the "hands" pick up the components to be mounted. The beam then moves to position over the board, guided by infrared sensors that feed back the exact location of the board with respect to the station. The "hands" rotate to the correct orientation, place the components onto the board and then solder them in. An assembly cycle consists of the number of mounting cycles needed to fill the board completely. At the end of an assembly cycle, the beam moves back to its quiescent position.

1. Develop an object model for this system.
2. Develop an operation model and object interaction graph for the **start_assembly** operation. Hierarchically decompose the suboperations invoked by the **start_assembly** operation so that all the necessary operations on the **Beam** class are specified.
3. Develop a visibility graph for **Beam**.
4. Construct a class description for **Beam**.

7-4 GEOGRAPHICAL INFORMATION SYSTEM

A geographical information system maintains information on the properties of resources or features "attached" to some region, such as a city or campus, in physical space. Such information systems are commonplace in urban and regional planning agencies and communications network management departments, and are starting to appear in other spatially dispersed administrative entities such as university campuses and corporate sites.

1. Develop a basic object model for a city. Model the city from the viewpoint of a tourist. Compare with the models developed for the geographical information system described in [16].
2. Consider how this system might be employed by a taxi driver to find an optimal route (where optimal can be defined as shortest distance or least amount of time) from a hotel location to a tourist attraction. Note that street congestion, as well as length and direction, will affect the traveling time. Because street congestion conditions will have to be updated periodically, assume there exists a system comprised of monitoring stations and a clearing house that broadcasts this information.

   Refine the object model for this application.
3. Develop an operation model and object interaction graph for the **find_route** operation. Hierarchically decompose the suboperations invoked by the **find_route** operation so that all the necessary operations on the **Street** class are specified.

4. Develop a visibility graph for **Street**.

5. Construct a class description for **Street**.

6. How would the object model (operation model, etc.) have to be changed if the shortest *bus* route was desired?

7-5 RENTAL SYSTEM

A rental system is used by an agent to track the allocation of resources for the temporary use of customers. A resource is allocated to a customer for a certain duration of time called a rental period. A rental period will be a multiple of some time unit such as hour, day, and so on. Different resources will have different fees (including zero fee) per time unit.

Resources can be reserved for rental periods in the future. Both reservations and current allocations can be canceled before the rental period expires. The rental system may also provide waiting lists for resources that are allocated or reserved, and there is the possibility of a cancellation freeing up the resource.

Once the rental period has ended, two actions are possible. The resource must be returned, at which time the fee for the rental will be due, or the rental agreement can be renewed. A resource should not be renewed if there is a waiting list or a future reservation that might overlap with the renewed rental period. If the resource is neither returned or renewed, the customer will be liable for overdue charges.

For each rental, customer information (such as an address where the customer can be located) must be maintained so as to be able to track down the resource if it is needed urgently during the rental period or if the resource is not returned or renewed after a suitable grace period.

Such a system could be the basis of any of several rental systems: theater seat, place in a university course, hotel room booking, car hire, or library system.

1. Develop a *reusable* object model for a rental system.

2. Brainstorm a set of operations for the agent entering the rental information. Develop an operation model schema for each operation.

3. Develop a life-cycle model for the rental system operations.

4. Develop object interaction graphs for the rental system operations **renew_rental** and **request_resource**.

5. Develop a visibility graph for **Rental**.

6. Construct a class description for **Rental**.

7. Develop an implementation of the rental system life-cycle model.

7-6 GRAPHICAL PROGRAMMING LANGUAGE

The aim is to develop a tool for editing and running programs written in a graphical language.

A program consists of a **Start_statement**, followed by a sequence of statements and ending in a **Stop_statement**. Each statement type has a particular graphical representation called a **view**. The tool supports the insertion, deletion, and replacement of statements. In addition, some statement types have a specialized set of functions.

- **Std_Deviation_Node** and **Average_Node**

    - Add formal input parameter
    - Remove formal input parameter

- **If_statement**

    - Add branch
    - Remove branch

- **Loop**

    - Insert statement

A program is well defined when each statement is fully connected, that is, each has actual input parameters for the formal input parameters. Only statements terminated with output nodes can show the value calculated. The user can also check the well-definedness of the program currently being edited. A program can be executed only when it is well defined.

A sample program appears in Figure 7.1.

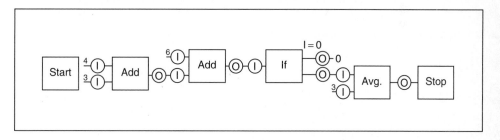

Figure 7.1   Sanmple GPL Program

The BNF grammar of the programming language is given subsequently.

<Program> ::= <ProgramHeader> <Statements> <ProgramStop>

<ProgramHeader> ::= <Start_statement>

<Statements> ::= (<Statement>)*

<Statement> ::= (<If_statement> | <Loop> | <Simple_statement>)

<Loop> ::= <While_exp> <Statement>* <End_while>

<Simple_statement> ::= <Add_Node> | <Mult_Node>|
<Average_Node> | <Std_Deviation_Node> |
<Input_Node> | <Output_Node>

<Add_Node> ::= <Data_parameter> x <Data_parameter> -> <Data_parameter>

<Mult_Node> ::= <Data_parameter> x <Data_parameter> -> <Data_parameter>

<Std_Deviation_Node> ::= <Data_parameter>* -> <Data_parameter>

<Average_Node> ::= <Data_parameter>* -> <Data_parameter>

<Input_Node> ::= -> <Data_parameter>

<Output_Node> ::= <Data_parameter>

<ProgramStop> ::= <Stop_statement>

In summary, the tool should support the following functions:

- Create a program.
- Select and copy a program section to the copy buffer.
- Select and insert a program section from the copy buffer into the current program edited.
- Insert/delete a statement.
- Replace a statement with another statement.
- Check the well-definedness of a program.
- Run a program by pressing the **Run** view.
- Stop the execution of a program by pressing the **Stop** view.

Analysis.

1. Develop an object model for this example. Pay particular attention to the relationships between programs, statements, and views. Define the system interface.
2. Develop

   (a) The life-cycle model for this system considering the relationship between **Run, Stop** and the well-definedness of the program.
   (b) An Operation model for the following functions:
   - Create a program.
   - Copy a program/section of program to copy buffer.

- Replace a statement with another.
- Check the well-definedness of a program.
- Run a program.

Design.

1. Develop object interaction graphs for

- Create a program.
- Copy a program/section of program to copy buffer.
- Select a program/statement from the copy buffer.
- Check the well-definedness of a program.

2. Define visibility graphs for the program, statements, and their respective views, **Run** and **Start_statement** views and program nodes.

Implementation.

Define the class specifications for create a program, copy to buffer, and select from buffer.

Enhancements.

1. A program has other views besides the graphical view (e.g., assembler code, machine code) that can be simultaneously shown. Extend the object model, object interaction graphs, and visibility graphs for this enhancement. What effect does this have on the **create_program** functionality?

2. Optimize the copy to buffer and select from buffer operations so that the copy to buffer is a shallow copy and the select from buffer is a deep copy. What effect does this have on the visibility graphs?

3. Extend the language to be multithreaded. A program is defined as

$$<Program> ::= <Run> <Threads> <Stop>$$
$$<Threads> ::= <Thread>*$$
$$<Thread> :: = <Start\_thread> <Statements> <Stop\_thread>$$

Pressing **Run** executes all threads. Pressing **Stop** stops the execution of all threads. Pressing **Start_thread** starts the execution of one thread. Pressing the **Stop_thread** stops the execution of its thread. When the **Run** is pressed, there must be no executing threads.

(a) Extend the object model for this example. Extend the life-cycle model.

(b) Define operation models for **Start_thread** and **Stop_thread**.

(c) Extend the object model to distinguish between executing and nonexecuting threads.

(d) Amend the object interaction graphs to reflect this change.

(e) Extend the inheritance graph to include **Thread**, **Start_thread**, and **Stop_thread**.

(f) What are the similarities between programs, threads, and statements?

  (g) Extend the visibility graphs for **Run** and **Stop** for multithreading.

  (h) Does multithreading have any effect on the copy to buffer optimization?

7-7 ATM

Certain examples have acquired canonical status in the system development method community. A cruise control system for a car and an elevator controller are two common ones. For object-oriented methods, the ATM problem is popular. It has been developed using OMT in Rumbaugh et al. [93] and Responsibility Driven Design in Wirfs-Brock et al. [108].

We have found this to be a suitable problem for a 1.5-day Fusion workshop as described in section 10-2.2. Although it exercises all the notations of Fusion, it is particularly good for practicing life-cycle modeling.

Requirements.

An ATM is a machine through which bank customers can perform several of the most common financial transactions. The machine consists of a display screen, a bank card reader, numeric and special input keys, a money dispenser slot, and a receipt printer. When the machine is idle, a greeting message is displayed. The keys will remain inactive until a bank card has been entered. When a bank card is inserted, the card reader attempts to read it. If the card cannot be read, the user is informed that the card is unreadable, and the card is ejected.

If the card is readable, the user is asked to enter a personal identification number (PIN). If the PIN is entered correctly, the user is shown the menu that contains a list of the transactions that can be performed: deposit funds into an account, withdraw funds from an account, transfer funds from one account to another, and query the balance for an account.

For the deposit transaction, the customer must specify the account where the deposit is to be made and the amount of the deposit. The withdraw transaction requires the customer to specify which account the withdrawal is to be made from and the amount to be withdrawn. The amount must not exceed the limit on the card or cause the account to become further overdrawn than permitted. The transfer transaction requires the source and destination accounts as well as the amount to transfer. No transfer may exceed the balance of the source account. The withdrawal limit on the card is not relevant to the transfer transaction. Finally, the balance inquiry transaction requires the user to supply the account number for which the balance is to be displayed.

If an incorrect PIN is entered the user is given up to two additional chances to enter the PIN correctly. Failure to do so on the third try causes the machine to keep the bank card. The user can retrieve the card only by dealing directly with the bank. The user can select a transaction and specify all relevant information. When a transaction has been completed, the system returns to the main menu. At any time after reaching the main menu and before finishing a transaction (including before selecting a transaction), the user may press the cancel key. The transaction being specified (if there is one) is canceled, the user's card is returned, and the machine once again becomes idle. If a withdrawal transaction is selected, the user is asked to specify the amount of the withdrawal. If the account contains sufficient funds, the funds are given to the user through the cash dispenser. If a balance inquiry is selected, the balance is not displayed but is printed on the receipt.

7-8 CONFERENCE SYSTEM

The following requirements are a generalized version of a problem statement distributed at the 1991 OOPSLA Conference. A worked solution to the original statement appeared in the analysis and design column of the Journal of Object-Oriented Programming [91], [92].

Requirements.

A conference is held at regular intervals to bring together experts from various disciplines to discuss topics of interest. No permanent body exists that is responsible for the conference. Financial support for the conference is obtained from one or more sponsoring professional organizations. The conference itself is put together and run by volunteers from the professional "community" who are enlisted in committees to manage various tasks. At minimum, two committees are usually required.

The program committee is responsible for deciding on the technical content of the conference. The program committee has a subcommittee responsible for the selection of tutorials given during the conference.

The organizing committee handles financial matters, local arrangements, invitations, and publicity. It should ensure that interested members of the community are invited to participate and attend. Given a fixed level of sponsorship, the organizing committee must ensure that sufficient people attend the conference so that the financial break-even point is reached without exceeding the maximum dictated by the facilities available.

An information system should be designed to support the activities of both the program committee and an organizing committee involved in arranging a conference. Such an information system could serve equally well the organizers of a trade show or hobbyists convention. The involvement of the two committees is also analogous to two organizational entities within a corporate structure using some common information.

Lists of the activities of the program and organizing committees follow:

Program Committee Activities.

- Prepare a list to whom the call for papers/tutorials is to be sent.
- Register the letters of intent received in response to the call.
- Register the contributed papers.
- Distribute the papers among those undertaking the refereeing.
- Collect the referees' reports and select the papers for inclusion in the program.
- Group selected papers into sessions for presentation, and select chairs for each session.

- Schedule sessions, and notify the authors of selection.
- Register proposals for tutorials.
- Distribute the proposals to members of the tutorial review committee.
- Collect committee reports, and select the tutorials for inclusion in the program.
- Schedule the tutorials, and notify the authors of selection.

Organizing Committee Activities.

- Prepare a list of people to invite to the conference.
- Issue priority invitations to past attendees and members of the sponsoring organization(s).
- Ensure all authors of each selected paper or tutorial receive an invitation.
- Ensure authors of rejected papers or tutorials receive an invitation.
- Avoid sending duplicate invitations to any individual.
- Enlist sponsoring organization(s).
- Ensure that enough people attend conference to break even financially.
- Ensure that the attendance does not exceed the maximum dictated by the facilities.
- Ensure that the final copies of the papers are received one month in advance of the conference for printing. One way to do this is to program "reminder" letters into the system.
- Register attendees before and during the conference.
- Print a badge for each attendee on their arrival at the conference.
- Generate a list of attendees for each tutorial, ensuring that attendees do not register for concurrent tutorials.
- Generate a final list of attendees.

7-9 ELECTRONIC WHITEBOARD

Computer Supported Cooperative Work has received much attention recently. The aim of this project is to design a shared electronic whiteboard whereby a group of people can participate in a computer-mediated conversation.

Requirements.

The interface to the electronic whiteboard creation tool is a window that displays a list of potential participants, a list of invitees, and several buttons for constructing the invitee list, creating a whiteboard with these users and specifying the type of whiteboard required.

To initiate a conversation (i.e., a group of users sharing a whiteboard), a user first generates a list of would-be participants. When a conversation is created, each user in the list is asked if they wish to join in the conversation (a list of all the invitees is supplied with the invitation). It is assumed that the initiating user wishes to participate in the conversation, and so they do not receive an invitation.

When every user has responded to the invitation, (or *timeout* seconds have elapsed, whichever is sooner), an interface to the shared whiteboard is created for each user who has accepted (and for the creating user).

The initiator of the conversation decides on which interface should be used: a simple text-based interface that allows the participants to exchange messages, or a more elaborate "scrawl" interface with facilities for drawing as well as text entry. All participants are provided with the same type of interface, and it is not possible to change the type of interface during the conversation.

In the text-based interface, the participant is provided with two windows: one for editing messages and the other for displaying received messages. When the send message button is pressed, the text in the editing window is broadcast to all the participants and displayed in the received messages window. The name of the sender is displayed with the message.

The scrawl interface provides one main window. Everything that the user draws or writes on the whiteboard is broadcast to the other participants. A menu allows the user to vary the form of input: "scrawl" allows the user to draw with a pen, "airbrush" is analogous to a spray can, "text" allows the user to enter text, and "eraser" allows the user to clean portions of the whiteboard.

Apart from entering text and graphics, both types of whiteboards can be cleared and saved to and restored from a file.

Once a whiteboard has started, participating users may leave, and new users may be invited to join. The list of current participants can also be displayed. When users are invited to join an existing conversation, they again have the option to accept or refuse, and a list of the current participants is provided. The conversation continues until the last participant leaves, or until the initiator "closes" the conversation. If the initiator leaves the conversation (rather than closing it), the conversation continues among the remaining participants. A user may be involved in more than one conversation at any given time.

CHAPTER

8

Fusion and Other Methods

8-1 INTRODUCTION

Fusion was developed because existing object-oriented methods did not meet the requirements of industrial software projects. It was not, however, developed from scratch. The previous "generation" of object-oriented methods was synthesized into a method that better met the requirements.

This chapter looks at Fusion in the context of some other object-oriented methods. We begin by introducing a set of criteria for assessing methods. The next four sections describe in detail four important object-oriented methods that provided many of Fusion's core features. Each description is followed by an assessment against the criteria. The next section references some other methods that have influenced Fusion. Finally, we discuss the rationale behind Fusion, and how these other methods have influenced it. We conclude with an assessment of Fusion.

8-2 CRITERIA FOR ASSESSING METHODS

There are several comparisons of object-oriented methodologies, [9], [34], [36], [81], [64], [100], [103], but there is no agreed way of comparing or evaluating different methods.

The criteria given subsequently assess methods from the practical perspective of industrial projects wishing to use a method. Each role in a project (e.g., software

developer, manager, maintainer, etc.) has a different perspective on the requirements for a method. The following criteria we use to reflect these differing needs.

- *Does it make it easier to develop a system?* The method should provide a step-by-step guide for getting from requirements to code. There should be checks for assessing when each step has been successfully completed. If multiple models are used then their interrelationship should be clear. It should be possible to get an overall view of the system and also detect inconsistencies.

- *Does the method make the system easier to maintain?* The method should allow the important decisions to be recorded. Thus the models should be intuitive, concise, and scaled up for large developments.

- *Does it help produce software with good object-oriented structure?* The method should help the design of inheritance hierarchies and run-time structures. Two crucial problems are designing control flow and dynamic object creation.

- *Does it assist project management?* Like all software technologies, the object-oriented approach requires careful management. The method should have a systematic process with defined deliverables.

- *Can it be given effective tool support?* CASE tools help automate software development. Simple drawing tools require the notations to have a defined syntax. More powerful tools, such as those that allow requirements to be traced to code, depend on the semantics of the notations being defined.

In the next sections we describe four different important and established methods: Object Modeling Technique (OMT) [93], Booch [14], Objectory [58], and CRC [11]. The ECO example is used as a vehicle for illustrating the methods. In each section we provide a short assessment of the method against the criteria.

8-3 OBJECT MODELING TECHNIQUE

Figure 8.1 presents an overview of the OMT process. It is divided into three phases: analysis, which is concerned with modeling the real world; design, which decides on subsystems and overall architecture; and implementation, which encodes the design in a programming language.

8-3.1 Analysis

There are three models in the analysis phase: the *object model*, the *dynamic model*, and the *functional model*. It is recommended that they be produced in this order. In Figure 8.1, the arrow from the functional model back to the object model indicates that there is an iteration to verify and refine the models.

Object Model.

Figure 8.2 shows part of an OMT object model for the ECO example. The OMT object model is meant to capture the static structure of a system by showing the classes in the system, relationships between the classes, and the attributes and operations that

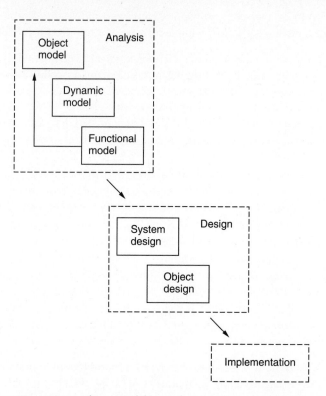

Figure 8.1 Object Modeling Technique: Process Overview

characterize each class. It is the most important of the three models. The notation is an extended entity-relationship diagram, which describes objects, classes, and relationships. In addition it can display methods and invariants. Binary relationships are shown with labeled lines; ternary and higher relationships use relation diamonds. Symbols on the ends of the relationship lines show the cardinality of the relationship.

Dynamic Model.

The dynamic model uses state machine diagrams to capture the dynamic behavior of each class. Each state machine shows how the class objects respond to *events*. An *event* represents an instantaneous external stimulus; a *state* is an abstraction of the attribute values and relationships of an object. The state machine transitions show how events cause an object to change state and perform operations.

Figure 8.3 shows a state machine for the **Loading_bay** class. The **Loading_bay** has three states and responds to events **check_in_drum**, **end_check_in**, and **load_bay_empty**. Associated with each state transition there may be an instantaneous operation, called an *action*. For example, **check_in_drum** causes the action, send event **update_manifest** to the objects that can receive it.

Activities may be attached to states. An *activity* is an operation that takes time to complete. Whenever a **Loading_bay** object enters the **END OF DELIVERY** state

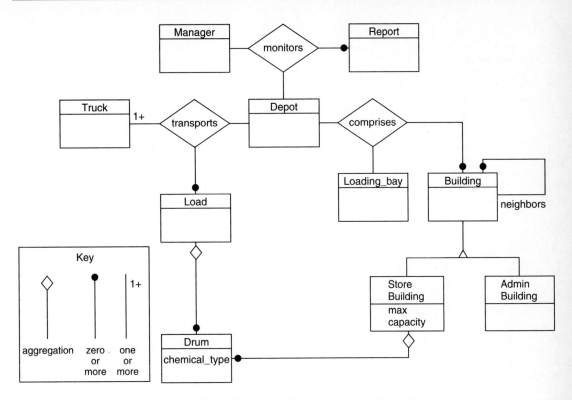

Figure 8.2 Object Modeling Technique: Object Model

the activity **compute allocation** is performed. On exiting from the state the events **drums to be returned**, and **allocation of drums** are generated.

State machines suffer from state explosion. That is, the number of states grows rapidly with the size of the application. OMT recommends the use of Harel notation, [50], which introduces two combinators on machines (viz. nesting of machines and the product of machines). These help overcome the state explosion problem and provide a more intuitive descriptions of larger machines.

Functional Model.

The functional model shows what has to be done by a system. It uses data flow diagrams (DFD) [37] to show how outputs are computed for inputs. The purpose of the functional model is to specify the computations without regard for the order in which the values are computed. Figure 8.4 shows a DFD for checking in a drum. The sources, sinks, data stores, and the values on arcs represent objects and the nodes are processes. For a given application there will be a hierarchy of DFDs, in which the behavior of each higher level node is defined by a lower-level diagram. A higher-level process corresponds to an operation on a complex object and a leaf node process represents a method on an object.

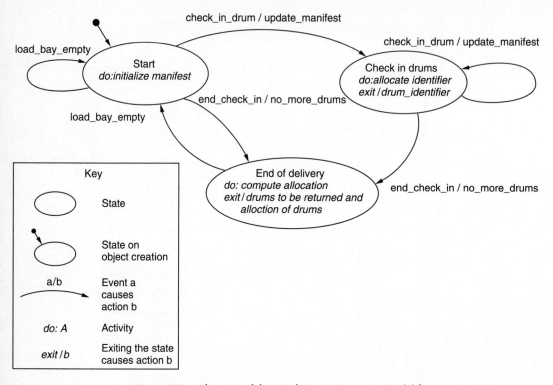

Figure 8.3   Object Modeling Technique: Dynamic Model for Loading_bay

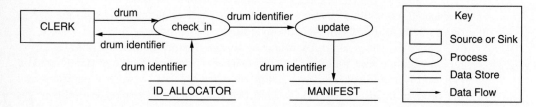

Figure 8.4   Object Modeling Technique: Functional Model for Checking in a Drum

Analysis Process.

Analysis concentrates on modeling the world. The method gives advice on identifying appropriate classes and associations between them. Attributes are added as necessary. The object model is refined using inheritance. The dynamic model is built by considering the events coming into the system and its responses; these are formalized with the state diagram. Then the functional model is built by examining input and output values (which are parameters of events) and showing dependencies using data-flow diagrams; this process may uncover additional, internal, values.

As with any realistic development process, OMT analysis is iterative. The functional model can reveal extra objects and methods that have to be incorporated into the other two models. All three models should be compared with the requirements. The phase is completed when all the models are consistent and capture all the requirements.

8-3.2 Design

The design phase builds on the analysis models. However, it does not introduce any models of its own. Instead, it consists of heuristics or guidelines for carrying out the design. There are two stages: the *system design* and the *object design*.

The system design breaks the system into subsystems, allocates processes to processors, and commits to the overall architecture (e.g., batch vs. interactive). The issues that arise include resource management and organization of data stores. OMT suggests various architectural approaches, but does not constrain the designer to them.

The object design stage decides on algorithms for methods. The analysis models are combined to determine the methods of each class. Data representations are chosen, and the inheritance graph may have to be adjusted to reflect design decisions. Relationships must be encoded in a way suitable for their use. Finally, the design is partitioned into modules suitable for the target programming language.

8-3.3 Implementation

The implementation step converts the object design into code. Guidelines are given for how different aspects, such as the implementation of relationships, may be encoded in various object-oriented languages. The method also covers such issues as programming style and how to design classes for reuse.

8-3.4 Assessment

- *Does it make it easier to develop a system?* The analysis stage provides a step-by-step process, and each step is supported by many heuristics. However, there are few rules for discovering inconsistencies between models.
  Because there are no design models, design is essentially a process of coding the analysis models. The large gap between analysis and code can make this a daunting task.

- *Does the method make the system easier to maintain?* The object model can be used to record much structural information. The dynamic model captures the behavior of individual classes. The functional model is less successful because DFDs are essentially operational and are thus not good for specifying behavior. In practice, some OMT users omit the functional model.
  The models contain features for scaling up for larger developments.

- *Does it help produce software with good object-oriented structure?* Inheritance in analysis, design, and implementation is fully treated by OMT. Object interaction is not supported by an explicit model; neither is dynamic object creation.

- *Does it assist project management?* The deliverables from the analysis phase are well defined. However, because there are no design models, knowing when the analysis phase is complete and when design should begin can be a problem.

- *Can it be given effective tool support?* OMT is supported by several CASE tools. The absence of a rigorous semantics limits them mainly to diagraming support.

The primary strength of OMT is its analysis phase. It has a well-defined process, and all the models use concise and understandable notations. The relationship between the three models is not clear. They are developed more or less independently, and it can be difficult to get the overall picture.

The main weakness is that the design stage lacks the step-by-step approach of the analysis phase. It is less clear where to start and what to do next, but it does embody some useful heuristics.

8-4 BOOCH

Figure 8.5 gives an overview of the Booch process. Booch acknowledges that analysis and design cannot proceed in isolation of each other, and advocates a piecemeal approach; keep improving the design until you are satisfied. Booch calls this "round-trip gestalt design" and suggests this is the foundation of object-oriented development. Thus the Booch process is descriptive (saying what you *may* do) rather than prescriptive (saying what you *should* do).

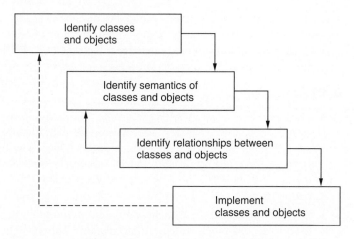

Figure 8.5   Booch: Process Overview

8-4.1 Process Steps

The first step is to identify the objects and classes that form part of the system. Then the interface for classes is constructed (this is "identifying the semantics") followed by finding relationships between the classes. The discovery of relationships may cause new interfaces to be added, so these two steps are iterated until a satisfactory state is obtained. Then the implementation stage decides on the representation of class internals (attributes and behavior); this in turn may result in having to apply the entire process to the behavior of a single class.

8-4.2 Notations

Because of the descriptive nature of the process, we discuss the notations without a process ordering. There are six notations: *object diagrams*, *class diagrams*, *timing diagrams*, *state diagrams*, *module diagrams*, and *process diagrams*.

Class Diagrams.

Class diagrams show classes and their relationships. A class diagram is a notational variation of entity-relationship diagrams. *Inheritance*, *instantiation*, and *use* are standard relationships. There is also an "undefined" relationship arrow, to show that a relation exists but that its kind has not been fixed.

To deal with complex diagrams, the notation allows *class categories* that group classes into namespaces. Each category is itself a class diagram, and the classes it exports to other categories, or imports from other categories, are so labeled.

Drafts of class diagrams are produced during the initial stages of the development and are completed when identifying the relationships among classes.

Object Diagrams.

An object diagram shows objects and their relationships. Whereas class relationships are mostly static, object relationships are dynamic; during the life of a system described by a few tens of classes, some millions of objects may be created and destroyed. An object diagram exhibits the behavior of a "typical" object by showing the objects and the relationships between them. In this instance "relationship" means that the objects can send messages to each other.

The object diagrams can be annotated in several ways. The *visibility* of one object from another can be shown; this distinguishes between visibility by scope, slot, or parameter, and independently whether the referenced object is shared or not. The relationship lines can be made directed and labeled with the names of the messages that they represent. Finally, messages can be marked with synchronization information (Booch deals with multiple threads of control, not single sequential systems).

Booch places particular emphasis on discovering the "key mechanisms" of a design. A *mechanism* is any structure whereby objects work together to provide some behavior that satisfies a requirement of the problem. Figure 8.6 is an object diagram showing the key mechanism involved in getting a status report on the depot. Objects are represented by an amorphous blob icon. Like class diagrams, drafts of object diagrams are produced during early stages of development and completed during the identification of the relationships among classes and objects.

Timing Diagrams.

Object diagrams show possible message communication between objects, without showing control flow. State diagrams show timing information for *single* objects. To show timing of message sends, the object diagram may be annotated with sequencing information, or pseudocode can be added to it.

Booch also suggests using timing diagrams to display ordering information. A timing diagram has time as the *x*-axis and the different objects as the *y*-axis; a line represent the flow of control between objects, as in Figure 8.7. The notation is similar

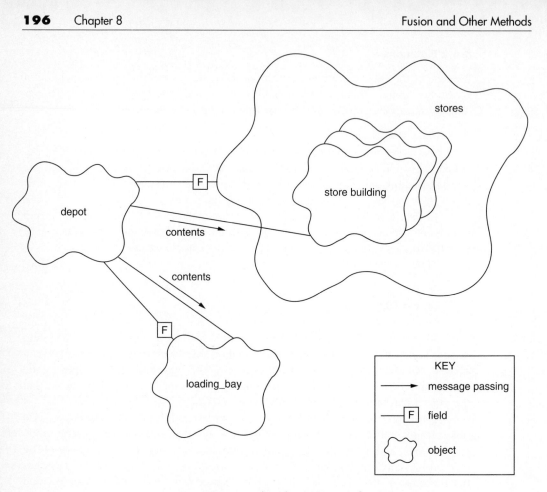

Figure 8.6 Booch: Object Diagram for depot_status

to that used in hardware design to indicate the flow of signals in a circuit. Object creation and destruction can also be shown on timing diagrams.

State Diagrams.

State transition diagrams show how the instances of classes move from one state to another under the influence of events and what actions result from such state changes. Booch notation is very similar to that used in OMT (section 8-3.1). Like OMT, Booch recommends the use of Harel notation to overcome the state explosion problem.

Module Diagrams and Process Diagrams.

Booch distinguishes between the logical and physical views of a system. The models described previously are used to document the logical view of a system; they deal with issues such as which classes exist and how they collaborate. The physical view describes the concrete hardware and software components of the system, and

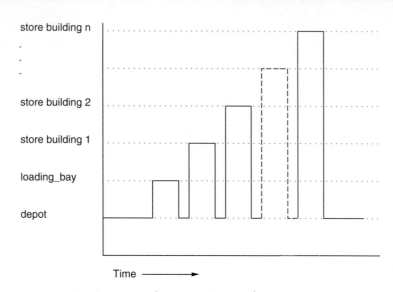

Figure 8.7   Booch: Timing Diagram for depot_status

deals with issues such as where classes should be declared and the allocation of processes to processors.

Module and process diagrams are simple graphs giving a physical view of the system under development. A *module diagram* shows the allocation of classes and objects to modules. It also shows the compile-time dependency relationship between modules. A *process diagram* shows processors (annotated with the process which they run), devices, and the communication connections between them. Module and process diagrams are produced during the implementation phase.

8-4.3 Assessment

- *Does it make it easier to develop a system?* The method comprises a set of notations together with a very ill-defined and loose process. There is little help for the developer if he gets stuck.

- *Does the method make the system easier to maintain?* Booch's notations are very comprehensive and can be used to document almost any aspect of a system. The main problem is that the notations tend to be verbose and their semantics vague.

- *Does it help produce software with good object-oriented structure?* The Booch method contains a wealth of information on the semantics of object orientation. The key mechanism concept explicitly addresses the flow of control issue. Object creation and deletion can also be shown.

- *Does it assist project management?* The Booch models constitute a well-defined set of deliverables. However, the lack of process limits the help that the method gives the project manager.

- *Can it be given effective tool support?* Booch is supported by several diagramming tools. The absence of a rigorous semantics limits them mainly to diagramming support.

The main strength of Booch is that it has notations to cover all aspects of an object-oriented system. However, the notation is complex and information can be fragmented and duplicated across models. A major weakness in Booch is the absence of a defined process for developing systems.

8-5 OBJECTORY

Figure 8.8 shows the three phases of Objectory: requirements, analysis, and construction.

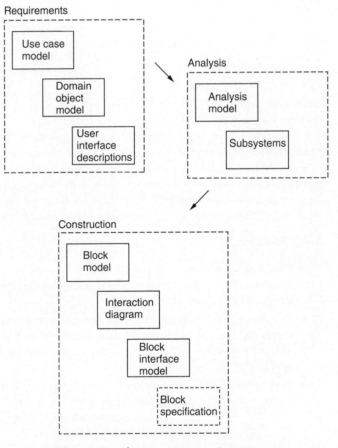

Figure 8.8   Objectory: Process Overview

The Objectory method is based on the notion of *use case*. A use case is a dialogue (i.e., a sequence of transactions), between the system and a user, which is carried out to achieve some goal. Because other systems can also be "users," Objectory employs the term *agent* to cover all system users, human and mechanical. Use cases attempt to capture the functionality of the system by representing what agents should be able to do with it. All the other models are built as a result of considering the use cases, and consequently they provide a link between the phases of Objectory.

8-5.1 Requirements

The starting point is a natural language requirements statement that is used to build three models.

Use-case model: This model shows the agents and the use cases in which they participate, as in Figure 8.9. Each use case should be documented by a textual description, which shows the sequence of events, and explains how the objects in the domain object model participate. Figure 8.10 describes the **delivery** use-case.

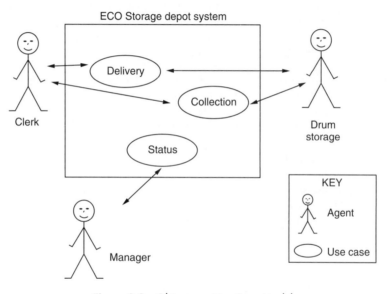

Figure 8.9   Objectory: Use Case Model

Domain object model: This model supports the use cases by defining the concepts with which the system works. The notation is similar to an entity-relationship model and shows object instances, classes, and associations. The associations include inheritance and acquaintance (i.e., one object *holds a reference* to another). The domain object model may be regarded as a preliminary version of the analysis model developed in the next phase.

User interface descriptions: These descriptions are sketches of the windows that the users will see on the screen. This model helps involve the user in the development process. Other system interfaces should be defined by describing their protocols.

The clerk tells the system that the **loading_bay** is now empty, so a delivery may begin. The clerk then gives the system the details from the manifest, and starts checking in the drums. As each drum is checked in, the system issues an identifier for the drum.

When there are no more drums to be checked in the clerk tells the system. The system then informs the clerk of any discrepancy in the delivery, *vis-à-vis* the manifest. The system computes in which store buildings the drums are to be stored and sends the allocation to **Drum** storage.

Finally, the system tells the clerk, which, if any, drums cannot be stored and so must be returned from whence they came.

Figure 8.10   Objectory: Documentation of Use-Case Model

The use cases can be analyzed and structured into a hierarchy showing how they relate. For example, one use case, *A*, *extends* another, *B*, means that *A*'s interactions include *B*'s at some point.

8-5.2 Analysis

The analysis phase refines the requirements models to produce an ideal description of the system (i.e., one that assumes no bounds to the speed or capacity of the implementation platform). The analysis model is a form of entity-relationship model. It is built up incrementally by considering what objects and classes are required for each use case.

The relationships between classes are *inheritance* and *extends*. Class *A* extends class *B*, if *A* behaves like *B* but with some additional behavior. *Acquaintance* is a directed relationship between objects. In an acquaintance relationship one object holds a reference to another object. Aggregation is treated as a special kind of acquaintance relationship. If one object can send stimuli to another then there is a *communication* acquaintance from the first object to the second.

A *control* object "ties together" the other objects participating in a use case. Control objects unite courses of events and carry on communication with other objects; they have transaction-related behavior that isolates entity objects from interface objects. Typically they only survive during the performance of the use case with which they are associated. An *entity* object models information and behavior associated with the system that persists beyond the completion of a single use case. An *interface* object is responsible for presentation of a system at its interface to agents. Figure 8.11 presents an analysis model for the **delivery** use-case.

Subsystems: These are groups of objects with similar behavior. They are used to reduce complexity and structure the system for further development. The criteria for partitioning includes strong coupling between objects and resilience in the face of predicted changes to the system.

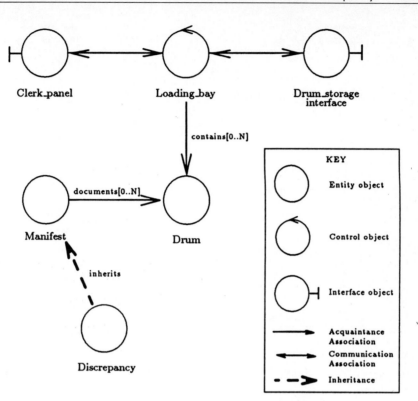

Figure 8.11   Objectory: Analysis Object Model

8-5.3 Construction

In this stage the analysis models are refined. Object communication is more precisely defined, and the characteristics of the implementation environment are considered. Four models are produced.

Block model: This model shows the blocks of the system. A *block* is an abstraction of a code module. Each block is formed from one or more analysis objects.

Interaction diagrams: These are *timeline* diagrams for each of the use cases developed previously. They show how the blocks participate in each of the use cases by sending messages or asynchronous events to each other or to the system. Figure 8.12 shows an interaction diagram for the **delivery** use case. In this example all the objects communicate by messaging.

Block interfaces: These show the operational interface of each block. Each block interface is formed by extracting all the operations for a block from all the interaction diagrams.

Block specification: This specification is an optional model, which shows the internal behavior of blocks as state machines (cf. OMT and Booch). Objectory uses

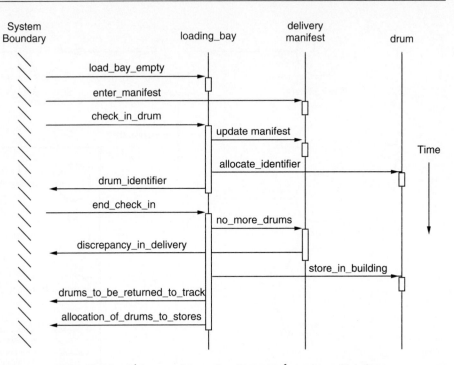

Figure 8.12 Objectory: Interaction Diagram for delivery Use Case

a graphical notation and also a nonstandard variant of the Comité Consultatif International Telegraphique et Telephonique (CCITT) standard language Specification and Description Language (SDL) [1], a state machine-based programming notation used in the telecommunications industry.

The final stage is to implement the block specifications for the target system. Objectory provides heuristics for various programming languages and relational databases.

8-5.4 Assessment

- *Does it make it easier to develop a system?* Use cases provide a lot of assistance in developing the various models and knowing when to move on. A weakness is the absence of checks for ensuring that the models are complete or consistent. There is a discussion of metrics for the requirements phase.

- *Does the method make the system easier to maintain?* The use-case model and timeline diagrams are simple and intuitive. The entity-relationship models are nonstandard but similar to those used in other methods. There are no special facilities for large-scale models.

- *Does it help produce software with good object-oriented structure?* The interaction diagrams provide some support for thinking about flow of control. However, object creation is not addressed.

- *Does it assist project management?* Use cases provide a backbone for developing the other models. Therefore Objectory has a systematic process. The deliverables are also quite clear.

- *Can it be given effective tool support?* Objectory is supported by a diagramming tool. The absence of a rigorous semantics limits it mainly to diagramming support.

The main contribution of Objectory is the use-case concept. Although other methods use similar ideas, Objectory makes it the basis for the development process. A major weakness is that its models and notations are poorly defined. Consequently it can be difficult to discern the meaning of some models, and it is not possible to check for completeness or consistency.

8-6 CLASS RESPONSIBILITY COLLABORATOR (CRC)

CRC (Class Responsibility Collaborator) is an exploratory technique rather than a complete method. It was originally devised as a way of teaching basic concepts in object-oriented design. The CRC technique can be exploited in other methods (e.g., Booch). It is also the foundation for the responsibility-driven design method, [108], where it constitutes the first phase.

CRC deals primarily with the design phase of development. The process is anthropomorphic and drives development by having project teams enact scenarios and playing the parts of objects. Classes are recorded on index cards. The steps in the process are shown in Figure 8.13, and each step is considered in turn. A template for a CRC card appears Figure 8.14.

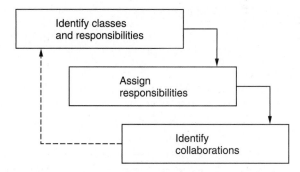

Figure 8.13   Class Responsibility Collaborator: Process Overview

8-6.1 Identification of Classes and Responsibilities

In this stage, the classes are identified. Guidelines include looking for nouns in the requirements document, and modeling physical objects and conceptual entities. Object categories are candidate classes. Grouping classes by common attributes gives candidates for abstract superclasses. The classes are written onto cards. The classes

Class Name	
Superclasses	
Subclasses	
Responsibilities	Collaborators
...	...

Figure 8.14   Class Responsibility Collaborator: Class Card

form the vocabulary for discussion. Subclasses and superclasses are also identified and recorded on the class card. The requirements are then examined for actions and information associated with each class to find the responsibilities of the classes. *Responsibilities* are the essential duties that have to be performed; they identify problems to be solved and are a handle for discussing potential solutions.

8-6.2 Assignment of Responsibilities

The responsibilities identified in the previous stage are allocated to classes. The goal is to distribute the "intelligence" of the system evenly around the classes, with behavior kept with related information. Information about one thing should appear in just one place; if necessary, responsibilities can be shared among related classes. Responsibilities should be made as general as possible, and placed as high as possible in the inheritance hierarchy. In the ECO example, **Depot** responsibilities might include store drums, notify if vulnerable, deliver load, hand over drum, and so on.

8-6.3 Identification of Collaborations

This stage identifies how classes interact. Each class/responsibility pair is examined to see which other classes would need to be consulted to fulfill the responsibility and which classes make use of which responsibilities. In the ECO example, the collaborators of the **Depot** include the **Store Buildings**, **Loading_bay**, **Load**, and so on. Figure 8.15 shows the completed CRC card for a **Depot**.

Depot	
...	
...	
notify if vulnerable accept deliveries report status fulfill collections	Store Buildings Loading_bay Load
...	...

Figure 8.15   Class Responsibility Collaborator: Depot Responsibilities and Collaborators

The cards for classes that closely collaborate are grouped together physically, as in Figure 8.16. Informal groupings like this aid understanding a design.

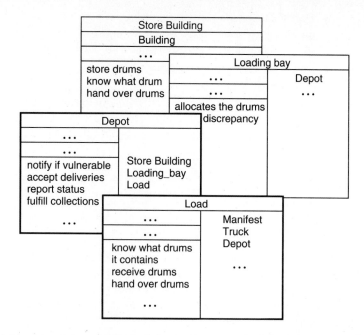

Figure 8.16   Class Responsibility Collaborator: Group of Closely Collaborating Classes

8-6.4 Refinement

The design process is driven toward completion by considering execution scenarios. Each member of the design team takes the part of a class in enacting the scenario. This process uncovers missing responsibilities and collaborators. The restricted size of the index cards helps stop classes becoming too complex. If a card becomes too cluttered, then it is reviewed. The outcome can be simplified statements of responsibilities, new subclasses or superclasses, or even new classes.

The output of the design is a set of classes that are related through inheritance. The hierarchy is refined with common responsibilities placed as high as possible in the graph. Abstract classes cannot inherit from concrete ones, and classes that add no functionality can be discarded.

8-6.5 Assessment

In assessing CRC it should be remembered that CRC is a technique and does not claim to be a method.

- *Does it make it easier to develop a system?* As an exploratory technique it is very powerful, but it bridges only part of the gap from requirements to code.

- *Does the method make the system easier to maintain?* The index cards are the only record of the decisions taken and are clearly inadequate for maintenance purposes.

- *Does it help produce software with good object-oriented structure?* It helps with the design of inheritance structures and is a powerful technique for designing object interaction. It does not deal with object creation.
- *Does it assist project management?* Only so far as the game playing helps team building.
- *Can it be given effective tool support?* Interestingly enough, it is not amenable to computer-based tools. One of the originators, Cunningham, originally developed the method using hypercards, but found index cards more portable and system independent.

CRC is a powerful technique that is best employed as part of another method.

8-7 OTHER METHODS

Numerous other object-oriented analysis and design methods have been documented in the literature or are being offered by consultants and CASE companies. In 1992 the Object Management Group began a comparative study of over twenty methods [3]. Clearly, space does not permit a discussion of all them. Most involve some variation of the ideas that have been discussed earlier (i.e., entity-relationship object modeling, state machines, scenarios, etc.).

Coad-Yourdon is an important method intended primarily for developing management information systems [27], [28]. The method has a well-defined process covering analysis and design. The analysis phase is based on developing a form of extended entity-relationship model, called the OOA model. State machines are used as auxiliary models for defining class behavior. The OOA model is used as input into the design phase, where it is further elaborated. The method also supplies criteria for evaluating designs.

Other important methods are Martin-Odell [78], OSA [41], and Shlaer-Mellor [96], [97]. A summary of some of these methods, and others, is contained in [34].

Formal Methods.

Formal methods are an approach to software engineering that is based on the application of discrete mathematics (i.e., set theory, logic, etc.) to computer programming. Mathematically inspired specification languages allow the essential properties of a system to be captured at a high level of abstraction. Several different formal specification languages have been developed. VDM [63] is a state-based language that explicitly uses pre-conditions and postconditions to specify operations. Z [99] is a modular language based on set theory. Both languages have been used in the development of nontrivial commercial systems.

Recently there has been work on extending formal methods for object-oriented systems. Object-Z [39] and Z++ [67] are object-oriented extensions to Z. Fresco [107] incorporates VDM into a Coad-Yourdon like methodology for developing Smalltalk programs. The technical challenges of dealing with object-oriented type systems, message passing, dynamic binding, etc., mean that object-oriented formal methods are not yet a mature technology.

All formal methods suffer from the problem that they are very costly to introduce because of the high level of mathematical maturity that they require of the user. Currently, therefore, formal methods are really only viable in circumstances where the cost of defects is very high. In the longer term, however, formal methods have the promise of radically improving the way software is produced.

In the next section we explain the rationale behind the Fusion method and show how it relates to other methods.

8-8 FUSION

The Fusion method integrates the best aspects of several methods. Figure 8.17 shows the principal influences on Fusion. In addition to object-oriented methods, formal methods have been influential. We now look at the analysis, design, and implementation phases in turn.

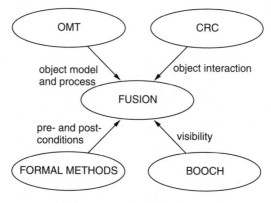

Figure 8.17   Influences on Fusion

8-8.1 Analysis

The main inspiration for the analysis phase is OMT. The three analysis models are used to give orthogonal views of the system and to provide the basis for the process. The major influences on the models are the following:

Object model: Apart from relatively minor notational differences, the object model in Fusion is similar to that in OMT and other methods.

Operation model: This model is analogous to the functional model in OMT. The OMT dataflow diagram notation is theoretically inappropriate and has proved unsatisfactory in practice. Fusion has adopted pre-condition and postcondition specifications from formal methods to specify declaratively what a system does.

Life-cycle model: The use of regular expressions to describe life cycles is adapted from Jackson System Design [57]. Textual descriptions are used because they are more compact.

Fusion incorporates checks for consistency and completeness because there is an underlying semantic foundation for the three analysis models.

The reader should note that the notion of object during analysis is different from that usually employed. Many methods permit analysis objects to exhibit dynamic behavior and have a method, or event, interface; this is not the case in Fusion, where analysis objects have no interface and no dynamic behavior. This is an important distinction. We believe it is inappropriate to assign an interface to an object until the analysis phase has finished and the overall desired system behavior is known. Local decisions taken about object interfaces are likely to be invalidated by the later global decisions regarding the overall system and its behavior.

Fusion also does not use state machines during analysis because analysis objects do not exhibit dynamic behavior. There are other reasons for not using state machines early in the life cycle. Most importantly, state machines describe mechanisms and therefore invite the analyst to indulge in design. State machine descriptions can also get very cumbersome, as even the Harel notations do not fully overcome the state explosion problem.

8-8.2 Design

The Fusion design stage is based on the CRC and Booch methods. An important characteristic of Fusion is that all the important design decisions can be documented using the following design models:

Object interaction graphs: CRC does not provide an appropriate record of the design process because communication information is scattered across index cards. Object interaction graphs provide such a notation.

Visibility graphs: It is necessary to decide how one object knows of another's existence. Booch documents this by adding visibility information to object diagrams. In Fusion, this is documented separately on visibility graphs. Most other methods pay little attention to this aspect of design.

Class descriptions and inheritance graphs: Fusion uses a simple template notation for documenting the syntax of classes and graphs for recording inheritance.

The design models provide Fusion with a systematic process for the design stage. The process is derived from CRC, with the advantage that the exploration of interactions is goal driven from the operational model schemata. The other advantage of Fusion is that it is possible to form the initial versions of the class descriptions by simply collating information from the object model, object interaction graphs, and the visibility graphs.

8-8.3 Implementation

In most applications, the class descriptions can be directly implemented. The semantics for each class are extracted from the documentation accompanying the object interaction graphs and the visibility graphs. In some circumstances it may be desirable to record class semantics in a language-independent way. Extended state machine notations, such as SDL or Objectcharts [30] can be used for this purpose. Objectcharts are a declarative notation that combine pre-conditions and postconditions with Harel state machine diagrams. Such a step does not require any extensions to the analysis or design phases.

8-8.4 Assessment

As is discussed in the introduction, Fusion has been developed to meet the needs of software development teams. This is how we assess it against the criteria used for the other methods.

- *Does it make it easier to develop a system?* The process is systematic and takes the developer from requirements through to code. The rigorous nature of the method means that it possible to detect inconsistencies between models.

- *Does the method make the system easier to maintain?* The models can record all the key decisions made during development. However, it is still up to the developer to document the motivation and reasoning for the choices taken.

- *Does it help produce software with good object-oriented structure?* The method provides models specifically for designing control flow and dynamic object creation. It is the developer's responsibility to ensure that the decisions are well founded.

- *Does it facilitate the management of project teams?* The systematic development of analysis and design models provides the basis for project management.

- *Can it be given effective tool support?* The syntax and semantics of the notations are fully defined. These are necessary for CASE support.

Of course there are drawbacks and limitations to using Fusion. The principal drawback is that the method requires a strong commitment to being systematic and rigorous, which may not always be appropriate. The limitations on Fusion arise from its focus on the particular needs of the technical software developer using an object-oriented programming language.

One such limitation is that the method needs to be modified for use on the development of systems that employ a different object model. For example, in Open-ODB [4], an object-oriented database, methods are not attached to objects. This does not affect the analysis phase of Fusion, but the design phase has to be modified. For example, object interaction graphs have to allow methods that are not bound to an object. This kind of change is reasonably straightforward, and we believe that Fusion can be readily adapted to different object-oriented platforms of this type.

Another limitation is that Fusion is restricted to the development of the sequential components of systems. The architectural design of a system as a group of co-operating sequential programs has to be done outside of Fusion. Once the overall architecture is known then Fusion can be used to develop each of the components. This limitation is an inconvenience rather than a major disadvantage as many systems have a simple and predictable architecture. Recent work to deal with architectural concurrency [31] has shown that it is relatively straightforward to extend Fusion into this domain.

Not all limitations can be dealt with so easily. For example, developing applications for distributed object-oriented systems (e.g., [2]) involves issues that need more than minor changes to Fusion, or indeed, any of today's methods. This is a topic for future research.

Overall we believe that Fusion represents a state-of-the-art object-oriented development method. However, because we are not disinterested, it must be for others to provide a truly objective assessment.

8-9 SUMMARY

This chapter has explained how Fusion relates to other methods.

- Fusion aims to meet the needs of technical software developers. It was developed because no one existing method met these needs.
- OMT, Booch, CRC, and formal methods were the major influences on Fusion.
- OMT has a systematic analysis phase. The design phase is defined by a set of heuristics rather than a process.
- Booch provides detailed notation for describing object-oriented systems, but the process is informal.
- Objectory has a systematic process based on use-case scenarios. Its notations and concepts are informally defined and can be difficult to understand.
- CRC is a technique for design that can be combined with other methods.
- Fusion is a systematic and rigorous method. It is applicable to the development of the sequential components of systems.

CHAPTER

9

Reuse

9-1 INTRODUCTION

One of the benefits of object-oriented technology is its superior technical support for reuse of software components. The aim of this chapter is to examine the effect that the goal of reuse has on the software development life cycle. In contrast to previous chapters, where a detailed and systematic method for going from requirements to code is developed, the approach of this chapter is to highlight additional issues pertaining to reuse that must be considered in each phase of the life cycle. Practical guidance is given on how to use the Fusion method in the reuse context.

The first part of the chapter begins by classifying the reuse issues relevant to the object-oriented approach (section 9-2). This is done both from the technology and management viewpoint. The next section continues by discussing the features of object-oriented technology that assist reuse and some of the limitations (section 9-3).

The next three sections address distinct development contexts with respect to reuse: developing components for reuse (section 9-4), system development with reuse (section 9-5), and reengineering (section 9-6). In development for reuse, the role of reusable analysis and design models as well as code is discussed. In development with reuse, various technical conflicts that impede the integration of separately developed subsystems are considered along with some solutions in the form of standards for documentation and quality control. Also discussed are requirements for infrastructure support for reuse. Finally, reengineering is viewed from the perspective of being a combination of development *for* and *with* reuse. Each of these sections concludes with an assessment of the state of the art and implications for production software development. The chapter concludes with a brief summary of the major points presented.

9-2 REUSE CLASSIFICATION

Software reuse can be viewed from many different perspectives. To assess the effect of the object-oriented approach on reuse in context, this section briefly summarizes the aspects of reuse that are relevant. This is done from both the technology and management viewpoints.

9-2.1 Technology Viewpoint

Software reuse has always been a part of most user's and developer's lives. For example, reuse occurs in

- Repeated executions of a program with different inputs
- Repeated invocations of a routine within a given program
- Reuse of expertise of personnel
- Code and design scavenging
- Importing of library routines

It is the last item, the selection and integration (but not modification) of existing modules in the construction or maintenance of programs, which we are addressing here, and on which we consider the impact of the object-oriented approach. Component libraries are a common form of code and design reuse. Some well-known examples are reuse of subsystems (e.g., math functions, user interface, communications, memory management, and database) and reuse of "small" abstractions such as buffers and complex numbers.

Reuse should be conceived in terms of the entire software development life cycle. When early life cycle workproducts are reused, there is a high probability of reusing downstream workproducts as well [10]. Although extensive research into code reuse techniques has been carried out, far less has been done for equally labor-intensive workproducts such as requirements specifications, designs, test plans, and documentation. For more information on the spectrum of general reuse techniques, an up-to-date review is given in [66].

The object-oriented approach to reuse spans a large range of abstraction, from analyses through designs and implementations. There are object-oriented libraries available now that essentially duplicate what is available in standard subroutine libraries, though (as will be discussed in the next section) with several advantages over the earlier forms. More important, reusable object-oriented analysis and design models have been developed for a wide variety of domains thus paving the way for realizing some of the sought-after benefits of reuse. Such analyses and designs are called *frameworks* or *domain architectures* and are discussed in detail in section 9-4.2.

9-2.2 Management Viewpoint

The technical aspects outlined earlier provide us with just one view of reuse. There are also many issues involved with the management of a project that is either developing or reusing software components. To help identify some of these, it is helpful to explore a typical reuse scenario.

In Figure 9.1 a simple producer/consumer scenario is shown. There are managers like Mr. P., who is a producer of reusable components. On the other side there is another manager Mr. C., who is a consumer. Julie P. and Joe C. are workers. In a typical reuse scenario Mr. P.'s real job will be to produce things. In the example these things are houses. Some of the components produced are suitable candidates for inclusion in the reuse library. The first point this picture brings out is that to build the houses the components will probably have little bits on them so that they lock together (i.e., specific features), ideal for the building of houses. In making the components suitable for reuse they have to be made generic. In general the thing that will be reused will normally not be the thing that you built for your own use.

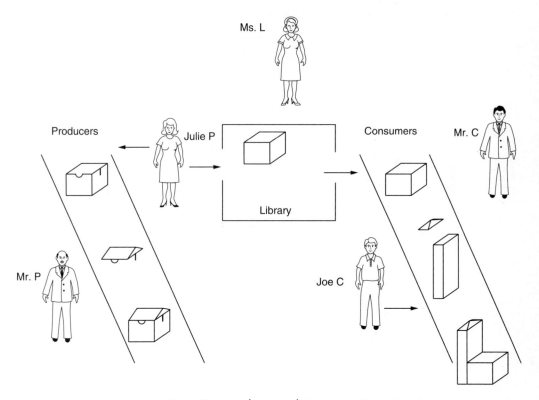

Figure 9.1 Producers and Consumers Reuse Scenario

Special attention has to be given to components that go into the reuse library. For example, if Joe C. takes a component out of the library and it turns out to be no good, he is likely to stop using the library and build the component himself. Consequently, Mr. P. has several conflicts to manage. He has the desire to get his houses out on time, and this conflicts with the cost of producing generic components for the library. For reusable and high-quality components, Julie P. has to be good at her job and have a thorough knowledge of the application domain.

Looking at the consumer side of the reuse scenario there are some other issues involved. The consumers want to build churches. To enable Joe C. to use components out of the library he has to know what is in the library. Ms. L., the librarian, has the job of promoting and publishing the contents of the library. She also has the job of providing maintenance contracts that are required because the producing project will come to the end of its natural life. Someone will have to be around to maintain their contributions in the library and that is the librarian's job.

Joe C. may sometimes feel a bit reluctant about taking things out of the library because of the "not invented here" syndrome. A related issue is that Joe C. is probably getting paid for building components that make churches rather than for reusing components. If he tells Mr. C. that he reused 10,000 components to build a church, the reaction Joe C. gets is likely to be different from the one he would get if he had built the components himself. In the latter case he is likely to get much praise. So there is an issue here to do with the reward structure.

This reuse scenario can easily be specialized to relate to the software development context, and there are clearly many nontechnical issues involved in obtaining the benefits of reuse. Reuse will not just happen. It requires a conscious investment by the production team. The company or organization also has to know how it is going to get the return on that investment. Although the object-oriented approach has technical capabilities to support reuse, this example illustrates that planning and management are involved in getting the benefits of reuse.

The key impediments to achieving reuse can be summarized in terms of the management issues that have to be tackled by Mr. P., Mr. C., and Ms. L.

- Producers

  - Cost of producing more generic components
  - Schedule conflict between developing a class for a product and making it reusable
  - Support and maintenance costs of reusable classes (primarily an issue for the reuse librarian)

- Consumers

  - Knowledge about what is available
  - "Not invented here" syndrome
  - Reward mechanisms for reusing code

- Reuse librarian

  - Acquisition of new assets and cataloging
  - Promotion and publicity of the library assets
  - Quality control (documentation, maintenance, etc.)

This chapter looks at the technical issues of using the object-oriented approach to achieve the goals of reuse. This is done from the perspectives of producers, developing components *for* reuse, and consumers, involved in system development *with* reusable assets. In chapter 10 further insight is given into the general management task of introducing object-oriented technology into a project.

9-3 REUSE FEATURES OF OBJECT-ORIENTED APPROACH

The object-oriented approach provides several features and techniques that reduce the complexity inherent in many software development projects. This section examines some of these with emphasis on how they can improve on existing approaches to reuse.

9-3.1 Features that Support Reuse

Real-world modeling is supported by the object-oriented approach. From the reuse perspective, classes are usually the most stable elements of a problem domain. Hence, programs structured around classes are more robust in the face of changing requirements. Reuse of components in successive releases of a single product and within product families is more likely with classes than with functional units.

Encapsulation aids reuse by encouraging clients to depend on the interface an object provides while being shielded from modifications to its implementation and from its interactions with other parts of a system. Encapsulation thus minimizes the exposure of clients to changes in implementation and frees them from being locked into a single implementation of a specific behavior. Finally, encapsulation makes libraries easier to understand because all information relating to a specific component can be self-contained.

Inheritance supports incremental refinement of data types, hence providing explicit support for specialization of behavior not envisaged by the original developer. In addition, by providing documentation of design rationale and organization of the data types, inheritance can increase the comprehensibility of the design of a library.

The probability of reuse is enhanced when components can be easily extended to cope with slightly different requirements on behavior. A major problem with traditional subroutine libraries is the extremely limited support, namely, through parameterization, for customizing behavior. Parameterization restricts customizations to those originally envisioned by the developer. More flexibility (at the cost of increased complexity) may be achieved by providing many parameters or alternatively many small routines that cover the same requirement space. In contrast with the subroutine approach of achieving generality through high degrees of parameterization, inheritance supports generality through simplification; a more general component is one that has less specific behavior (i.e., fewer methods [71]).

Polymorphism permits the same message to be handled by a set of data types related by inheritance. Polymorphism aids reuse by allowing newly specialized components to be used in the same environment as old components without having to modify the calling environment.

Parametric types also aid reuse by allowing the definition of a family of classes with the same interface and implementation that differ only in a type specified as a class parameter. An example of this technique finds most extensive use in the development of typesafe "container" classes, examples such as Tree, Stack, Set, List, Vector, and Map. For this category of classes, parametric types reduce complexity because specialized container classes do not have to be constructed for each possible occupant.

9-3.2 Impediments to Reuse

It is wise to ask at this point if there are any side effects of these features that could *impede* reuse. Paradoxically it is inheritance, widely viewed as the fundamental technique supporting reuse, for which the answer is yes.

The increased reusability of class hierarchies consisting of many of fine-grained components must be balanced against the higher complexity of such hierarchies. The kind of change that inheritance supports best is incremental refinement of existing types. Large-scale changes such as addition of substantially new semantics (e.g., persistence) to an existing hierarchy either greatly increase complexity (if achieved using multiple inheritance as in Figure 9.2) or must be obtained through modifying the original classes.

Reuse by inheritance requires the reuser to have a deeper understanding of the reused parts than if they were just calling subroutines. This is because the attributes of the superclass may be accessed and modified by the subclass. Consequently, it is the responsibility of the developer of the subclass to preserve any superclass invariants on the attributes. Hence, using inheritance requires a larger up-front investment on the part of developers to become familiar with their tool kit. Proposals for documentation standards and tools to cope with some of these problems are discussed in section 9-5.2.

Another problem arises when inheritance is used purely for implementation reuse. This occurs when an inheritance relationship has been introduced into a program to promote code reuse but a supertype/subtype relationship does not really exist. Clients (both subclasses and external users) assume that the related classes can be used polymorphically.

With respect to reuse, inheritance has to be used with care. On the one hand, it enables developers to make extensive use of existing components when coping with new requirements; conversely, clients can be exposed to a source of instability that discourages them from depending on a hierarchy of classes with the same degree of confidence as a class interface. Some approaches to design and implementation that minimize this conflict are outlined in sections 9-4.2 and 9-4.3.

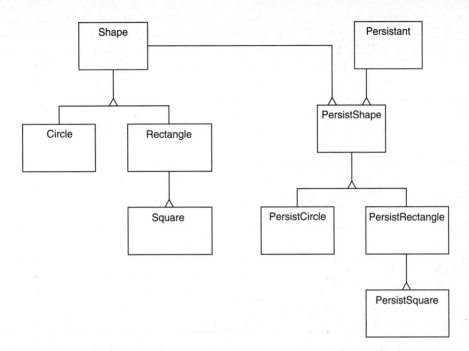

Figure 9.2   Introducing Persistence Using Multiple Inheritance

9-4 DEVELOPMENT OF COMPONENTS FOR REUSE

This section examines the impact that the goal of developing assets for reuse has on the processes and techniques presented in previous chapters. It also identifies the types of reusable artifacts that may be produced. The analysis, design, and implementation phases of Fusion are each considered in turn and at the end of the section an overall assessment is given of current reuse practices.

9-4.1 Analysis

Reusable components not only satisfy the immediate needs of the current development but those of the future as well. Therefore, the analysis phase needs to provide activities explicitly that lead to the building of models that characterize the classes and functionality typical of a *domain*, or group of related products, rather than that of a specific *system*. In addition to being the starting point for developing a reusable design, such domain models can also be input to the analysis of a specific system.

Development of Domain Models.

As discussed in section 9-3.1, one advantage of the object-oriented approach is that there is potentially a direct mapping between the most stable elements in the problem domain and the unit of abstraction in the solution domain. The goal of object-oriented systems analysis is to produce models of the problem domain and requirements on the system under development. Therefore, some of the products of object-oriented analysis *are* what one would obtain from a domain analysis. One difference, however, is that a domain model should account for and be able to express *variants* as well as *invariants*. To make use of the Fusion analysis models for expressing domain properties, we must determine the invariant and variant aspects of domains in general and then adapt the analysis models to express that information.

Two models are produced during analysis: the object model, which captures the structure of the information in the system, and the interface model, which describes the effect of system-level operations on this structure. By definition, the features of the object model for a particular domain (i.e., the object classes and their relationships) are unlikely to vary much. However, the stability of an object model is strongly dependent on how carefully the domain is scoped. Reports have been published of extensive restructuring of class hierarchies owing mainly to expansions of the domain [8].

In contrast, the system operations specified for a particular system are subject to a fair degree of variation. One way to arrive at an interface model for a domain would be to generate a more complete set of system operations by considering scenarios from several different applications.

Domain Analysis Process.

The process for doing domain analysis subsumes that of a single system analysis. Differences in the processes appear in scoping and capturing the range of variation present in a domain. The following domain analysis process, proposed by Prieto-Diaz, provides a reasonable approach [89].

1. *Scope domain.* List the type of applications being considered and the amount of information being consulted.
2. *Generate or collect information.* There are two basic approaches to domain analysis: inductively generalize from specific instances or deduce abstractions from first principles. The former is the much more common approach.

    To proceed inductively, information about the domain must be collected. Sources of domain knowledge are similar to that which might be drawn on when developing single systems: human experts, technical literature, existing systems, customer surveys, and current and future requirements.
3. *Analyze and abstract.* The collected information is then analyzed to yield the set of canonical objects (domain vocabulary) that are present in all or most systems in the domain.
4. *Construct analysis models.* Finally, the invariant and variant properties are captured and represented in a domain model.

Note that before undertaking domain analysis, several domain properties must be considered in determining whether it is economically justified or even necessary. For example, the maturity and complexity of a domain has a bearing on whether it is a good candidate for domain analysis. A domain that is new or unstable for whatever reason is probably not a good candidate for domain analysis or reuse. A very mature domain, such as mathematics, will have many example systems and it will be clear what the canonical objects are. Similarly, complex domains (e.g., medical diagnosis) will require more effort than more straightforward ones (e.g., payroll automation).

9-4.2 Design

There are two main types of reusable object-oriented designs: abstract classes and frameworks. These are both described before considering process issues relevant to reusable designs.

Abstract Classes.

An *abstract class* is a reusable object-oriented design for a component. It specifies the interface of a class and the tree of subclasses that can be derived from it. Abstract classes fully specify behavior, not implementation; they cannot be instantiated, only subclassed from.

While the most valuable part of abstract classes is the interface they provide, they may provide some implementations of the methods contained in its interface without restricting choices about representation for its descendants. The methods of an abstract class can be classified as abstract, template, or base methods [61]. An *abstract* method is unimplemented by an abstract class, whereas a *template* is implemented in terms of one or more abstract methods. A *base method* is fully implemented.

Abstract classes can be used in two ways. First, they can fully specify the behavior of a set of classes that differ only in implementation. Second, they can be found at the root of a tree of classes, each class adding behavior to that specified by its parent. A matrix class, for example, might typically have several implementations dependent on the efficiency considerations of dealing with different forms of matrix (dense, sparse, etc.).

Frameworks.

A *framework* is a reusable object-oriented analysis and design for an *application* or *subsystem*. An application framework provides a template for an entire application. Domain specific examples include frameworks for graphical editors and compilers [102]. The Model-View-Controller from Smalltalk-80 provides an example of a nondomain-specific framework for developing interactive applications [47]. A subsystem framework provides a set of services that are relatively independent of the rest of the system. Subsystems can be distinguished (from an applications' viewpoint) on the basis of domain of use. For example, an application subsystem provides services relevant to a specific domain such as network management, whereas a general service subsystem would be useful across domains [76]. Another distinction can be made with architecture subsystems that are pervasive across domains. Examples include operating systems and interprocess communication [19], [109].

A framework embodies the invariant part of a domain analysis with its choice of classes from the problem space and with a design for a set of interacting classes that provides the solution to a range of applications within that domain. Both the problem and solution space classes will include abstract classes. The solution encompasses the class hierarchy and the factoring of functionality between interacting classes (Figure 9.3).

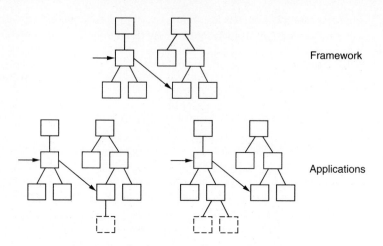

Figure 9.3 Frameworks Support Range of Domain Applications

Frameworks often include a library of concrete subclasses that provide solutions to the requirements of several particular applications (i.e., several variants) within the domain. The Unidraw framework for graphical editors, for example, has been instantiated as a simple drawing editor, an electronic schematic capture editor and a user interface layout tool [102]. Considering the requirements of these various applications refined the design of the invariant part of the framework.

Design Process Considerations.

The process for developing a reusable design will vary in part depending on the maturity of a domain. Different approaches to "finding the objects" have been recommended for domains exhibiting different degrees of maturity: exploratory for unknown domains and prescriptive for well-understood domains [105]. Many developers have observed that a natural path to develop such designs is by generalizing from existing examples.

Unfortunately, object-oriented languages support specialization (via subclassing), not generalization. Backfitting generalizations can be very expensive, because any client that depends on a specific design will also have to be modified. Different proposals have arisen to address this problem. They fall into two categories: introducing new object-oriented language features [75], [87] or developing tools to automate both the identification of generalizations and propagation of restructuring updates [21], [73], [84]. As new language features require a much greater investment to be adopted, tools seem to hold more promise, although those currently in existence are solely research prototypes.

The key issues to address in minimizing the need to perform class surgery are

- Develop an approach to design in which generalization is an explicit goal. Just as problem domain objects can be generalized by considering a more complete set of system operations, the design of more general solution space objects can be driven by generalizing the suboperations comprising system operations.

- In general, "good" designs are more reusable, so designs should satisfy the rules set out in section 4-6. Further guidance on the development of abstract classes and frameworks can be found in [60].

- The main point, however, is that *iteration* is required to arrive at truly reusable abstractions. Iteration of a design involves testing it by using it to develop solutions to particular problems. This has been found to be necessary even for relatively well understood domains (e.g., virtual memory management [61]).

9-4.3 Implementation

The form in which most frameworks and collections of utility classes are instantiated are object-oriented code libraries. Object-oriented analogs of traditional subroutine libraries such as abstract data types, geometrical objects, tasking, input/output, communications, and mathematical routines have been developed as well as frameworks for operating systems, drawing editors, network management applications, and user interface subsystems. Frameworks are composed of collections of abstract classes and a library of subclasses that satisfy the requirements of some particular applications in the domain captured in the framework.

As we indicated earlier, inheritance can compromise encapsulation and hinder reuse. A partial solution to the problem comes about by revisiting one of the original motivations for the object-oriented approach, separating the interface of an object from its implementation. For example, separation of interface and implementation is achieved in C++ by using abstract classes to provide the interface and subclasses of the abstract class to provide the implementation. Public inheritance (which is visible to clients) can also be used to express a *public* statement of a subclass's conformity to its superclass's interface. *Private* inheritance can be used to obtain code reuse, although this should be used judiciously. Another approach is to reuse the class by declaring it as a component instead of a superclass.

The particularly fine-grained control over the relationships between classes in a hierarchy provided by languages such as C++ adds to the number of decisions and assumptions class designers must make. It has been observed that noninvasive inheritance in C++ (i.e., inheritance without modifying the base class) can be difficult to achieve [20]. This means that changes will probably have to be made to the base class to remove simplifying assumptions not satisfied by a derived class.

9-4.4 Assessment of Development *for* Reuse

The object-oriented approach has encouraged the development of an increasing number of reusable libraries and frameworks in a variety of domains. However, processes for developing such reusable analyses, designs, and components are currently not well articulated or systematic. To minimize disruption to reusers of components and frameworks, therefore, adequate time for design iteration must be allocated in the beginning of development. As for who should develop the reuse assets, there are two main alternatives: product developers or specialists in reusable component development.

Within a single domain, product developers will be better placed to develop reusable assets as a result of their familiarity with the domain. In the context of a single product, the up-front cost of making a component more reusable must be balanced against possible maintenance costs later in the product's lifetime. In the context of a product family, the up-front cost of making components more reusable (or developing a reusable framework) will be amortized over the cost of multiple products. This requires organizational support for rewarding efforts that yield benefit in the long term. Specialists will have greater expertise in processes and techniques for reuse. However, they also require an even higher level of organizational support than that required for reuse within product families.

Another factor to consider in determining how much effort should be expended in developing a reusable asset is the *extent* to which it will be reused. The possibilities are reuse within a given domain in the development of a single product (i.e., maintenance or successive releases) or product family, or across domains. The analysis of likely reuse scenarios can help to determine this [10]. Estimates of the number and type of component variants that are likely to be required should guide development. This ensures that effort proportional to potential return is expended in producing and consuming reusable components.

There are very few models for estimating the cost of developing or using reusable software, especially the huge undertaking of developing a framework or highly generalized component library. Developing such a model clearly requires some idea of the life cycle of reusable software development. Typically, several iterations of a framework will be required before it can be considered stable enough for application developers to depend on it. It has been recommended, therefore, that framework development should be kept independent from product development and must not be on the product's critical path [62].

9-5 SYSTEM DEVELOPMENT WITH REUSE

This section examines the impact that the goal of developing a system with reusable assets has on the processes and techniques presented in previous chapters. It also considers problems in using and integrating separately developed systems and proposes solutions in the form of standards for assets and tool support to assist with retrieving and understanding them.

9-5.1 Development Process Issues

When doing software development with reuse, the degree to which it is necessary to follow the complete development cycle as presented in previous chapters depends on what is available. Two situations are considered here: the configuration of a framework and the integration of a subsystem.

Framework Configuration.
If a framework exists, there is a spectrum of how it can be reused.

- *Configuration*. The reuser employs a high-level tool to configure a framework for a specific application. User interface builders are the best-known examples of such tools.
- *Black box*. The reuser need only understand the external interface of the components. Frameworks that can be configured can also be used programmatically in a black-box fashion.
- *White box*. The reuser must have an understanding of the functional factoring if not the complete implementation of the framework. Most frameworks fall in this category.

These different approaches clearly differ in the degree of investment required by the reuser. If there are only components available, then the standard development cycle is followed with the modification that a look-ahead approach should be followed so that components that satisfy the functional requirements are identified as early as possible.

Subsystem Integration.

Problems in integrating separately developed subsystems have always been a technical impediment to wide-scale reuse. Clearly, integration costs will also diminish the productivity gains expected from reuse. Reports show that these problems do not disappear as a result of using object-oriented libraries. In fact, integration difficulties have been known to add a third to a project's overall development time [12]. There are some standard style conflicts in object-oriented software that include the following:

- Development of monolithic inheritance hierarchies versus a forest of trees.
- Different approaches to the implementation of name space control.
- Run-time-type query and garbage collection.
- The control of composite objects (e.g., bottom-up or top-down). Conflicts can arise when different choices are made about how a particular composite should be controlled. For example, a top-down versus bottom-up order of event handling is a common difference between windowing systems. In a windowing system, top-down control enables uniform enforcement of the style of component attributes but makes delegation of control to individual components convoluted.
- Group and compound operations. Subsystems typically aim to provide a complete, orthogonal set of primitive operations from which group operations may be composed. Sometimes for efficiency or safety, group operations are required that provide atomic execution of all or none of the primitive operations. Group operations, however, may be required at different levels of an application, and it would overly complicate a subsystem to try to anticipate all the different combinations that will be needed.

Some of the choices to be made, for example, those having to do with coding style, can be dealt with in a single organization by establishing standards for assets held in a reuse library.

Software obtained from external sources is less amenable to the standards approach except when the standard emanates from an official body. Subsystems acquired from external sources can be suspect on a whole variety of issues that have legal ramifications, such as responsibility for the correctness, reliability, and integrity of the software. Traditionally, obtaining components from external sources is more acceptable if they can be acquired in source form. It can then at least be subjected to local quality control processes. Source licensing, however, is very costly and usually only occurs when the application or subsystem implements a well-established standard (e.g., X Window servers).

9-5.2 Reuse Infrastructure

For a component to be reused, the effort required to reuse it must be less than that to build it from scratch. Developers need a way of finding and understanding components that can be easily tailored and that meet their requirements. This implies that an investment in a reuse *infrastructure* is a prerequisite to achieving reuse.

This section discusses two facets of such a reuse infrastructure: standards for software assets and tool support for asset retrieval and understanding. Neither facet is particularly well supported in current software production environments.

Asset Standards.

Standards for documenting and ensuring the quality of software assets aid reuse by

- Minimizing difficulties in integrating separately developed subsystems
- Assisting the process of understanding class specifications and interactions
- Combating "not invented here" syndrome among developers by increasing trust in "foreign" components

Traditional forms of documentation for subroutine libraries include manual pages and header files. Complex subsystems generally provide more extensive documentation in the form of tutorials. Both forms of documentation rely on natural language to document the semantics of component behavior.

Researchers have argued that safe use of inheritance (i.e., ensuring that client expectations about the behavior of subclasses are satisfied) requires the implementation language to provide support for formal documentation of the semantics of the interface of a class as well as its syntax. In the Eiffel environment, for example, assertions can be documented that specify what a class must do, independently of how it does it [80]. This is done by using preconditions and postconditions to specify semantic properties of individual methods, and class invariants to express global properties that must be preserved by all methods on instances of a class. These assertions can be checked at run time.

In Figure 9.4 part of an Eiffel declaration for a **Stack** class is given. Preconditions are introduced by the keyword **require**. The **push** method, for example, may not be called if the stack is full. Postconditions are introduced by the keyword **ensure**. The **push** method ensures that

- The stack is not empty after a push.
- The method **top** returns the element just pushed onto the stack.
- The number of elements in the stack has been increased by one.

```
class STACK [T] export
        nb_elements, empty, full, push, pop, top
feature
        nb_elements : INTEGER;
        ⋮

        push(x : T) is
              – Add x on top
        require
              not full
        do ⋯
        ensure
              not empty;
              top = x;
              nb_elements = old nb_elements + 1
        end; – push
        ⋮

        invariant
              0 ≤ nb_elements; nb_elements ≤ max_size;
              empty = (nb_elements = 0)
end – class STACK
```

Figure 9.4   Eiffel Specification of Assertions

The **invariant** clause introduces a set of assertions that must be preserved by all methods operating on the stack. For example, the number of elements on the stack must always be between 0 and a declared maximum **size**, and the **empty** method returns **true** when the number of elements in the stack is zero.

Proposals have been made for similar capabilities to be added to C++ [26], [71]. In the absence of runtime checking, such specifications serve to document the intended semantics of class interfaces, providing guidance to subclass developers. An example of such a specification for a Calendar class is shown in Figure 9.5.

The example places constraints on the values of private data in the **legal** clause and similar constraints on the behavior of instances of the class in the **axioms** clause. For example, the attribute **mon** is constrained to legal values for months, between 1 and 12 inclusive, and the **date** can only take on values that are legal for the **days_in** the selected month. The legality constraint is never violated throughout an object's lifetime. The **axioms** characterize behavioral properties of object instances. The **require** and **promise** are preconditions and postconditions indicating the conditions that must hold before an operation begins and the conditions that will hold after it finishes, respectively. In the example, it is required that the value of the **m** parameter to the **reset** method must have a value between 1 and 12. After an invocation of this

```
class Calendar {
    int mon, date;
    int days_in(int month);
    legal:
        mon >= 1 && mon <= 12;
        date >= 1&& date <= days_in(mon);
public:
        int month( ) const {return mon; };
        Calendar( ) : mon(1), date(31) {/* ··· */ };
        void reset(int m);
axioms :
        [int m; require m >= 1 && m <= 12; promise month( ) == m] reset (m);
};
```

Figure 9.5   Semantic Specification of a Calendar Class

method, the promise is made that there is an equivalence between **m** and the value returned from an invocation of **month**.

Frameworks require further documentation of how objects interact to satisfy high-level requirements and behavioral invariants. The reason for this is that, in contrast to functionally decomposed systems, object-oriented systems will not have high-level functions that map directly to the functional requirements. Nor is this information easily extracted from the code because object-oriented languages emphasize the inheritance relationship.

In Fusion the object interaction graphs specifically capture this information, and the full documentation for a framework architecture should include the following:

- Object interaction graphs to document the run-time behavior of objects to support specific functionality
- Class descriptions to provide a specification of the method interface, and class attribute and visibility reference structure of classes in the framework
- Inheritance graphs presenting a complete picture of the class/subclass structures
- Data dictionary documenting the terms, concepts, and constraints applicable to the framework

Examples of these models are given in Figure 9.6. Further examples can also be found in chapter 4.

A major impediment to component reuse is that nonfunctional properties may not be adequate for a specific application. Information about such nonfunctional properties (such as a component's time and space complexity, precision, failure modes, and assumptions about concurrency) becomes even more important in object-oriented libraries because of the ability to have many plug-compatible implementations of the same interface.

Developers are also reluctant to rely on reusable components if they have no indication of their quality. A well-reused component is likely to have higher quality in

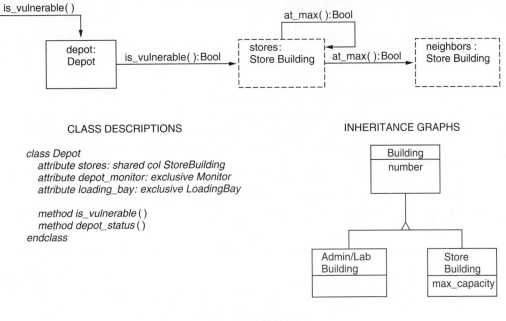

Figure 9.6 Fusion Asset Documentation

terms of performance and defect density but still may not be chosen by a developer if those attributes are not made explicit. A process for ensuring that reusable components are maintained and, in the best cases certified, would go a long way to reducing suspicion of externally acquired components. At a minimum, quality attributes should be part of the documentation. The packaging of components with validation suites would also help in establishing trust.

Asset Retrieval and Understanding.

Support for retrieving assets is needed by experienced developers (who are aware of and understand the assets) to refresh their memory and by neophyte developers to help them develop an understanding of the tool kit. There are two types of tools currently available which assist with the retrieval of reusable assets: *information retrieval* systems for accessing documentation, such as that described in the previous section, and *browsers*, which provide a variety of different views of source code.

The separation of these two approaches is suboptimal and probably stems from a long-standing dichotomy within the software engineering community concerning the relevance of natural language documentation of software assets. Attempts have been made to combine these approaches to provide richer views of asset collections [53]. This minimizes the human intervention required to integrate information present in documentation and source code. No commercial tools exist that provide this kind of multidimensional support for asset retrieval and browsing.

9-5.3 Assessment of Development *with* Reuse

It might seem that the biggest barrier to be overcome in creating and sustaining a reuse culture is the effort required to populate a repository with truly reusable assets. It is clear, however, that substantial barriers remain even for developers who are committed to reuse.

The establishment of a reuse *infrastructure* is the first step to eliminating some of the barriers to development with reuse. Currently, tool support for such an infrastructure is in a very primitive state.

9-6 REENGINEERING

This section addresses the development context in which a requirement exists to reuse workproducts that are not structured around objects. Before progressing to the issues involved in this type of development, a definition of reengineering and related terms is first presented. A summary of a systematic process for reengineering an existing system to an object-oriented structure is then given. Finally, some of the problems that were addressed in a case study of reengineering a three-dimensional modeling package are discussed.

9-6.1 Definition of Terms

The various terms related to reengineering are defined as follows (taken from [23]):

- Forward engineering is the traditional process of moving from high-level abstractions and logical designs to the physical implementation of a system.
- Reverse engineering creates representations of a system in another form or at a higher level of abstraction. There are two subareas of reverse engineering:

  - *Redocumentation* is the creation of a semantically equivalent representation within the same abstraction level from the subject system. CASE tools that advertise reverse engineering functions are really performing redocumentation.
  - *Design recovery* recreates design abstractions from a combination of code, design documentation, personal experience, and knowledge about problem domain.

- Restructuring is transformation from one representation to another at the same level of abstraction while preserving the system's external behavior. The elimination of goto's is the canonical example of restructuring.

- Reengineering is composed of reverse engineering and forward engineering or restructuring. In contrast to restructuring, reengineering may involve modifications to functionality or implementation technique.

As mentioned earlier, reengineering is frequently performed to enable the reuse of existing components. The reverse engineering phase identifies the components and restructuring or forward engineering will encapsulate or generalize them to make them more reusable.

9-6.2 Reengineering Development Process

There are a variety of development situations that involve reengineering of some form or another, ranging from the simple addition of new functionality using a new implementation technology to the complete introduction of a new technology. Three scenarios are considered in recent work where an outline reengineering process is proposed [59]. The first situation deals with a complete change of implementation technique but with no change in the system functionality. Second, a situation is considered in which there is still no change in functionality but only a partial change in implementation technique is required. Finally, reengineering is considered where there is also a change in functionality. The following process outline summarizes the most general case in which there is to be a partial reimplementation with a change in functionality.

1. *Identify part of system.* It is necessary to identify the part of the system that is to be reimplemented as well as the agents that interact with it.

2. *Prepare analysis models.* Based on documentation (including requirements specifications, manuals, design models, source code, and database schema) produce analysis models of the component to be reengineered. This emphasizes *what* the component does rather than *how* it is currently implemented.

3. *Map analysis models to existing system.* The map should satisfy the following constraints: For each analysis component and each relationship in the analysis models, there must exist one element in the system documentation that is consistent with the source code.

4. *Incorporate new requirements.* Change the analysis models according to the new requirements. The analysis models will then consist of three subsets representing respectively: new objects, old objects involved with new functionality, and old objects.

5. *Evaluate interface of new component.* The interface between the part to be exchanged and the remaining part of the old system has to be fully defined.

6. *Design new subsystem.* The new component and its interface to the old system is designed.

7. *Modify old system.* Add an interface to the old system so that the agents can interact with the new system component.

9-6.3 Assessment of Reengineering

Software development projects that decide to introduce object-oriented technology will typically be faced with a reengineering problem. Green field (or clean slate) developments that do not involve legacy code are rare in practice. It is also unusual, and probably unwise, for an existing product to be completely reengineered using a new technology in one go. Consequently, component reengineering provides a low-risk migration path.

The reengineering development process outlined earlier is based on the premise that object-oriented analysis models can be used to characterize a system that has been designed using non-object-oriented techniques. Dependant on the quality and level of documentation of the legacy software, significant effort may be required to uncover appropriate analysis abstractions. Several iterations may also be required to establish an appropriate interface between the old system and the new component.

Fusion provides a systematic forward engineering development process. Although several reengineering experience reports have been published only tentative process frameworks have been proposed.

9-7 SUMMARY

- Reuse is often cited as a key factor in motivating a switch from functional to object-oriented development. For reuse to be realized, it must be an explicit goal of all the activities comprising the software development process.

- Producers of reusable components must keep their focus on the needs of several systems.

- Consumers of reusable components must be provided with access to components that are easy to find and understand, and that can easily be tailored to the needs of specific systems.

- The establishment of a reuse infrastructure is the first step to eliminating some of the barriers to development with reuse.

- Systematic processes for developing reusable analyses, designs, and components are not well established. More practical metricated experience must be gained with reuse in general and the object-oriented approach to it before vast improvements in productivity can be expected to be routine.

- Reuse is still not established in the standard practice of software developers and the need for tools to support the processes of development for and with reuse is only beginning to be addressed by CASE vendors. Development without such tools or accompanied by peripheral tool building activities will diminish the economic and technical rewards of reuse.

Management
of a Fusion Project

10-1 INTRODUCTION

In this chapter we consider how Fusion can be successfully introduced and used by a project. The material is based on experience of introducing advanced software engineering methodologies into projects in Hewlett-Packard. The chapter is intended for project managers and engineers who need to understand the management implications of using Fusion. Technology transition is primarily a project management issue and some of the material, especially that relating to good practice, may already be familiar to the reader. However, in the presentation we emphasize the relationship between project management and Fusion.

We first consider how to go about introducing Fusion into a project (section 10-2). Then we explain how the method integrates with the overall software development process (section 10-5). Finally, we discuss how the method directly affects project management (section 10-6).

10-2 WAYS TO INTRODUCE FUSION INTO A PROJECT

A project should evaluate the benefits and the costs of a new technology before adopting it. If a change is judged beneficial, the timing and mode of introduction have to be carefully planned.

It is better to introduce change at the beginning of a project. Many start with an investigative phase, during which potential technologies for the project are explored.

This is the ideal time to investigate the introduction of Fusion. If it is considered important to adopt the method midway through a project, it should be introduced via a low-risk activity. That activity should be treated as if it was a new project and should follow the process described below. Large-scale attempts to introduce a new technology late in the life cycle of a project should be avoided, because they run a high risk of failing.

Experience of transferring new software technologies leads us to suggest a three-step approach.

1. *Needs assessment.* Review the project's software development process and its business needs.
2. *Training.* Train the project in the new technology.
3. *Planning of transition.* Plan the use of the method on the actual development.

Figure 10.1 illustrates this approach and shows the major inputs to each step and the review questions to be settled after each step is completed. Each step is considered in turn.

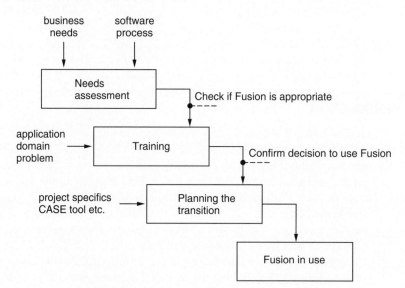

Figure 10.1 Steps Involved in Introducing Fusion

10-2.1 Needs Assessment

There can be no hard-and-fast rules for deciding whether a project is ready to use a new technology. In the case of Fusion the following issues should be considered:

Business Case: The success of a project usually depends on attributes such as quality, time-to-market, development costs, performance, and so forth. The software process should be attuned to helping whichever of these is considered critical.

Fusion helps improve software quality, particularly through the articulation and communication of design information. Therefore, the method will be of most immediate benefit to projects whose success depends on these characteristics. For example, Fusion is beneficial to a project embarking on the design of a family of products, since it improves quality and allows design alternatives to be explored. A project involving collaboration between teams on different sites can also expect to benefit because of the importance of the communication of design information. Fusion can also improve time-to-market by reducing design rework. However, this benefit is not so immediate because it requires expertise and fluency with the method.

The use of the method may not help every goal to be attained. For example, it will be of less help to a project that has to reengineer large amounts of unstructured and undocumented legacy C code.

Project Management.

Use of a new method involves changing the way that a project produces software. The change will initially increase the demands on the management of the project. The biggest risk in adopting a new software method comes from making a change without, first, having a managed software process in place. The Software Engineering Institute [56] has a model for assessing process maturity. If a project is at the lowest level of maturity, with an ad hoc process, the chances of a successful technology transition are very small. Their studies show that using improved methodologies only becomes a key issue for projects with a process that is defined, repeatable, and measured. Thus the successful introduction of Fusion requires project planning to be routine and not the exception.

Starting out on a small project is better because the project management task is simpler. Small teams are more adaptable and can learn more quickly because intraproject communication constitutes a much lower overhead than on big teams.

Technical Background.

Adopting a new method requires mastering a process and a whole set of notations. There is a limit to how much can be absorbed in one go. Consequently, the project's technical expertise is directly linked to the likelihood of success. Relevant expertise includes knowledge and use of object-oriented programming languages, structured methods, CASE tools, inspections, and systematic testing. It must be feasible to learn and employ all the new skills in the time available. Section 10-2.3 discusses how Fusion can be phased in so as to ease the problems associated with learning a new technology.

Support for Change.

Both the project, and its management, must support the change. Management support is vital and must not be neglected. They should understand the benefits, and how the distribution of effort across the software life cycle is changed. Management should also be aware, in advance, of the costs involved in making the transition, particularly the investment in training.

The project team should be sufficiently enthusiastic so as not to abandon Fusion at the first problem that is encountered. In no circumstances should change of method be imposed on a project.

Resources.

The ease with which a new technology can be adopted depends partly on the level of resources available to help during the transition. Before starting, the sources of training and consultancy should be identified. Access to the experience of projects that have already used an object-oriented method can also be very helpful. It is also necessary to identify and evaluate available CASE tool support for Fusion (see section 10-4).

An effective way to assess needs is to hold a two- or three-day review meeting, as part of the overall planning process for the project. The review should *not* focus directly on Fusion but consider the broader issue of defining a software process to meet the project's business needs.

The review should be conducted by a small team not directly involved in the project; it should include at least one independent software consultant. The key members of the project, including the manager, should all participate. They should present the current software process and all proposed changes. Senior management should contribute by explaining the business needs. The reviewers should familiarize themselves with the technical nature of the software needed for a new product and see demonstrations of current relevant products. To assess project morale, the reviewers should meet with some of the project team in their work environment.

At the end of the meeting, the reviewers should present feedback on the software process. This should then be discussed with the whole project and a set of recommendations be drawn up. The review should conclude with a presentation of the final recommendations to the appropriate line manager. If it is recommended to use Fusion, the issue of training needs to be addressed.

10-2.2 Training

There are two ways to organize training for a new technology. One approach is to stage a series of organization-wide courses and ensure that all software engineers, project managers, and so forth, attend the course. This is sometimes known, rather unkindly, as the "sheep dip" principle. Everybody has to pass through the experience irrespective of their need for it.

It is preferable to adopt a *project-centered* approach in which the training is organized for intact project teams at the most appropriate point in their life cycle. The project-centered training should be in two phases. The first phase should be general training on Fusion, the second phase should apply the method to the problem domain of the project.

Training Course.

All the project, including the project manager, should be trained in the use of Fusion. A course from an in-house, or external, training and consultancy organization is an easy way to learn. Three-and-a-half or four days is the appropriate duration for a course, which should include plenty of opportunity for reinforcing learning by doing exercises. Ideally, there should be no more than fifteen or twenty participants per course. The training should practice the process steps of the method by carrying out the development on a small lab project.

The course can try to simulate some aspects of real-life development by doing the laboratory work in teams. This allows for feedback sessions in which the solutions can be compared with each other.

A prerequisite for such a course is an understanding of the object-oriented approach. A short one- or two-day course can provide the background. The CRC method [11] is an excellent way of getting across the basics of the new paradigm.

If a course is not commercially available, this book can be used as the basis for self-help group training. The self-help study can be organized as a series of led discussions, over a period of several weeks. It should concentrate on the analysis, design, implementation, and case study chapters. All participants should read all chapters. However, for each phase of the method, one or two participants should be assigned the task of becoming local experts. The job of the local experts is to lead a discussion by short presentations on aspects of the method. The presentations need not be highly polished, but should aim at getting the basic ideas across. The experts should seek the involvement of the other team members, and not be afraid to identify those topics that they personally find difficult or obscure. After the series of discussions has finished, and there is a reasonable level of confidence in understanding Fusion, the next step is to attempt a short lab project. The lab project should be carried out by small teams in an intensive two- or three-day period. Regular feedback meetings should be scheduled to discuss the outputs from the analysis, design, and implementation phases. The schedule should be planned in advance, and adhered to. In this way some insight can be gained into the practical difficulties that may arise when using the method. Chapter 7 contains some ideas for possible lab projects.

There is often a need for training in C++ or the object-oriented programming language that is to be used. The training can be provided before or after Fusion. Giving the programming training first is usually preferred as it is a more incremental approach and, therefore, lower risk. Experience with the programming language can be gained earlier, and the language can provide a firmer foundation in objects for appreciating the method. The danger is that the project may never get around to taking training in analysis and design.

Workshop.

The second phase in Fusion training should happen about four weeks after the course to try out the method on a problem taken from the application domain of the project. A familiar problem, typical of the domain, should be chosen. The aim is to get an understanding of how the method will apply in practice and to provide a basis for deciding how Fusion is to be used. If possible, a consultant should be brought in to facilitate the workshop. The workshop should begin with a short overview of Fusion and then proceed into the project. The workshop should be done in teams, with feedback sessions as in the training course.

Before embarking on the transition to using Fusion, the lessons of the training should be reviewed and any other needs identified.

10-2.3 Planning the Transition

The transition must be based on the principle of minimizing risk. Ensure that early mistakes do not jeopardize the entire enterprise. Allow experience to develop by proceeding in small steps. The following guidelines should be used when planning the transition:

- Identify those components of the software that are most amenable to the use of Fusion. Choose one or two low-risk components to apply the method to first.
- Do not plan to do *all* the analysis, followed by *all* the design, followed by *all* the implementation. Build up confidence by taking a small part through to code as soon as possible.
- Realize that the whole project team need not be directly involved in using the method. Those not analyzing and designing can participate through reviewing.
- Encourage the development of "champions" for the method. A champion can become very effective by acting as mentor and unofficial consultant to the rest of the team.

Before considering how Fusion fits into the overall product development process we consider how the method can be modified to fit particular contexts.

10-3 ADAPTATION OF FUSION

Although Fusion is intended to provide significant benefits without being difficult to use, it is unrealistic to expect that it can be readily adopted by every project whatever its circumstances. In this section we consider modifications that can be made to the method to ease the transition.

10-3.1 Lightweight Fusion

A project may not always be able to adopt Fusion in one step. Schedule pressure, or some other reason, may not permit the necessary amount of time to be spent becoming fully conversant with all of the method. In these circumstances it is appropriate to introduce some parts of the method straight away, while leaving other parts for later.

Figure 10.2 outlines a lighter weight version of Fusion. In the analysis phase, the operation model schemata are simplified and the life-cycle model is replaced by scenarios. This has the effect of producing less precise specifications of system behavior. In the design phase, visibility is specified in less detail. These simplifications mean that less effort has to be put in learning the method. The cost is that some design decisions are no longer made explicitly and are therefore not documented. The decisions still have to be made, but this happens implicitly during implementation. Therefore, lightweight Fusion provides a reduced amount of support for the maintenance phase.

10-3.2 Combining Fusion with Other Methods

An immediate switch to Fusion may not be a realistic option for an organization that has already invested in another object-oriented method. In this situation, it may be

Phase	Model	Recommended Change
Analysis	System object Model	No change
	Operation model	Ensure *Description* is fully informative Keep *Reads, Changes, Sends* Omit *Assumes* and *Result*
	Life-cycle model	Replace by scenarios
Design	Object interaction Graphs	No change
	Visibility graphs	Restrict type of reference to *lifetime* (i.e., permanent or dynamic)
	Class descriptions	Omit information on visibility, lifetime, and mutability of object attributes
	Inheritance graphs	No change
Implementation		No change

Figure 10.2   Lightweight Fusion

possible to supplement the existing method with aspects of the Fusion. The purpose of doing this would be to strengthen the existing method. This has to be done with some care to avoid ending up with the worst of both worlds.

As an example of how this might be done, consider how Fusion might be used to supplement OMT [93]. As is discussed in chapter 8, a weakness of OMT is the absence of a process for the design phase. Figure 10.3 shows a set of modifications to OMT, in which Lightweight Fusion is used for design. The change to the analysis phase is to replace dataflow diagrams with the more descriptive notation of schemata. For the design phase, lightweight Fusion is used except that the dynamic model state machines have to be consulted when constructing object interaction graphs. This is because the analysis state machines will have already determined some class interfaces.

Phase	Model	Notes on Notation	Notes on Process
Analysis	Object model	OMT E-R notation	As for OMT
	Dynamic model	OMT state machines	
	Functional Model	Lightweight Fusion schemata	
Design	Object interaction graphs	As for Lightweight Fusion	As for Fusion, but use functional model *and* dynamic model to construct object interaction graphs
	Visibility graphs		
	Class descriptions		
	Inheritance graphs		
Implementation		Fusion plus OMT heuristics	

Figure 10.3   Incorporation of Fusion into OMT

The benefit of using a modified form of Fusion is that it reduces the amount of material that has to be learned. However, the adaptation can bring extra risk.

The main danger arises because there is no standard to follow. Consequently, it is recommended that a modified form of Fusion only be used as a temporary expedient.

10-4 SELECTION OF CASE TOOL

The choice of CASE tools is the final issue to be settled before starting to use Fusion. Like other methods, it can benefit from tool support. Tools can provide two kinds of support: support for *diagrams* and support for *semantics*. A tool for Fusion needs to be able to draw and modify diagrams simply and effectively. But diagrams are not enough; there should be an underlying meaning for the diagrams, on which tools can perform consistency checks and computations. A tool should help automate the Fusion process. In particular,

- When turning schemata into object interaction graphs, it should be possible to offer as-yet-unimplemented schemata and draw initial diagrams (with at least the appropriate classes).
- Initial visibility graphs can be computed from the object interaction graphs.
- Initial class descriptions can be computed from the system object model, object interaction graphs, visibility graphs, and inheritance graphs.
- Changes later in the process should be reflected back to models developed earlier, with appropriate controls to prevent ad hoc changes.
- The life-cycle model can be compiled automatically into skeletal code for state machines.
- Conversion of class descriptions to programming language class headers should be automatic (and customizable to the language).

Some CASE tools are configurable, which means they can be tailored to support different methods. As well as offering diagram editing facilities, they often incorporate a repository and a language for manipulating semantics. Configurable tools protect investment of the suppliers and purchasers as they are not tied to a single method. They also mean that the tool can be modified to fit the needs of the local environment. To summarize, some criteria for evaluating Fusion tools are the following:

- Does the tool give diagramming support for all the models?
- Does the tool provide any semantic support?
- Can the tool be tailored to take account of local conditions?
- Can the tool work with other tools that handle other aspects of the development process (e.g., database, configuration management system, version control system, etc.)?

10-5 SOFTWARE DEVELOPMENT PROCESS

In real-life use, Fusion has to fit it into the wider context of producing products. An idealized model of a product development process is shown in Figure 10.4. Cameron

[18] uses a similar model to show how object-oriented methods relate to the development of management information software.

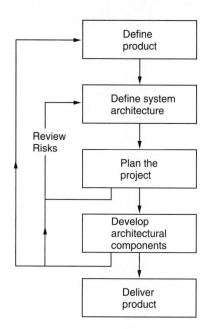

Figure 10.4   Process for Developing Software Products

Referring to Figure 10.4, the first step in the process is to define the product. It is vital for the product definition to be stable before a lot of effort is spent on development. Once the requirements for the product have been established, the next step is to define the software architecture for the system. In this context, the term architecture means major software (and hardware) components. Next, the project is planned. If it is not possible to decide whether some component should be done in hardware or software, the plan must include an activity for making the decision. The plan should also schedule and resource all the activities needed to produce the architecture and be resilient to risk. Next, the architectural components are developed, and the risks regularly reviewed. On completion of each component, it may be necessary to update the architecture. Finally, once all the components have been developed, the product can be delivered. The next sections consider each step of the process in more detail.

Definition of Product.

Product definition depends on having an understanding of the marketplace and the business strategy of the organization. Consequently, this task lies mainly outside of the scope of this book. However, in one important respect the object-oriented approach can make a significant contribution to the task of product definition through rapid prototyping. A prototype is a software model that is used to reduce risk by obtaining information at an early stage in the development of a product.

By building and reviewing prototypes it is possible to get early feedback on the user interface and functionality of a product. The essence of rapid prototyping is speed of production rather than code quality. Generally, a development method is not appropriate to the construction of rapid prototypes because they are not products and should be discarded after evaluation. It is a mistake to try to shorten development times by enhancing and delivering a rapid prototype. This policy is often disastrous because a rapidly produced prototype generally makes a hacked-up product.

The rapid prototyping process must be carefully managed. Reviewers of a prototype, being human, are capable of many views on what is good, what is bad, and what might be better. Considering their comments and updating the prototype leads naturally to another set of comments and, of course, a subsequent prototype to be reviewed. There must always be some criteria for terminating the iteration. Maude and Willis [79] discuss in detail how rapid prototyping can be used to reduce risk.

The object-oriented approach supports prototyping through reusable frameworks and indirectly through interactive programming environments. Once an abstract class has been built, different concrete classes can be derived by supplying implementations for the abstract methods. This allows prototypes to be constructed very cheaply to explore various design alternatives. Interactive programming environments with features such as incremental compilation, dynamic type systems, and garbage collection greatly increase the speed with which prototypes can be built and evaluated.

Definition of System Architecture.

A *system architecture* structures a system into its major sequential components that communicate via dataflows and events. An architecture can be represented by a dataflow diagram as shown in Figure 10.5.

Sometimes an architecture can be obtained by adapting one from similar applications. For example, compilers are often architected as multipass pipelines. In general, there are several prototypical architectures (e.g., real-time system, batch processing, interactive system, transaction manager, etc.).

If there is no preexisting knowledge, the architecture has to be designed considering the application domain and the implementation platform. The development of architectural components is done in a subsequent step.

Planning of Project.

The plan should include activities to develop the entire architecture. It should also produce an outline plan for the development of the components and identify any that are to be prototyped.

Focus on the critical success factors by identifying the risks. A *risk* is the possibility of damage, injury, or loss that involves an element of choice. The risks should be identified and ranked in order of priority. The priority of a risk is the product of the probability that the risk will happen and the magnitude of the potential loss. Thus a high-priority risk can arise from something with only a medium chance of happening that would inflict moderate damage. Each risk needs to be considered and a plan

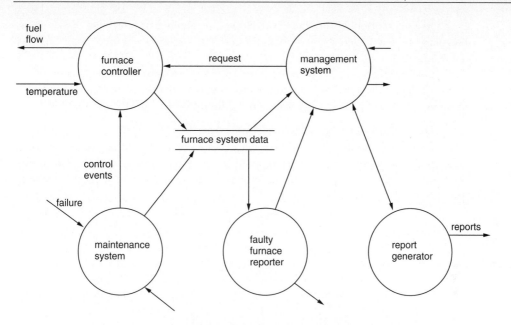

Figure 10.5   Example of System Architecture

established to resolve it. Each risk plan should then be integrated into the overall project plan to make it more resilient. Figure 10.6 shows the process for assessing risks.

---

1. Identify and rank the following risks:

- What can go wrong?
- What will be the magnitude of the damage?
- What are the chances that it will happen?
- Produce a "top-ten" risk list.

2. Complete the following for each risk in the list:

- If the risk is well-understood include actions to

    - Reduce chances of a risk occurring.
    - Reduce impact if it does happen by having contingency plans.

- Otherwise include an action to obtain more information, followed by a checkpoint to decide what to do about the risk.

3. Modify project plans to incorporate risk management activities, wherever possible dealing with big risks early.

Figure 10.6   Review of Project Plan for Risks

As the components are being developed, maintain a "top-ten" list of risk items. Regularly review progress in resolving the risks and identify any new risks that may have arisen.

Risk management is not a cookbook approach to project management. It requires judgment to understand and analyze the potential problems facing a project. A fuller account of risk management is to be found in Boehm [13] and Ould [85].

Development of Architectural Components.

Fusion fits into the overall process as a technique for developing object-oriented sequential components of the system architecture. The analysis, design, and implementation phases correspond to the left-hand arm of the classic V-model software process, as in Figure 10.7.

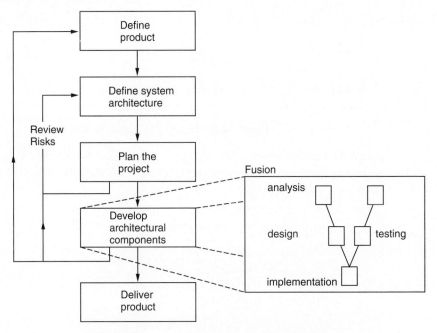

Figure 10.7 Development of Software Components

In principle, a development using Fusion should conform to the *waterfall* model, in which each phase from analysis through to testing is completed before the next is started. Of course, this is only an approximation to reality. Normally, backtracking is necessary because of requirements, changes, or errors found late in the development. Thus there must be a mechanism to ensure the consistency of updates to the various analysis and design models.

It is sensible to develop the components incrementally, especially if customers are likely to want early access to working systems. Another advantage of incremental development is that system integration can be done in small stages, thus avoiding the problems that can arise from a "big-bang" integration. As much as possible of the analysis for all the increments should be done in advance of implementation. This reduces the risk of the evolution failing because of an apparently small change in functionality requiring a massive internal restructuring of the software. It is preferable if each increment lasts no longer than six to nine months.

Development of the increments can be overlapped, with the analysis of one increment starting before a previous increment has been completed, as in Figure 10.8. Because it is quite possible for one phase to cause a change to a Fusion model produced in a previous phase, care must be taken to ensure that the propagation of changes between the different developments is carefully managed. Incremental development also needs a disciplined approach to documentation.

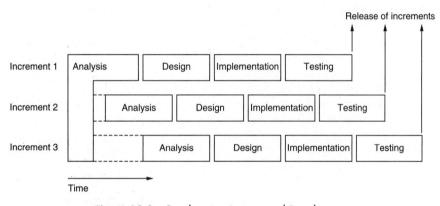

Figure 10.8   Overlapping Incremental Development

10-6 PROJECT MANAGEMENT

Software development is inherently difficult to manage, because software is complex, invisible, and readily changeable. The complexity makes software difficult to understand. Invisibility means the inner workings of a program are hidden; consequently it is hard to measure either software quality, or progress in a software development. It is also easy to change a program, whatever its size, but extremely difficult to work out what the consequences are, especially for large programs. In this section we consider how Fusion can help ameliorate these issues.

Managing the Development.

The object-oriented approach reduces the complexity of software by structuring it into class inheritance hierarchies. Fusion takes this further by recording much more of the structure. It also allows the key decisions behind the structure to be made explicit. All this information is recorded in the Fusion models. Managing the production of these models is therefore an effective tool for managing the development itself.

The key models produced during a development are the following:

- *System architecture*. Decomposes the system into its major sequential components

- For each sequential component a
  - *Specification.* Comprises the object model and the interface model
  - *Object-oriented architecture.* Comprises the object interaction graphs, the class descriptions, and the inheritance graphs
- *Data Dictionary.* Documents all the terms and concepts used in the other models

These models evolve as the development proceeds. At some point, the models become stable and then crystallize into their final form. This process has to be controlled as at every point in time the true status of each work product must be clear. This can be achieved by keeping the models under change control. This allows a single authorized version to be defined and stops conflicting versions of the system from developing. The change management of interfaces is particularly important. At all times, the provider and all the users of a class must conform to a common definition of the class interface and behavior.

To ensure the quality of the models, a *design team* should be established with the responsibility for controlling the evolution and maintaining correctness. The team should be in charge of applying the appropriate quality checks to new additions, ensuring that changes are consistent and are propagated to the entire project. They must also ensure that the implementation is developed according the specification and architectural models. The architectural models must satisfy their specification, and the implementation must satisfy the models.

The design team should be composed of skilled and experienced designers. One of the team's main tasks is to gain and keep the confidence of the rest of the project. Without this, the models will fall into disrepute and will not be used.

Deliverables.

The main deliverables from a project are the system itself together with its user documentation and validation tests. The final versions of the system architecture together with the component specifications and architectures constitute the technical deliverables from the project. Without this documentation, postdelivery stages of the life cycle will be unnecessarily expensive.

All deliverables should be worked on as soon as the schedule allows. In this way the documentation will be produced during the active life of the project rather than after the event when the information is much more difficult to glean.

Quality Management.

There are two complementary approaches to quality management. One approach is to build in quality by using a disciplined process to minimize the number of defects that are introduced during development. The other approach is to remove defects from software before it is shipped, by using checks to find and fix any defects that have been introduced.

The systematic and rigorous process in Fusion contributes to reducing the number of defects that are introduced during construction. The method also helps defect removal because each stage of the process has associated quality checks on the models. These should be used as exit criteria for walkthroughs and formal inspections.

Section 5-9.2 contains more on quality assurance techniques for object-oriented software.

Distribution of Effort and Work Breakdown .

The use of Fusion increases the amount of effort required in earlier phases of development. More effort is spent on analysis and design than is the case if no method is used. This should be more than offset by the reduced time during testing and integration, and, of course, by less time to perform enhancements and do maintenance.

This different distribution must be recognized by the project and its management. Consequently, progress cannot be properly measured by the number of lines of code produced. Instead, the completed and reviewed analysis and design artifacts should be used as milestones.

During implementation, the class structure of the design architecture can be used as the atomic unit of allocation. However, work units have to be groups of classes that consider the following:

- *Usage relations*. These provide functional subsystems that can be easily tested.
- *Inheritance relations*. The developer of a subclass may need to know how the superclass is implemented.

Allocating classes to different people to develop makes it vital that class interface definitions be agreed and maintained. This should be the responsibility of the design team.

Estimation and Tracking.

An object-oriented architecture can be used as the basis of effort estimation and progress tracking. Effort estimates can be based on the inheritance graphs [54] [68]. The estimates are based on the assumption that the effort to produce a class grows linearly with the number of (nonabstract) methods and class attributes. The effort to produce the entire software is estimated by summing the effort to produce all the classes in the architecture. By keeping records of actual costs, the process can be refined so as to improve the reliability of the estimates. Project progress can be tracked similarly. However, until there is the automatic collection of data by CASE tools, project estimation and tracking is likely to remain an imprecise art.

10-7 SUMMARY

The main points of the chapter are the following:

- The introduction of Fusion needs to be planned. A project should evaluate the benefits and the costs of a new technology before adopting it. If a change is judged beneficial, the timing and mode of introduction have to be carefully planned.

- Fusion fits into the overall software development process as a method for developing object-oriented sequential components of the system architecture.
- Fusion aids good project management by defining models whose production can be managed.

APPENDIX

A

Fusion Process Summary

The Fusion method is presented in this book as a rational development process [86]. Each notation used has been introduced in turn outlining its logical purpose and its relation to other aspects of analysis, design, and implementation. It must be remembered, however, that the method presented is an "idealized" view. It describes a logical and systematic way of developing object-oriented software. In practice, development does not proceed in such an orderly manner. Individual aspects of the system may be explored and developed before expanding on other parts. Requirements may not be fully known before development beginning. Presenting the development process in a rational manner makes it easier to illustrate the dependencies and relationships between different phases in the development. The reader should realize that actual software development does not mirror such a rational process but that the documentation produced reflects, and in some sense "fakes," the rational process.

In this appendix all of the process steps which have been introduced for analysis, design, and implementation are summarized. Figure A.1 provides a route map for the method and shows the dependencies between the models produced.

A-1 ANALYSIS

Analysis is about describing *what* a system does rather than *how* it does it. Separating the behavior of a system from the way it is implemented requires viewing the system from the user's perspective rather than that of the machine. Thus analysis is focused

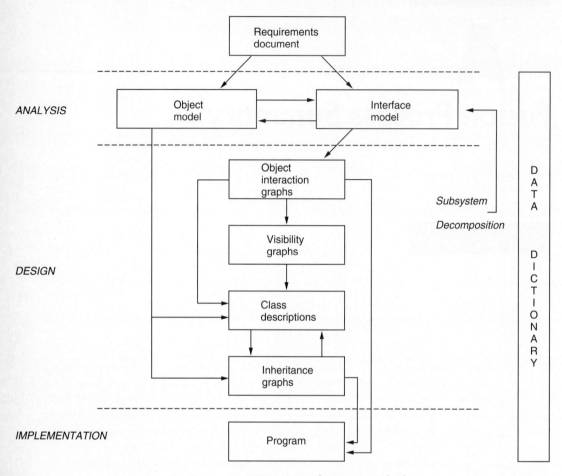

Figure A.1   The Fusion Method

on the domain of the problem and is concerned with externally visible behavior. Full details of the analysis process are given in chapter 3.

Step 1: Develop the Object Model (section 3-4)

The purpose of the object model is to capture the concepts that exist in the domain of the problem and the relationships between them. It can represent classes, attributes, and relationships between classes.

1. Brainstorm a list of candidate classes and relationships.
2. Enter classes and relationships into data dictionary.
3. Incrementally produce object model looking for
   - Generalizations modeling "kind of" or *is-a* relationships.
   - Aggregations modeling "part of" or *has-a* relationships.

- Attributes of classes.
- Cardinalities of relationships.
- General constraints that should be recorded in the data dictionary.
- Derived relationships that should be recorded in the data dictionary but that do not appear on the object model.

Step 2: Determine the System Interface (section 3-5)

A system cooperates with active agents in its environment. Agents invoke system operations that can change the state of the system and can cause events to be output.

The system interface is the set of system operations to which it can respond and the events that it can output. An entry is required in the data dictionary for every agent, system operation, and output event.

1. Identify agents, system operations, and events.
2. Produce the system object model. The system object model is a refinement of the object model developed in the first step of analysis.

   - Using information from the system interface, identify classes and relationships on the object model that pertain to the state of the system.
   - Document system boundary to produce the system object model.

A useful technique for establishing the interface boundary is to focus on scenarios of usage. For each scenario consider

1. The agents who are involved.
2. What they want the system to do.

Timeline diagrams can be used to represent scenarios. Note that timeline diagrams are a helpful tool for identifying the system boundary, but they only provide a snapshot of system behavior.

Step 3: Develop an Interface Model (section 3-6)

The interface model is made up of a life-cycle model and an operation model.

Life-Cycle Model (section 3-6.1).

The life-cycle model defines the allowable sequences of interactions in which a system may participate. The life-cycle model is defined in terms of regular expressions that are a means of describing sequence patterns.

1. Generalize scenarios and form named life-cycle expressions.
2. Combine life-cycle expressions to form life-cycle model.

Operation Model (section 3-6.2).

The operation model defines the semantics of each system operation in the system interface.

For each system operation

1. Develop the **Assumes** and **Results** clauses.

   - Describe each aspect of the result as a separate subclause of **Results**.
   - Use the life-cycle model to find the events that have to be output in **Results**.
   - Check that **Results** does not allow unwanted values.
   - Add relevant system object model invariants to **Assumes** and **Results**.
   - Ensure **Assumes** and **Results** are satisfiable.
   - Update data dictionary entries for system operations and events.

2. Extract **Sends**, **Reads**, and **Changes** clauses from the **Results** and **Assumes**.

Step 4: Check the Analysis Models (section 3-7)

There are two aspects to checking the analysis models; they should be complete and consistent. A model is complete when it captures all the meaningful abstractions in the domain. Models are consistent when they do not contradict each other. A model can be checked for internal consistency and also for those areas where it overlaps with other models.

Note that the following checks are not exhaustive but provide guidelines for checking the analysis.

1. *Completeness against the requirements.* Reread the requirements document carefully. Check that

   - All possible scenarios are covered by the life cycle.
   - All operations are defined by a schema.
   - All static information is captured by the system object model.
   - Any other information (e.g., technical definitions and invariant constraints) are in the data dictionary.

2. *Simple consistency.* These checks deal with the areas of overlap between the models of analysis. Check that

   - All classes, relationships, and attributes mentioned in the object model appear in the system object model. All other concepts (e.g., predicates) must be defined in the data dictionary or some referenced source.
   - The boundary of the system object model is consistent with the interface model.
   - All the system operations in the life-cycle model have a schema.
   - All identifiers in all models have entries in the data dictionary.

3. *Semantic consistency.* These checks attempt to ensure that the implications of the models are consistent.

   - Output of events in life-cycle model and operation model must be consistent. The schema for a system operation must generate the output events that follow it in the life-cycle model.
   - The operation model must preserve system object model invariant constraints. If there is an invariant concerning a relationship or class, then any operation that can change them must respect the invariant in its schema.

- Desk check scenarios using the schemas. Choose examples of scenarios and define the state change that each should cause. Then "execute" the scenarios, using the schemas to define the behavior of each system operation. Check that the result is what is expected.

A-2 DESIGN

During design, software structures are introduced to satisfy the abstract definitions produced from analysis. Full details of the design process are given in chapter 4.

Step 1: Object Interaction Graphs (section 4-2)

Develop object interaction graphs for each system operation in the operation model. The object interaction graphs show how functionality is distributed across the objects of a system.

1. Identify relevant objects involved in the computation.
2. Establish role of each object in computation.

- Identify controller.
- Identify collaborators.

3. Decide on messages between objects.
4. Record how the identified objects interact on an object interaction graph.

   Check the following:

1. *Consistency with analysis models.* Check that each of the classes in the system object model are represented in at least one object interaction graph.
2. *Verification of functional effect.* Check that the functional effect of each object interaction graph satisfies the specification of its system operation given in the operation model.

Step 2: Visibility Graphs (section 4-3)

For each class define a visibility graph. These show how the object-oriented system is structured to enable object communication. Visibility graphs are constructed as follows:

1. All the object interaction graphs are inspected. Each message on an object interaction graph implies that a visibility reference is needed from the client class to the server object.
2. Decide on the kind of visibility reference required taking into account:

- Lifetime of reference.
- Visibility of target object.
- Lifetime of target object.
- Mutability of target object.

3. Draw a visibility graph for each design object class.

Check the following:

1. *Consistency with analysis models.* For each relation on the system object model check that there is a path of visibility for the corresponding classes on the visibility graphs.
2. *Mutual consistency.* Check that exclusive target objects are not referenced by more than one class and that shared targets are referenced by more than one class.

Step 3: Class Descriptions (section 4-4)

Class descriptions are the specifications from which coding begins. They specify the internal state and external interface required by each class.

Extract information from the system object model, object interaction graphs, and visibility graphs to build class descriptions.

Each class description records the following:

1. Methods and parameters from the object interaction graph.
2. Data attributes from the system object model and the data dictionary.
3. Object attributes from the visibility graph for the class.
4. Inheritance information (included after next stage) from the inheritance graph.

Check the following:

1. *Methods and parameters.* Check that all methods from object interaction graphs are recorded.
2. *Data attributes.* Check that all data attributes from the system object model are recorded.
3. *Object attributes.* Check that all visibility references are recorded.
4. *Inheritance.* Check that all inherited superclasses are recorded.

Step 4: Inheritance Graphs (section 4-5)

Here we build the inheritance structures, looking at the classes to identify commonalities and abstractions.

Identify superclasses and subclasses. Construct inheritance graphs. Look for the following:

1. Generalizations and specializations in the object model.
2. Common methods in object interaction graphs and class descriptions.
3. Common visibility in the visibility graphs.

Step 5: Update Class Descriptions (section 4-4)

Update the class descriptions with the new inheritance information. Check the the following:

1. *System object model.* Check that the subtype relations are preserved.

2. *Object interaction graphs.* Check that all classes are represented in an inheritance graph. A naive assumption is that each class in the object interaction graph is in the inheritance graph. This is generally the case, but we also need to consider that the class structure may be reorganized because of the introduction of new abstract classes.

3. *Visibility graphs.* Check that all classes are represented in an inheritance graph. Abstract classes can be defined for common structure between classes in the visibility graphs.

4. *Class descriptions.* Check that updated class descriptions implement all the functionality of the preliminary ones and respect the inheritance graphs.

A-3 IMPLEMENTATION

The final stage of Fusion is mapping the design into an effective implementation. This transition is relatively straightforward as the majority of complex design decisions have already been made. Full details of the implementation process are given in chapter 5.

Step 1: Coding

System Life Cycle (section 5-10).
For life cycles with no interleaving

1. Translate life-cycle regular expression into a (nondeterministic) state machine.
2. Implement the state machine.

   For life cycles with interleaving

1. Implement interleaving-free subexpressions.
2. Link the resulting state machines.

Class Descriptions (section 5-3).

1. *Specify representation and interface of the classes.*
   - *Attribute declaration.* The attributes of the class descriptions will usually be slots of the named class. Attribute qualifiers are added to specify the *mutability* and *sharing* as appropriate.
   - *Method declaration.* The methods of a class description are implemented by code in the class named (i.e., as member functions, routines, etc.).
   - *Inheritance.* The **isa** clauses of class descriptions name the parents of classes.

2. *Implement method bodies.* Most of the information required for the implementation of method bodies is contained in the object interaction graphs and the data dictionary. The main issues to deal with are *error handling* and *iteration*.
   - *Error handling.* An error is defined as *the violation of a precondition*. Each method promises to achieve its postcondition if it is invoked with its precondition **true**. It is also obliged to invoke any further methods with their preconditions **true**.

Appropriate code has to be written to manage both *error detection* and *error recovery*.

- *Iteration.* Code to deal with iterations that arise from invoking methods on collections will have to deal with two cases:

    - A method is invoked on all the objects in a collection.
    - A method is invoked on a subset of the objects in a collection.

Data Dictionary (section 5-5).

1. Implement functions, predicates, and types that are both found in the data dictionary and used by methods.
2. Ensure assertions are respected by adding any necessary code to all affected methods.

Step 2: Performance (section 5-7)

This is not strictly a step in the implementation process. Remember the following:

1. Performance cannot be obtained as an afterthought. It must be considered throughout the analysis, design, and implementation process.
2. Optimizing rarely executed code is ineffective.

So,

1. Profile your system in as many ways as you can.
2. Optimize the "hot spots."

Storage Management (section 5-8).

Unless the implementation language provides *garbage collection*, you must ensure that when there is no further use for an object, any resources it uses can be reclaimed by the system.

Step 3: Review (section 5-9)

1. *Inspections.* A cost-effective technique for the detection of defects in software. Remember that in object-oriented software the static analysis of the flow of control is complicated by the following:

- Object-oriented languages emphasizing the inheritance relationship rather than the control relationship. There is no direct mapping between functional requirements and high-level functions.
- The smaller size of data structures, access functions used to implement classes, and classes as a whole.
- The dispersal of method specifications and implementations among the classes.
- Dynamic binding making it difficult to determine which code is actually executed for a method invocation.

Inspections should, in addition to tracing the flow of control, focus on detecting typical flaws in object-oriented systems. Confirm that all subclasses implementing a specific method conform to the method specification.

2. *Testing.* Complementary technique to inspections for exposing defects in software. Test cases for classes should include the following:

- Checking state observation and manipulation.
- Applying algebraic properties such as associativity and identity preservation to member function invocation.
- Checking that destructors in C++ are consistent with the corresponding constructors.
- Checking proper use of initialization.
- Checking that casting in C++ is being used in safe ways.
- Trying to trigger exception-handling capabilities via extreme boundary value inputs.

APPENDIX

B

Fusion Notation Summary

Object Model Notation

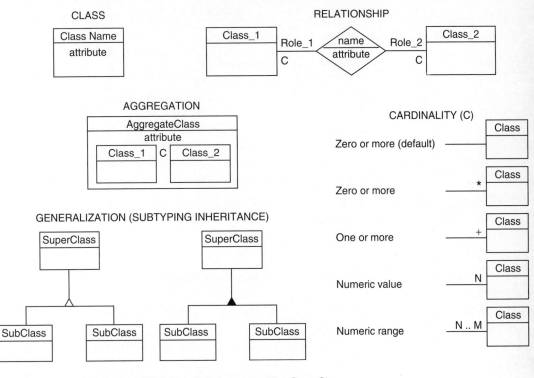

Interface Model Notation

Life-Cycle Model

life cycle [*Name* :] *Regular_Expression*

(*LocalName* = *Regular_Expression*)*

Regular_Expressions:Name		Any event name (operation), local name, or output event
	Concatenation	$x.y$
	Alternation	$x\|y$
	Repetition	
	Zero or more	x^*
	One or more	x^+
	Optional	$[x]$
	Interleaving	$\|\|$
	Grouping	(x)

Operation Model

Operation:	*operation identifier*
Description:	*<text> Description of operation*
Reads:	*<supplied values> <state components>*
Changes:	*<supplied values> <state components>*
Sends:	*<agent communication>*
Assumes:	*<assertions> (preconditions)*
Result:	*<assertions> (postconditions)*

Object Interaction Graph Notation

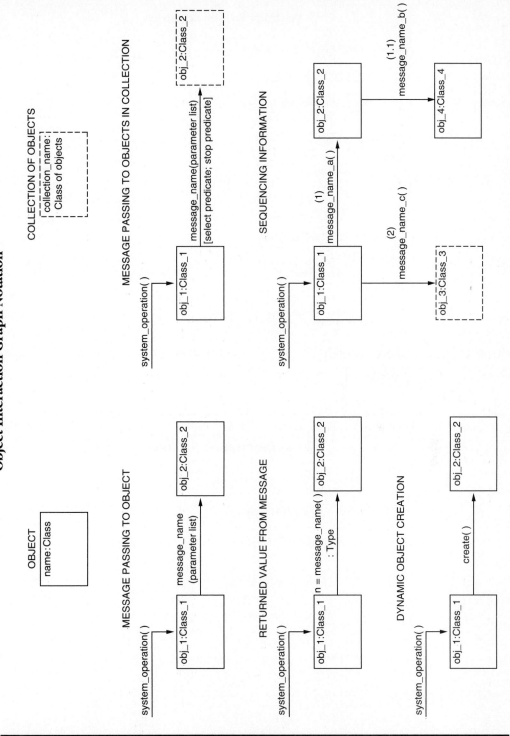

Visibility Graph Notation

VISIBILITY REFERENCE ARROWS

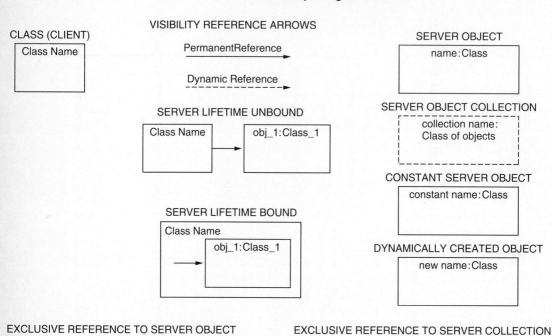

CLASS (CLIENT)

Class Name

PermanentReference

Dynamic Reference

SERVER OBJECT

name:Class

SERVER LIFETIME UNBOUND

Class Name → obj_1:Class_1

SERVER OBJECT COLLECTION

collection name:
Class of objects

CONSTANT SERVER OBJECT

constant name:Class

SERVER LIFETIME BOUND

Class Name
obj_1:Class_1

DYNAMICALLY CREATED OBJECT

new name:Class

EXCLUSIVE REFERENCE TO SERVER OBJECT

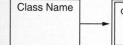

Class Name → obj_1:Class_1

EXCLUSIVE REFERENCE TO SERVER COLLECTION

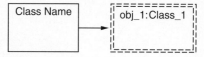

Class Name → obj_1:Class_1

Class Description Notation

class *<ClassName>* [isa *< SuperClassNames>*]

    // for each attribute

    [attribute] *[Mutability]<a_name>* :*[Sharing][Binding]<Type>*
        ⋮
    //for each method

    [method] *<m_name>* *<arglist>*[:*<Type >*]
        ⋮
endclass

Inheritance Graph Notation

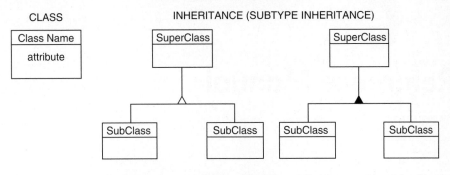

CLASS   INHERITANCE (SUBTYPE INHERITANCE)

SubClasses may overlap (nondisjoint)   Subclasses partition SuperClass
Possibly more SubClasses

APPENDIX

C

Reference Manual

C-1 INTRODUCTION

This appendix is a reference manual for the notations of Fusion; we assume the reader is already familiar with them from the body of the book. Each notation of Fusion is discussed, in approximately the order in which they are encountered in the process, giving first its syntax and then its semantics. Each (legal) use of a Fusion notation is given a well-defined meaning.

C-1.1 Roadmap

The *analysis* stage of Fusion builds the object model (section C-2) and the interface model (section C-3). The object model defines classes and their relationships (including inheritance), whereas the system behavior is defined by the interface model.

Information is also collected in the data dictionary (section C-4), a nondiagrammatic record of data about the system, such as constraints on numbers, nonclass types, shared functions, and so on.

The *design* stage of Fusion constructs object interaction graphs (section C-5), which describe how the system behavior can be built out of interacting objects, and visibility graphs (section C-6), which show how the objects have access one to another. Then inheritance graphs (section C-7) show how classes are related by inheritance. Class descriptions (section C-8) are then developed to summarize the properties of classes.

C-1.2 Naming Convention

The names of Fusion types and classes are conventionally written with an initial uppercase letter: hence **Depot**, **String**. The same name written with an initial lowercase letter refers to a variable of that type. This convention allows the omission of type names in various circumstances. Where implicitly typed names are used, they have the syntax

$$TypedName ::=$$
$$Name_1 \text{ ``:'' } Type$$
$$|\quad Name_2$$

where a $Name_1$ is an ordinary name, and a $Name_2$ is the name of a known type with its initial letter reduced to lowercase.

Names in Fusion can consist of letters, digits, and underbars in any combination, subject to not forming a reserved word or a number. Names may contain spaces; any component of such a name cannot be a reserved word.

In this appendix, names starting with capitals are also used for nonterminals in grammatical descriptions.

C-1.3 Syntactic Descriptions

Where the syntax of items is described, the variant of extended BNF described in Figure C.1 is used. "|" is least binding, juxtaposition next binding, "**" and "++" more binding, and "+" and "*" most binding.

el | e2	"el" or "e2"
[e]	optional "e"
e*	zero or more "e"
e**s	zero or more "e" separated by "s"
e+	one or more "e"
e++s	one or more "e" separated by "s"
n	nonterminal symbol "n"
attr n	nonterminal symbol "n" with attributes "attr"
"t"	terminal symbol "t"
(e)	grouping of syntatic components

Figure C.1   Syntactic Notation

In some places, quote marks appear as literal items in the grammar. To avoid confusion, the opening and closing quote marks are defined once as follows:

$$LQuote ::=$$
$$\text{````''}$$

$$RQuote ::=$$
$$\text{``''''}$$

End-of-line comments are introduced by the character pair "//".

C-2 OBJECT MODEL

The object model is a modified form of entity-relationship diagram.

C-2.1 Object Model Syntax

An object model is a diagram whose components are *class boxes* and *relationship diamonds*, connected by *subtype arcs* and *role arcs*.

Classes.

A class box is a rectangle containing the name of a class. A class may also contain *attributes*. If a class contains attributes, they are separated from the class name by a horizontal line drawn across the box; the class name appears above the line. Attributes are represented by names. See the example in Figure C.2, where **value** is an attribute of **SampleValue** and **last_stamped** is an attribute of **TimeStamped**.

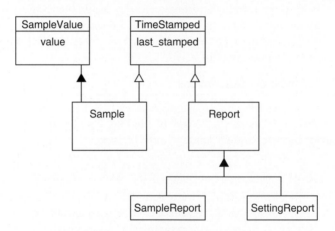

Figure C.2   Object Model with Subtypes

Subtyping.

Subtyping is shown using the subtype triangle symbol, △. The triangle may be *outlined* or *solid*.

A *lower* subtype arc connects a class to the base of a subtype triangle. An *upper* subtype arc can connect the apex of a subtype triangle to a class. Every subtype triangle must have exactly one upper arc and at least one lower arc. Subtype arcs and triangles are not named. Figure C.2 shows both kinds of subtyping.

The class at the upper end of the arc is the *base-*, *parent-*, or *super*class; those at the lower end are *derived-*, *child-*, or *sub*classes.

Although subtype triangles are usually shown vertically, it may be necessary to rotate them to keep diagrams clear; the important distinction is that between the sharp end (for the parent) and the blunt end (for the children).

The descriptions of Fusion diagrams refer to *arcs* in many places. An arc is just a line joining the shapes on the diagram; our normal style is to make arcs out of joined horizontal and vertical line segments, but this is not a requirement of the method.

Some arcs are directional. They bear an arrow at their *head*, the end pointed to. The other end, the *tail*, is plain.

Aggregation.

Classes and relationships can appear nested within *aggregate* classes (but not within relationships). Arcs can cross such enclosing class boundaries. The classes and relationships inside the aggregate are the *parts* or *components* of the aggregate.

Cardinalities can be attached to classes in aggregations; they are written on the outside top left of the component class box.

Relationships.

A relationship is represented by a diamond, $\diamond$, containing its name; Figure C.3 is an example. The diamond may also contain attributes, as for classes.

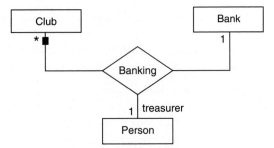

Figure C.3   *Cardinality Example*

A relationship may be linked to any nonzero number of classes by *role arcs*; the number of arcs is called the *arity* of the relationship. The arcs emerge from the vertices of the diamond (relationships of arity greater than four are discouraged for other reasons). Role arcs may be named. The class end of each role arc may carry a *cardinality*, which is the symbol "+", the symbol "*", a natural number, or two natural numbers separated by the symbol "..".

A role arc may also carry a *total* marker, ■, written at or near the class end of the arc.

Constraints.

Class and relationship boxes can contain at most one attribute with any given name.

A relationship cannot have two role arcs with the same role names. An unnamed arc is taken to be named by the class at its end. (It follows that a binary relation on a single class must have at least one of its role arcs named.)

C-2.2 Object Model Semantics

The meaning of the object model is expressed in terms of sets of objects (for classes) and sets of tuples (for relationships).

Objects.

The elements of class sets are called *objects*. Objects have *identity*; two objects can be *equal* (have the same values for their attributes) without being *identical*. Objects are *mutable*: that is, the values of their attributes can change. The number and type of their attributes is, however, fixed.

Classes and Subtyping.

Each class box represents a named set of objects. Boxes with the same name represent the same set.

A class attached to a lower subtype arc is a subset of the class attached to the corresponding upper subtype arc. Each element of the subtype has all the attributes of the supertype. A *solid* subtype triangle means that different classes at the lower ends of the same subtype arc family are disjoint, and their union is the set at the upper end of the arc. (The parent class is then *abstract*, as it has no direct instances.) An *outline* subtype triangle does not make this commitment.

> There are four possible ways of restricting the subtyping, being the product of the choices exhaustive/possibly-incomplete and disjoint/possibly-overlapping. Fusion collapses the choices into two. Any further distinctions required must be made in the data dictionary.

It is possible for a class to be the base of several distinct subtypings. It is even possible for one class to be abstract in two different ways (e.g., people might be subclassed as male versus female or hemophilic versus not hemophilic), although such structures are likely to be confusing in practice.

Consider Figure C.2 again. **TimeStamped** is a supertype of both **Sample** and **Report**, and possibly of many other classes; it would be used to record time-stamp information and methods. Classes such as **TimeStamped** are sometimes called *mixins*; they exist to provide functionality for other classes rather than to have instances.

A **Sample** is a time-stamped sample value; it has all the properties of both of its parent classes. For example, a **Sample** has both a **value** and a **last_stamped** attribute. The only **SampleValue**s are **Sample**s. All **Report**s are time-stamped, and there are exactly two kinds of **Report**: sample reports and setting reports.

> Why make time-stamps multiply inherited classes rather than attributes? They might keep a time-stamp history, rather than a single value, so implementing them as attributes would be too confining. Making "being time-stamped" a relationship, rather than using inheritance, means that the cardinalities have to be made explicit. And using subtyping means that any time-stamped object may be supplied to a function or method expecting instances of **TimeStamped**.

Sharing of Parent Classes.

Multiple inheritance allows one class to be a subtype of some parent class in more than one way. Fusion regards this repeated statement of subtyping as having no additional effect: It does not mean that instances of the subtype contain multiple copies of instances of the repeated supertype.

Relationships.

A relationship with **N** role arcs represents a set of **N**-tuples. The elements of the tuple are labeled with the names of the roles. An element labeled with role **r** is a member of the class connected to the relationship by the arc labeled **r**.

Referring again to Figure C.3, **Banking** represents a set of 3-tuples, with the elements being labeled **Club**, **Bank**, and **treasurer**. The **treasurer** role is explicitly named; the other roles are named for their classes.

The relationship denotes some subset of the Cartesian product of the classes it relates. If a role arc carries a total marker, *all* objects in the marked class must appear in the relationship in that role; if there is no role marker, participation is optional. In the example, all **Club**s must participate in **Banking**, but there can be **Person**s and **Bank**s that do not.

The subset is further constrained by the cardinalities on the role arcs. If a role named **r** has cardinality **N**, this means that a given combination of objects filling the other roles is associated with **N** **r**-objects. In the example, any club-person pair determines exactly one bank, and every club-bank pair determines exactly one person.

A person-bank pair is associated with "*" clubs: cardinalities are *ranges* **N..M** rather than single numbers. **N** is a natural number and **M** is a natural number or the special symbol ∞ (infinity). The cardinalities **N**, *, and + then stand for the ranges **N..N**, **0..**∞, and **1..**∞, respectively.

A role arc without an explicit cardinality is deemed to have cardinality "*". This means that simply writing a relationship between classes does not force premature consideration of cardinality.

Note the difference in meaning between the cardinality "*" and the absence of a total marker. In the example, "*" means that a particular combination of *other* roles may be associated with zero (or more) clubs, but all clubs must participate in **Banking**. If we removed the marker, then there could be clubs not associated with *any* person-bank pairs.

Attributes.

Each attribute is typed, their types appearing in the data dictionary (see section C-4.5).

Class attributes denote variables associated with each object of the class in which they appear. An attribute possessed by a class is possessed by all of its subclasses.

Relationship attributes are associated with the tuples in the relationship (i.e., each tuple of the relationship is mapped to a tuple of attributes). There are no cardinality constraints on relationship attributes.

Aggregation.

An aggregate class denotes a set of objects, and each such object corresponds to a set of tuples. The elements of the tuples are objects of the classes within the aggregate. Thus each object of the aggregate class corresponds to a subset of the cartesian product of its component classes.

The product is restricted by any relationships contained in the aggregate, and by the cardinalities of the classes in the relationship.

- The tuples of each aggregate object must respect any contained relationship: if relationship **R** appears in aggregate **A**, then the tuples of instances of **A** must form a subrelation of **R**.

- For each class **C** of an aggregate **A**, the number of distinct instances of **C** appearing in an instance of **A** is given by the cardinality of **C** in **A**.

Instances of aggregates have the attributes that are given in the aggregate box.

Note that the same object can appear as part of many different aggregate objects: there is no notion of an aggregate "owning" its components. This is because aggregation need not correspond to a physical part-of relationship.

Multiple Appearance.

If two class boxes appear on the same diagram with the same name, they denote the same set; the class as a whole has the union of all the attributes of the individual boxes.

A relationship has a *full name* consisting of the name of its diamond followed by the names of its roles and the classes they connect to, in alphabetical order of role name. The **Banking** relationship of Figure C.3 thus has the full name

Banking Bank: Bank Club: Club treasurer: Person.

Two relationship boxes with the same full name are identified as denoting the same relationship, in the same way as classes; the entire relationship has the union of the attributes of its individuals.

C-2.3 Multiple Object Models

An object model may be broken apart into multiple diagrams. Arcs cannot cross diagram boundaries, but that effect is achieved by adding additional copies of the necessary class and relationship shapes.

The meaning of such a split diagram is the same as that of the original diagram.

C-2.4 Name Disambiguation

When a class has several attributes with the same name (because it has several parent classes with that name), an attribute name may be qualified with its *owning* class name using the notations **Attribute@Class** or **Class.Attribute**.

C-3 INTERFACE MODEL

This section describes the interface model, which is composed of a part of the object model (the *system object model*), a description of the behavior exhibited by that part (the *operation model*), and a description of the permitted sequences of system operations (the *life cycle*).

C-3.1 System Object Model

The system object model is a well-formed part of the object model. By *well-formed*, we mean that classes *outside* the system object model do not participate in relationships *inside* the system object model.

The *system boundary* separates the system object model from the rest of the object model.

The *system environment* consists of those system operations that may be performed on the system, and those operations that the system may perform on the outside world (mediated by messages placed into queues; see the operation model for more information).

The system object model is the basis on which the rest of the development is done.

C-3.2 Operation Model

The operation model is a precondition/postcondition style specification, as seen in Z or VDM.

Operation Model Syntax.

An operation model consists of a collection of *system operations*. Each system operation is described by a *schema* (or several *schemata*), which has the syntax

> *Schema* ::=
> > "**Operation**" ":" ["**reject**"] $Name_{schema}$ ["**.**" $Name_{tag}$]
> > ["**Description**" ":" *Text*]
> > ["**Reads**" ":" *Items*]
> > ["**Changes**":" *Items*]
> > ["**Sends**" ":" *Events*]
> > *PrePost**
>
> *PrePost* ::=
> > ["**Assumes**" ":" *Condition*]
> > "**Result**" ":" *Condition*

The $Name_{schema}$ (the *primary name*) is the name of the system operation being described. Where more than one schema is used, the different schemata are distinguished by providing the $Name_{tag}$ (the *secondary name*). A schema whose **Operation** part contains the keyword **reject** is a *rejection schema*; see section C-3.3. The **Description** is arbitrary text giving an informal summary of the meaning of the schema. (It is meant to be suggestive, not definitive; that job is for the **Result** clause.)

The **Reads** and **Changes** clauses are lists of objects and attributes. Each Item refers to something that can be read (or changed). If a clause is omitted, it is taken to refer to *no* items. The **Sends** clause records what events are sent to external agents.

> *Items* ::=
>> *Item*** ","
>
> *Item* ::=
>> *LQuote Text RQuote*
>> | ["**supplied**"] (*Variable* | *Object* | *Attribute* | *RelationName*)
>> | *TypedName* "**with**" *Condition*
>> | "**new**" *TypedName*
>
> *Variable* ::=
>> *Name* "**:**" *Type*
>
> *Object* ::=
>> *TypedName*
>
> *Attribute* ::=
>> *Object* "**.**" *Attribute*

Fusion allows an **Item** to be specified in an arbitrary user-defined way by enclosing the text in quotes. Otherwise an **Item** can be

- A **Variable**, naming a nonobject variable of the given type.
- An **Object**, naming an object and its class, possibly using implicit typing (section C-1.2).
- An **Attribute**, naming part of an object; when appearing in a **Changes** clause, it means that the other attributes of that object are not changed (unless they also appear in the **Changes** clause).
- A **RelationName**, naming a relationship from the object model.
- A **with**-description, identifying the object which satisfies a given condition.
- A **new** object, meaning that a new object is created by execution of the system operation. This **Item** can only appear in a **Changes** clause.

If a **Variable**, **Object**, **Attribute**, or **RelationName** is marked as **supplied**, then it is a parameter of the system operation; otherwise it is part of the system state.

The **Events** of a **Sends** clause show which events are sent to which external agents. Each item is the name of the agent with a set of the event names that it may be sent. The event names are also given, with their types, in the data dictionary.

> *Events* ::=
>> *Event*** ","
>
> *Event* ::=
>> *Agent* "**{**" *EventName*++ "," "**}**"

The **Assumes** and **Result** clauses are conditions—predicates in some suitable language. If the **Assumes** clause is omitted, it is taken to be **true**. The condition can mention only variables in the reads and changes clauses, and constants (including functions and relationships) from the data dictionary.

When a schema has repeated **PrePost**s, it is shorthand for several schemata, one for each **PrePost**. The schemata have the same header (the parts from **Operation** to **Sends**) as the shorthand schema, and they each have a different one of the **PrePost**s.

Constraints.

All schemata with the same primary name must have the same set of **supplied** items; that is, they must have the same names, and the types of those names must be the same. For these purposes, **Attribute** items are treated as their containing object.

(The other **Item**s can be different; thus schemata with the same primary name but different secondary names can affect different parts of the system state, or create objects of different classes, etc.)

Operation Model Semantics.

The operation model describes the effect of *system operations* on the *system state*. System operations are invoked by *events* sent to the system by external *agents*. An operation can send events back to agents, and alter the system state.

The system state is structured by the object model: it consists of all the objects that have been created since the system started, and all of the relationships that appear on the object model. Some objects are referred to by name, and some can only be referred to through the relationships they are involved in. When system operations are invoked, objects, etc., can be supplied by the environment or be named in the state.

A system operation is invoked when an event is accepted (see section C-3.3). The state space of the operation consists of

- Those objects named as part of the system state. These objects are the same on each invocation.
- Those objects supplied to it when it is invoked. These objects can be different (have different identities) on each invocation.
- Objects accessible via relationships. These can also be different on each invocation.

Objects become part of the named system state by being named in **Reads** and **Changes** clauses, and not marked as **supplied**.

Meaning of Schemata.

All schemata with the same primary name contribute to the definition of a single system operation, defined by preconditions/postconditions. The meaning of such a collection of schemata for a particular invocation of a system operation is as follows.

The **supplied** items in the **Reads** and **Changes** clauses are associated with the objects supplied by the system operation. Schemata with preconditions that are **false** with this binding of objects to **Item**s are discarded.

If no schemata remain, then the state of the system becomes *completely unspecified*; Fusion places no constraints on the effect of the operation. Otherwise, the state of the system after the operation has completed is unchanged, except for objects bound by **Changes** clauses. Their values are given by the conjunction of all the **Result** clauses of the remaining schemata.

> It may seem perverse to let the state become completely unspecified when a precondition is violated. Could not the chaos be confined only to the items in the changes clause? However, consider an analogous situation in a programming language: an array-bound violation when storing a value. This can affect *any* part of the state—including (on unprotected systems) operating system code. It is unwise to give any guarantee of safety whatsoever.

When a **Changes** clause has a **new** Item, then the state change of the schema includes a "new" object coming into existence. The TypedName gives the name used to refer to the object and its type. The **Result** clause must define the state of this new object.

> A formal interpretation can be made by associating with each class a set of objects that have been "created." Then the **new** means that this set has had another object added to it, and that the object so created can be referred to by that name in the **Result** clause.

A **Result** clause may need to refer to both the old and new values of variables. Unmarked names refer to the *new* values. Names are marked to refer to old values; a trailing apostrophe, a prefix **old**, or (in natural language text) the word Initial (and Final for the new values).

The message sending of the **Sends** clause appears in the **Result** clause as natural language text or by saying that the message is added to some queue of messages to the agent.

C-3.3 Life-Cycle Model

The system operations give the behavior of the system "in the small" (i.e., at the level of single operations). It is possible to give higher-level descriptions in terms of *sequences* of operations, using regular expressions.

Fusion identifies input events with the operations they cause; the restriction is historical rather than fundamental. A generalization would allow a single event to invoke different system operations at different points in the life cycle.

Life-Cycle Syntax.

The concrete syntax of lifecycles is described below. (The abstract syntax has ".", "|", and "||" as binary infix and "*", "+" as unary postfix. The translations are obvious, given that the binary operators are both associative.)

Life Cycle ::=

$\qquad$ "**lifecycle**" [*Name* "**:**"] *Regular*
$\qquad$ (*LocalName* "**=**" *Regular*)*

Regular ::=

$\qquad$ *RSerial*$^{++}$ "**||**"

RSerial ::=

$\qquad$ *RSeq*$^{++}$ "**|**"

RSeq ::=

$\qquad$ *RItem*** "**.**"

RItem ::=

$\qquad$ *Primitive* ["*****" | "**+**"]

Primitive ::=

$\qquad$ *OperationName*
$\qquad$ | "**#**" *MessageName*
$\qquad$ | *LocalName*
$\qquad$ | "**(**" *Regular* "**)**"
$\qquad$ | "**[**" *Regular* "**]**"

Regular may be written more concisely as:

Regular ::=

$\qquad$ (((*Primitive* ["*****" | "**+**"]) $^{++}$ "**.**") $^{++}$ "**|**") $^{++}$ "**||**"

LocalName definitions cannot be recursive; they are simply abbreviations.

Constraints.

OperationNames must be the names of operations, and MessageNames must be the names of output events. MessageNames can only appear in regular expressions immediately following an OperationName, and those regular expressions must be formed without using further OperationNames (directly or indirectly). Thus, if PressButton and ReleaseButton are operations, and Bleep and IssueMoney are events,

$\qquad$ PressButton. (#Bleep | ReleaseButton)

is illegal, but

$\qquad$ PressButton. (#Bleep | #IssueMoney)

is legal. (The constraint enforces the notion that output events are *generated* by system operations, and that a system operation cannot start until the previous one has completed.)

Life-Cycle Semantics.

The **Name**s of **RItem**s are system operation names or locally declared abbreviations. The behavior of the system is described by the set of sequences of **OperationNames** and **MessageNames** generated by the regular expression of the life cycle.

MessageNames following an **OperatioName** are the outputs of that system operation. The corresponding schemata must mention those **MessageNames** in their **Sends** and **Result** clauses.

A regular expression denotes a set of sequences. For life cycles, the elements of the sequence are the input and output events. The input events correspond to system operations. The regular expression notation is mostly conventional.

- The empty expression denotes the set containing only the empty sequence.
- A name (**OperationName** or **MessageName**) denotes the set with one element, that being the one-element sequence containing that name.
- "$R_1|R_2$" means either of R_1 and R_2; it denotes the union of the meanings of R_1 and R_2.
- "$R_1.R_2$" is left-to-right sequencing; it denotes the set whose elements are built by appending elements of (the meaning of) R_2 to elements of (the meaning of) R_1.
- "R^*" means zero or more repetitions of R; it denotes the set whose elements are the empty sequence, the meanings of $R.R$, the meanings of $R.R.R$, and so on.
- "$R+$" means one or more repetitions of R; it denotes the same set as $R.R^*$.
- "$[E]$" means that E is optional; it denotes the same set as "$(|\ E)$".
- $R_1\ ||\ R_2$ means the *interleaving* of R_1 and R_2; it denotes that set obtained by interleaving all the sequences denoted by R_1 with all of those of R_2.

Definition of Interleaving.

Once interleaving is defined on (pairs of) sequences, raising it to operate on sets (of sequences) is simple. The definition on sequences may be written

$$X\ ||\ \varepsilon = \{X\}$$
$$\varepsilon\ ||\ X = \{X\}$$
$$a : A\ ||\ b : B = a : (A\ ||\ b : B) \cup b : (a : A\ ||\ B)$$

where "$:$" is sequence prefix and "ε" is the empty sequence. Because Fusion output events are bound to the system operations that generate them, in the definition of interleaving we regard the elements of the sequence as consisting of system operation names *and all the output events immediately following them.*

Accepting and Rejecting Events.

Input events are generated by the system environment. An environment may generate sequences of events that are not in the set defined by the regular expression. If so, some events must be *rejected*, until the sequence is in the defining set.

To allow sequential (as opposed to predictive) implementation, events are accepted so long as they form an initial subsequence of some permitted element of the defining set. Any event that cannot extend such a subsequence is rejected. This allows the system to be implemented as a state machine, with the events driving the transitions between states. If the system operation of a rejected event has a *rejection schema*, then this defines the effect of the event. Otherwise a rejected event leaves the system state unchanged.

It does not matter if the precondition of the associated system operation is **false**; see Figure C.4. However, if the precondition of the rejection schema is **false**, the system state becomes unspecified, as usual.

		Event Accepted	Event Rejected
Normal	**true**	Operation executed	Not applicable
Precondition	**false**	Chaos reigns	Not applicable
Rejection	**true**	Not applicable	Rejection executed
Precondition	**false**	Not applicable	Chaos reigns

Figure C.4   Preconditions and Life Cycles

Interference of Expressions.

Two interleaved regular expressions with (input) events in common can *interfere* with each other by "stealing" each others events. Consider the simple life cycle (a.b||a).c, which denotes the set of sequences

$$aba'c, \ aa'bc, \ a'abc$$

where the **a** from the second operand of "||" has been dashed to show where it comes from. (Thus the second and third sequences are actually identical, and the set has just two elements.)

Interference makes implementation in terms of state machines more complicated. Without interference, state machines corresponding to the operands of the interleaving can be constructed and run independently. With interference, this is not possible. In our example, an incoming event **a** might be consumed by the state machine for **a.b** or the one for **a**. If the former, a following event **c** would be incorrectly rejected; if the latter, an incoming **b** would be incorrectly rejected. The two machines must communicate.

For this reason, we recommend that interleaved regular expressions do not share events.

C-4 DATA DICTIONARY

The data dictionary serves to collect information not available on the various diagrams of Fusion, and as a place to record information and constraints that cannot be placed on those diagrams.

Note that this syntax is suggested, and not mandatory; if the context in which Fusion is being used already has a data dictionary notation of adequate power, use that. In particular, collections of items of the same kind can be collected together into tables; see the entries for operations and agents for an example.

> *DataDictionary* ::=
> > *DataEntry**

> *DataEntry* ::=
> > *DataItem* ["**ref**" *DocumentReference*] ["**description**" *Text*]

Each **DataEntry** has a **ref** part, which refers to some reference material for the entry (e.g., part of the requirements document). It also has a **description**, which has informal (i.e., not dictated by Fusion) text that explains or defines the entry.

> *DataItem* ::=
> > *Attribution*
> > | *Predicate*
> > | *Function*
> > | *Method*
> > | *Assertion*
> > | *Class*
> > | *Relationship*
> > | *EventDef*
> > | *Operation*
> > | *AgentAndEvents*
> > | *TypeDef*

Each of these entry types is described subsequently. All entries can also be presented as *tables*, in which case they follow the general format shown below:

Name	Kind	Description
Name of entry	Keyword	Descriptive text

The entry name may include the owning class or relationship name, in the form **Class.Item**, for attributes and methods. Additional columns are added for entry-specific material, in which case they are labeled with the name of the appropriate syntactic category, for example, **Type**, **ArgList**.

C-4.1 Object Model Entries

The data dictionary records the *types* of the attributes of relationships and classes. It can also record the classes and relationships themselves.

> *Attribution* ::=
> > "**attribute**" *Name*$_1$ "." *Name*$_2$ ": " *Type*

This says that the attribute *Name*$_2$ of the class (or relationship) *Name*$_1$ has the given **Type**.

$$Class ::=$$
$$\text{``\textbf{class}''} \ ClassName$$

Notes the existence of the named class. Other information about the class appears on the diagrams, or as assertions (see section C-4.4).

$$Relationship ::=$$
$$\text{``\textbf{relationship}''} \ RelationshipName$$

Notes the existence of the named relationship. Other information about the relationship appears on the diagrams or as assertions (see section C-4.4).

C-4.2 Operation Model Entries

The data dictionary can record functions and predicates used in the operation model. We cannot prescribe a particular language for expressing conditions and expressions, but we recommend this for the definitions themselves.

$$Predicate ::=$$
$$\text{``\textbf{predicate}''} \ Name \ ArgList \ \text{``\textbf{is}''} \ Condition$$

$$Function ::=$$
$$\text{``\textbf{function}''} \ Name \ ArgList \ [\text{``:''} \ Type] \ \text{``=''} \ Expression$$

The **Name** of a **function** or **predicate** can also be an operator. The definitions of **Condition** and **Expression** are not given in this appendix (but see section C-4.8). It is permitted for a function to be defined several times, for example, on subtypes, or distinct argument types, subject only to consistency in its results: Two applicable definitions must not give different answers on the same arguments.

The **ArgList** syntax is shared by predicates, functions, and also methods in class descriptions (see section C-8):

$$ArgList ::=$$
$$\text{``(''} \ Arg^{**} \ \text{``,''} \ \text{``)''}$$
$$Arg ::=$$
$$Name \ \text{``:''} \ Type$$

A predicate delivers a **Boolean** result, by definition. The result **Type** of a function is given explicitly, unless it is obvious from the **Expression**.

C-4.3 Method Entries

The data dictionary should be used to record the headers, and perhaps the bodies, of methods.

$$Method ::=$$
$$\text{``\textbf{method}''} \ ClassName \ \text{``.''} \ Name \ ArgList \ MethodBody$$

$$MethodBody ::=$$
$$\text{``\textbf{is}''} \ Commands$$
$$| \quad [\text{``:''} \ Type] \ \text{``=''} \ Expression$$

Methods are associated with classes. They may deliver a result, given by an **Expression**, or simply have an effect on the state, given by **Commands**. The syntax of **Commands** is not given in this appendix. The **Type** of a result need not be given if it is obvious from the **Expression**.

C-4.4 Assertion Entries

The data dictionary can be used to record properties which apply *between* items, as well as *within* them. This is done by stating assertions.

> *Assertion* ::=
>> "**assert**" [*Name* ":"] *Condition*

C-4.5 Type Entries

The data dictionary records the meaning of type identifiers.

> *TypeDef* ::=
>> "**type**" *Name* ["**=**" *Type*]
>
> *Type* ::=
>> ["**col**"] *ClassName*
>> | *TypeExpression*
>
> *TypeExpression* ::=
>> *TypeName* ["**(**" *TypeExpression*** "**,**" "**)**"]
>> | *Enumeration*
>> | *OtherTypeExpression*
>
> *Enumeration* ::=
>> *Name*** "**|**"

A **TypeDef** defines that a **Name** denotes a type. If the **Type** is omitted, then the structure of that type is unspecified. Otherwise, the **Type** is either a class-based type (denoting either the set of members of the class, or a collection of objects of that type), or a nonclass type. Nonclass types are defined by parameterized **TypeName**s, or as enumerations, or as other types not specified by Fusion.

An enumeration introduces a new type and a named set of distinct constants of that type.

C-4.6 Event Entries

The data dictionary records the input events that the environment sends to the system, and the output events by which the system affects the environment.

> *EventDef* ::=
>> "**event**" ("**in**" | "**out**") *Name* [*EventArgs*]
>
> *EventArgs* ::=
>> "**(**" ([*Name* ":"] *Type*)** "**,**" "**)**"

Events **Name** carries information of the given **Type**. If **EventArgs** is omitted, or has no **Type** components, then the event has no internal structure. The **Type** can be named for convenient reference.

Each output event corresponds to a queue of sent messages; the only operation available on queues is to append another message. (Events and queues need not have a physical realization; they exist to formalize the idea that an operation can do something in a nonatomic way.) Input events immediately invoke system operations, if the life cycle permits.

C-4.7 Operation and Agent Entries

The schemata of operations are part of the data dictionary. An additional column, **Arguments**, is available in the tabular form, to show the items that are supplied by the environment when the operation is invoked.

Agents are also recorded in the data dictionary with the events that they can send or receive.

> *Agent* ::=
>> "**agent**" *Name* ["**sends**" *Events*] ["**receives**" *Events*]

The syntax of **Events** is given in section C-3.2.

C-4.8 Expressions

Fusion does not restrict the kinds of expression used in the data dictionary or in schemata. However, there are certain operations that should be available, and they are discussed here.

Equality and Identity.

The infix operator "==" is used to compare the *identity* of two references to objects: Do the references refer to the same object or not? The infix operator "=" is used to compare the *contents* of two objects, by comparing their attributes for equality.

If the equality of objects depends not only on their attributes, but on relationships in which they are involved, a definition for the equality operator should be supplied.

Operations on Relationships.

In Fusion, relationships change over time: New tuples are added, and old tuples removed. The infix operators **with** and **without** are used for the following:

> *Expression* ::=
>> *Relation* ("**with**" | "**without**") *Tuple*
>
> *Tuple* ::=
>> "**(**" (*Name* "**:**" *Expression*)** "**,**" "**)**"

The **Tuple** is a list of expressions labeled with the role-**Name** to which they belong. **Relation** is a relationship-valued expression. The name and number of the roles should be the same as that of the **Relation**. **with** adds the tuple to the relationship, **without** removes it.

To test whether an object participates in a relationship, use the infix form **has-Role**, where **Role** is the name of the role in the relationship being tested.

C-5 OBJECT INTERACTION GRAPHS

This section describes the syntax and semantics of object interaction graphs. These are a way of describing how the functionality of a system operation is implemented by collections of interacting objects. Each graph corresponds to a "typical" execution of a system operation.

C-5.1 Object Interaction Graph Syntax

An object interaction graph is a collection of *named boxes* linked by *labeled arrows*. Exactly one box—the *controller*—has an arrow coming into it that does not arrive from some other box; this arrow is labeled with the name of the *system operation* or *method* that the graph implements. The other boxes are called the *collaborators*. Every other arrow goes from one box to another.

The graph is connected; all boxes can be reached by traversing arrows tail to head, starting from the controller.

Each graph also has associated descriptive text, such as natural language narrative, pseudocode, or formal specification, to give meaning to the system operation and any associated methods. An object interaction graph example is shown in Figure C.5.

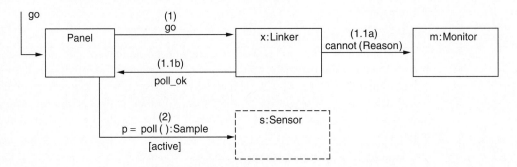

Figure C.5   Object Interaction Graph Example

Object Boxes.

An object box is either a rectangle with a solid outline (a *plain* box), or a rectangle with a dashed outline (a *collection* box). The object box is labeled with the object name and the name of its class. If the object is created during the execution of the graph, the label will also contain the keyword "**new**."

$$ObjectLabel ::=$$
$$[\text{"}\mathbf{new}\text{"}] \; TypedName$$

In Figure C.5, **Panel**, **x**, **m**, and **s** are object boxes. Only **s** is a collection. **Panel** is the controller; the other objects are collaborators.

Arrow Labels.

The arrow labels have three parts: the *sequencer*, the *method call*, and the *predicate*. The method call must always be present. The parts appear stacked in the order given.

ArrowLabel ::=
        [*Sequencer*] *Invocation* [*Predicate*]

Sequencer ::=
        "**(**" [*DottedNumber*] [*Decoration*] [*Multiplicity*] "**)**"

DottedNumber ::=
        Number^{++} "**.**"

Decoration ::=
        (*Prime* | *Letter*)*

Multiplicity ::=
        "*****"

Invocation ::=
        [*ResultName* "**=**"] *Name* [*ActualArgList*] ["**:**" *Type*]

ActualArgList ::=
        "**(**" *ActualArgs* "**)**"

ActualArgs ::=
        *ActualArg*** "**,**"

ActualArg ::=
        TypedName
        | *Type*

Predicate ::=
        "**[**" *SelectCondition* ["**;**" *StopCondition*] "**]**"

Figure C.5 shows several method arrows. There are two decorated sequencers, **(1.1a)** and **(1.1b)**. Only the **poll** arrow to **s** can have a predicate, here **active**. The message **cannot** has a single anonymous argument of type **Reason**.

Constraints.

- Only arrows leading to collection boxes can have predicates.
- If several boxes bear the same object name, they must bear the same class name.
- Method calls with the same **ResultName** must all appear on arrows with the same sequencer.
- Sequencers with **DottedNumber**s of the form **N.M** can only appear on arrows from object boxes entered with a sequencer **N**.

C-5.2 Object Interaction Graph Semantics

An object interaction graph represents a set of sequences of method calls. An execution of its system operation will result in one of those sequences being executed. A method call is either atomic, if it invokes no other methods, or compound, when it represents a set of sequences of method calls.

The state space of an object interaction graph is the objects that appear on it, plus the state space of any methods which that graph invokes. New objects may come into existence during the execution of a system operation described by an object interaction graph.

Solid boxes represent *objects*. Dashed boxes represent *collections* of objects. Such a collection is not *all* objects of that class, or some fixed subset, but is some relevant collection of objects of that class; the elements of the collection can change over time. The arrows represent method calls. The initial arrow represents the invocation of a system operation or method, and other arrows represent internal method invocations. Each collaborator represents an object known, in some way, to the controller. *How* the collaborators come to be known by the controller is specified by the visibility graphs (see section C-6).

Sequencing of Calls.

Each method call completes before control is returned to the caller. If the invoked object also makes method calls, then they must all complete before the invocation completes.

An arrow with a **Multiplicity** stands for an indefinite number of calls with the same sequencer. Arrows to collections automatically have **Multiplicity**. Calls labeled by sequencers with the same **DottedNumber** occur in an unspecified order, bearing in mind the completion requirement. Calls with *no* sequencer take place at any point, again subject to the completion requirement.

When calls with **Multiplicity** have the same sequencer, they may be interleaved.

Sequencers are ordered by the lexicographic order of their **DottedNumber**s. Let α be some (possibly complete) prefix of a **DottedNumber**, and β be some suffix. A method call with sequencer α starts before all calls with sequencers $\alpha.\beta$, and finishes after they have all finished. Two sequencers α_1 and α_2, neither of which is a prefix of the other, are executed in lexicographic order.

The existence of an arrow says that the given method call *may* happen, not that it *must* happen. Often arrows bearing the same **DottedNumber** will be mutually exclusive, because of their **Decoration**s, which supply additional constraints on invocations. Of two invocations with sequencers **NX** and **NY**, where **X** and **Y** are decorations with **X≠Y**, at most one will happen (i.e., the decorations allow grouping of invocations into exclusive sets).

In Figure C.5, the initial **go** message to **Panel** may first send a **go** message to the **Linker**, **x**. In turn this will *either* send a **cannot** message to **m** *or* a **poll_ok** message back to **Panel**. **x** cannot send both messages, as they have distinct decorations but the same **DottedNumber**.

When the **go** message to **x** completes, a **poll** message is sent to **s**. (This is described later.) When that completes, the initial **go** can complete.

If, instead, the **poll** sequencer had been **1.2b**, that would have shown that the polling was driven directly in response to the **poll_ok** message.

Meaning of Methods.

Each method invocation may alter object attributes and return a result. The meaning of the method should be given by téxt accompanying the graph. In particular, it is possible to give the meaning of a method by an operation model, in the same way as a system operation is described; this is an example of *recursive decomposition*.

The types of the arguments to a method are given by the parameters of the **Invocation**. If the method delivers a result, its type should be given with the trailing **:Type** notation.

The existence on some object interaction graph of a method arrow for some method **Do(Args)**, with a recipient object of class **C**, means that *all* objects of **C** can respond to **Do**, and that their class description will include the method **Do**.

In Figure C.5, **cannot** carries a **Reason** argument for **m**, and **poll** returns a **Sample** result (actually, *several* such results) from **s**.

The method **create** is special; it should be invoked on any **new** object in an object interaction graph. Usually the invoker is the creator of the object. The invocation parameters are the initialization information needed by the object; until **create** has been applied to an object, it is in an undefined state, and no other methods should be applied to it. **create** should be applied only to **new** objects.

Figure C.6 shows how the **Sensor**s referred to on figure C.5 obtain their **Sample** results: They are freshly **create**d with an **Integer** value, the **Sensor** reading.

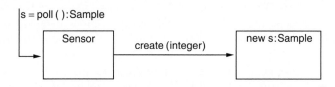

Figure C.6   Object Interaction Graph with **new**

Methods on Collections.

When a method is invoked on a collection, it is invoked on all the objects in that collection that satisfy the **SelectCondition** of the **Predicate**. The **SelectCondition** can refer only to information available in the invoking object before the invocation occurred. The methods are invoked in an unspecified order. Any invocation that results in the **StopCondition** becoming **true** will prevent further invocations. The **StopCondition** may refer to results returned by other invocations to objects in the collection.

An omitted **StopCondition** defaults to **false**. An omitted **Predicate** defaults to [**true**, **false**], so that all elements suffer the invocation. The name **client** refers to the object invoking the method, and the name **server** to the object suffering the invocation.

In Figure C.5, the **poll** message to the collection **s** will be sent to all of the elements of **s** that satisfy the predicate **active**. Each of these invocations delivers a **Sample** to the **Panel**.

Methods from Collections.

When a method is invoked by a collection, it means that some element of that collection may invoke that method. It does *not* mean that the collection itself invokes the method, nor does it mean that *all* of the selected elements invoke the method. Arguments to a method are evaluated per object.

Names.

When several boxes of the same name appear in a single object interaction graph, they denote the same object. (This may arise in preventing a confusion of arrows, for example, because the same object has a method invoked on it several times in the diagram.)

The names of arguments of calls refer to particular objects or values. The use of the same name means the same value or object. In particular, a **ResultName** may be used as an argument in a method call with a later sequencer.

Complex, Multiple, and Recursive Diagrams.

A graph is *simple* if no arrows come from collaborators; it is *complex* otherwise. Complex diagrams are constructed from simple ones, as described subsequently.

The behavior of a method may be further detailed by recursive decomposition, where a new object interaction graph is constructed for the method call (in the same way as for system operations).

The meaning of several diagrams taken together is the *consistent union* of the meanings of the diagrams; that is, the classes depicted have all the methods shown, and the meanings given to them by the various diagrams must be the same. The names of the objects on the diagrams are not important (at this stage).

It is possible to collapse diagrams together, by adding the method calls for implementing some method **M** on some recipient class **C** to the diagrams in which **M** and **C** appear. (Sequencers on the included diagram must be prefixed with the sequencer from the invoking diagram.) This is most useful when **M** appears on only one other diagram. Collapsing diagrams in this fashion identifies objects with the same name.

C-5.3 Relationship to System Operations

There must be an object interaction graph for each set of schemata with the same primary name.

The developer should be able to show that the behavior described by the graph is consistent with the behavior described by the corresponding schema, by considering the effects of the permitted sequences of method calls and showing that at least one of them implements the system operation. (Because the diagram is not a complete description, it can allow additional behavior. The annotations on the diagram must exclude all sequences that do not correctly implement the system operation.)

C-6 VISIBILITY GRAPHS

Visibility graphs show how objects obtain access to other objects. Objects have a *lifetime*; they come into existence when they are **new**ed, and they can cease to exist when no references to them remain. (Because there are no references to them, they cannot cause or suffer any method calls, so they can have no effect on the rest of the system.)

Server objects can be **bound** to client objects. The bound server forms part of the client and dies when it dies. No references to the server should remain in the system.

References hold over different periods. Fusion divides them into two classes: those that hold only during the invocation of a method and those that persist between methods.

C-6.1 Visibility Graph Syntax

A visibility graph is a diagram whose components are *client boxes*, *server boxes*, and *visibility arrows*. Figure C.7 shows three visibility graphs derived from the object interaction graphs of Figures C.5 and C.6.

Client Boxes.

A client box is a rectangle containing the name of a class. In the example, Panel, Sensor, and Linker are client boxes.

Servers.

A server box is a rectangle containing a server label, which names the instance in the box, the class of the instance, whether the server is created by the client, and whether the reference to the server is constant once initialized or not.

ServerLabel ::=
["**new**"] *Mutability TypedName*

The rectangle can be independently *single* or *double*, and have a *solid outline* or a *dashed outline*. Thus there are four kinds of server box.

A server may appear inside the client which references it, in which case it is said to be *bound*. Otherwise, it is *unbound*.

In Figure C.7, sensors, p, s, m, and panel are all client boxes. The only bound client is 1.

Arrows.

A visibility arrow is an arrow leading from a class box to a server box. The arrow may be a *permanent arrow*, which has a solid line, or a *dynamic arrow*, which has a dashed line.

When the server of an arrow is nested inside a client, the tail of the arrow need not be attached to the client box, as in the Panels reference to 1 in Figure C.7. The references to s and p are dynamic; all the others are permanent.

Constraints.

• Servers can be contained only in clients that refer to them.
• Dynamic references cannot refer to bound clients.

Simple and Compound Diagrams.

A simple visibility graph has exactly one client box, and all server boxes are at the end of at least one arrow from the client box.

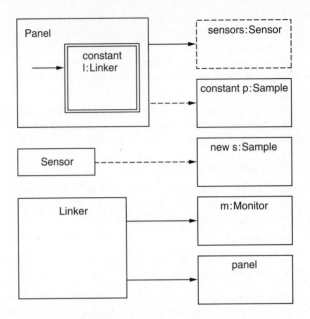

Figure C.7   Visibility Graph Example

A compound visibility graph is just several simple visibility graphs on the same diagram. Figure C.7 is a compound visibility graph.

C-6.2 Visibility Graph Semantics

An arrow means that the client at its tail has access to instances of the server at its head via a reference. The reference has the name of the server box.

If **new** is present in the ServerLabel, it means that (some method of) the client class creates instances of the server class.

Dynamic Versus Permanent References.

If the arrow is *dynamic*, then it means that client objects refer to server objects for the duration of a single method invocation (or less). Thus the reference is through a parameter, local variable, or intermediate computation.

If the arrow is *permanent*, then the access persists between method calls: Thus it is through a class feature. (Other possible cases, such as static variables, global variable, etc., can be modelled by classes with exactly one instance.)

In Figure C.7, the dynamic reference from Sensor to **new** Sample s appears because the poll method of Sensor creates a Sample. The dynamic reference p from Panel derives from the poll sent to the *collection* of Sensors.

Constant Versus Variable Server.

When the Mutability on a server is **constant**, the client always refers to the same server. (An implementations object-valued slot can be nonassignable.) The reference is fixed when the client is created. If the Mutability is **variable**, then the associated variable may be freely updated. If the Mutability is not given, it defaults to **variable**.

Note that the **Mutability** pertains to the *reference*, not to the server *object*. In Figure C.7, the **Panel** refers to the **Sample** object **p**. The reference is constant, so once established it does not change; it is also dynamic, so it persists only during a single method call.

Bound Versus Unbound Servers.

Servers inside the client box are *bound* to the client; they are regarded as part of it. (They may be aggregated inside it on the object model, for example.) Servers outside a client box are independent of the client and are said to be *unbound*.

If a client object is destroyed, then its bound servers may also be destroyed. There should be no other references to them when the client dies. If a bound reference is **variable**, then when the reference changes from one server to another the old server can also be destroyed.

In Figure C.7, the **bound** server l is part of the **Panel**. The reference is **constant**, so a **Panel** always refers to a single **Linker** via l. (**Linker** might well have been a component of a **Panel** aggregate on the object model.)

Collection Versus Singleton Servers.

If the server outline is dashed, it represents a *collection* of objects; if solid, *one* object. If a reference to a collection is **variable**, this means that the client can refer to *different collections* over time. If the reference is **constant**, the client refers to a *single* collection, but the collection may still contain different *elements* at different times.

Exclusive Versus Shared Servers.

If the server outline is single (shared), any number of other clients may refer to the server; if double (exclusive), this is the only reference to that server.

Because references can be **variable**, an exclusive reference can change over time, that is, it can refer to different servers at different times. The exclusivity of the reference does not need to hold during a method invocation. (Otherwise there would be no way to change an exclusive reference and retain a reference to the old object.)

In Figure C.7, the only exclusive reference is from **Panel** to l. Because the reference is also **constant**, we know that the *only* way to refer to the l object is through the **Panel**—there is no other way for the reference to escape.

C-6.3 Multiple Visibility Graphs

The meaning of multiple graphs is the consistent union of the meaning of the separate graphs.

There is no relationship implied by the use of the same name on different visibility graphs. For example, in Figure C.7, we cannot infer the the **Panel** referred to by a **Linker** is the same as the one in which it might be embedded. Statements like these can be made in the data dictionary.

C-7 INHERITANCE GRAPHS

Inheritance graphs reflect the inheritance (design subtype) relationships between classes.

C-7.1 Inheritance Graph Syntax

The syntax of an inheritance graph is that of an object model without relationships and aggregations.

C-7.2 Inheritance Graph Semantics

The meaning of an inheritance graph is that of subsetting; any element of a class at the bottom end of a subtype is a member of the class at the top of that same subtype arc, and has at least the attributes and methods of that supertype.

C-7.3 Multiple Inheritance Graphs

The meaning of several inheritance graphs taken together is that all the subtype relationships of the inheritance graphs apply at once.

C-8 CLASS DESCRIPTIONS

Class descriptions are generated by considering the object model, object interaction graphs, and visibility graphs; they collect in one place the properties of a *class* of objects from information about *instances* of those objects.

C-8.1 Class Description Syntax

A class description has the form:

$CDesc$ ::=
　　　　"**class**" *Name Inherit* Property** "**endclass**"

$Inherit$ ::=
　　　　"**isa**" *Names*

$Names$ ::=
　　　　Name^{++} ","

$Property$ ::=
　　　　Attribute
　　| 　*Method*

$Attribute$ ::=
　　　　["**attribute**"] *Mutability Name* ":" *Sharing Binding Type*

$Method$ ::=
　　　　["**method**"] *Name ArgList* [":" *Type*]

$Sharing$ ::=
　　　　["**shared**" | "**exclusive**"]

$Binding$ ::=
　　　　["**bound**" | "**unbound**"]

See section C-4.5 for a description of Type and section C-6.1 for the definition of Mutability.

C-8.2 Constraints

Property names cannot be duplicated; that is, a class description cannot have two attributes or methods with the same name, nor can a method and an attribute have the same name.

No two Args in the same parameter list can have the same name.

C-8.3 Class Description Semantics

The meaning of a CDesc is that the Name refers to a set of values which share certain properties. The properties are described by the body of the CDesc.

Inheritance.

The set denoted by a class description is a subset of all of the sets referred to in **isa** clauses.

This may be viewed either as *specialization* (where the **isa** classes "already" exist, and the current class is a piece of them) or as *generalization* (where the class already exists, and contributes elements to the definition of its **isa** classes).

Properties.

Each Property refers to a function that may be applied to a value from the set named by the class description; a property is either an *attribute* (usually implemented as a slot in a data structure) or a *method* (usually implemented as a procedure shared by all instances of the class).

The Attribute properties are projectors mapping class values into the given Types. The Sharing dictates whether the projected values may be obtained from any other class object or this one only.

Method properties refer to functions that need not be projections and may alter the contents of objects. Such functions are constrained to operate on arguments of appropriate types, and, if they deliver a result, deliver one of the indicated :Type.

Attribute Qualifiers.

If an attribute is marked **constant**, it cannot be assigned once its enclosing object has been initialized (by create). Otherwise it may be reassigned at any time. Any attribute may be marked **constant**. This is the same meaning as for Mutability on visibility graphs.

If an attribute is marked **exclusive**, its Type should be a class or collection. The attribute provides the only reference to the object it refers to. Otherwise there may be any number of additional references to that object. This is the same meaning as for exclusive versus shared objects on visibility graphs.

If an attribute is marked **bound**, its Type should be a class or collection. If the object containing the attribute becomes inaccessible, then the object referred to by that attribute also becomes inaccessible; it is regarded as part of the referring object. There should be no other references to the part when the whole becomes inaccessible. This is the same meaning as for bound versus unbound objects on visibility graphs.

Lifecycle Translation Algorithm

The process of translating a regular expression to a state machine can be expressed as a recursive algorithm. Each stage in the recursion takes a *start state*, **A**, an *end state*, **Z**, and a regular expression that describes the transitions from **A** to **Z**.

- An RE that is the name of an operation generates a transition to **Z** labeled with the operation name.

- An RE that is the name of another RE (a **Local Name**) generates the transitions of that RE from **A** to **Z**. (Because recursive definitions are not allowed in life cycles, this process must terminate.)

- An RE that is a bracketed expression **(E)** generates the transitions of **E** from **A** to **Z**.

- An RE that is a set of alternatives generates the union of all the transitions of those alternatives from **A** to **Z**.

- An RE that is a sequence $E_1.E_2$ generates transitions from **A** with E_1 to a new end state E_m. E_m has as its transitions those generated from itself, by E_2, to **Z**. (This is the only way new states are introduced.) An extended sequence $E_1 \ldots E_n$ is translated by right (or left; it does not matter) grouping the operations.

- An RE that is empty (i.e., is a sequence of no elements, generates the *empty* transition ε to **Z**. (The empty transition is taken without needing, or consuming, any event.)

- An RE that is a closure E^+ generates E-transitions from **A** to **Z** *and* to **A**.

- An RE that is a closure E^* generates all the transitions of E^+, plus the ε transition to Z.
- An RE that is an interleaving $E_1 || E_2$, generates *activate* transitions to the start states of all the state machines generated from the E_i, and *exit* transitions from the end states of those machines to Z.
- Finally, an RE that is an optionality $[E]$ generates the transitions of E plus an empty transition to Z.

The process starts by considering the entire life cycle regular expression with the standard start state **Initial** and end state **Final**.

Fusion Services

E-1 HEWLETT-PACKARD TRAINING AND CONSULTANCY SERVICES

E-1.1 Hewlett-Packard Customer Education

The HP Customer Registration Center can provide you with price, scheduling, and enrollment information, as well as information about on-site delivery of Fusion training.

To order Hewlett-Packard Customer Education classes in the U.S., call 1-800-HPCLASS (1-800-472-5277).

Outside the U.S. contact your nearest HP office.

United States

Hewlett-Packard Company
2101 Gaither Road
Rockville, MD 20850
(301) 258-2000

Hewlett-Packard Company
5201 Tollview Drive
Rolling Meadows, IL 60008
(708) 342-2000

Hewlett-Packard Company
5805 Sepulveda Blvd.
Van Nuys, CA 91411
(818) 786-5800

Hewlett-Packard Company
2015 South Park Place
Atlanta, GA 30339
(404) 850-2544

Canada

Hewlett-Packard Ltd.
5150 Spectrum Way
Mississauga, Ontario L4W5G1
(416) 206-4725
or (416) 206-3048

Europe/Africa/Middle East

Hewlett-Packard S.A.
150, Route du Nant-d'Avril
CH-1217 Meyrin 2
Geneva, Switzerland
(22) 780 81 11
or (22) 780 41 11

Japan

Yokogawa-Hewlett-Packard-Ltd.
3-29-21, Takaido-Higashi
Suginami-Ku, Tokyo 168
(03) 3335-8079

Latin America

Hewlett-Packard
Latin American Region Headquarters
5200 Blue Lagoon Drive
Miami, FL 33126
(305) 267-4220

Australia/New Zealand

Hewlett-Packard Australia, Ltd.
31-41 Joseph Street, Blackburn
Victoria 3130, Australia
(03) 272 2895

Asia Pacific

Hewlett-Packard Asia Ltd.
22-30 Floor Peregrine Tower
Lippo Centre
89 Queensway, Central
Hong Kong
(852) 848-7777

United Kingdom

Hewlett-Packard Customer Education
Nine Mile Ride
Wokingham
Berkshire RG11 3LL
UK
(0) 344 763136

E-1.2 Hewlett-Packard European Knowledge Systems Centre

Filton Road
Stoke Gifford
Bristol BS12 6QZ
UK
Tel: +44 (0) 272 228002
Fax: +44 (0) 272 311278
Email: dsb@hplb.hpl.hp.com

E-1.3 Hewlett-Packard Departement Ingenierie Informatique

Hewlett-Packard France
Z.A. du Bois Briard
2, avenue du Lac
91040 EVRY Cedex (FRANCE)
Tel: (1) 69 91 81 45
Fax: (1) 69 91 81 28
Email: philippe@hpfracti.france.hp.com

E-1.4 NTU Fusion Video Course

A Fusion video course, available from HP, has been produced by the National Technological University (NTU) in the United States. The course covers all aspects of the Fusion method. For more information contact Kellee Noonan:

Tel: (415) 857-4568
Email: noonan@hpcea.ce.hp.com

E-2 TOOL VENDORS AND CONSULTANCY

E-2.1 ProtoSoft Inc.

Developers of Paradigm Plus, an object-oriented CASE tool supporting Fusion and other popular object-oriented methods. Paradigm Plus is a configurable and customizable Meta-CASE tool.

Headquartered in Houston, ProtoSoft sells direct in the United States and has distributors and/or re-sellers in Europe (The Netherlands, Germany, Italy, The United Kingdom), Canada, Australia, and Japan.

ProtoSoft Inc.
17629 El Camino Real #202
Houston, TX 77058
Tel: (713) 480-3233
Fax: (713) 480-6606
Email: sales@protosoft.com

E-2.2 SoftCASE Consulting

SoftCASE Consulting is an independent consultancy specializing in meta-CASE and the specification and development of tailored CASE solutions. Using the GraphTalk meta-CASE tool from Parallax Software Technologies, SoftCASE Consulting is developing a CASE workbench supporting the Fusion method.

SoftCASE Consulting (Partners)
32 Canford Cliffs Road
Parkstone, Poole
Dorset BH13 7AA
UK
Tel/Fax: +44 (0)202 749643
Email: fusion@softcase.co.uk

E-2.3 ICON Computing, Inc.

ICON Computing specializes in education and consulting services in object-oriented technology. They offer a series of courses covering analysis, design, introductory through advanced implementation, and project management. The analysis and design courses include Fusion and other popular methods.

Headquartered in Austin, Texas, ICON provides services to clients across the United States and Europe.

ICON Computing, Inc.
11203 Oak View Drive
Austin, TX 78759
Tel: (512) 258-8437
Fax: (512) 258-0086
Email: info@iconcomp.com

E-2.4 Software Design & Build

One of the first British software consultancies to commit publicly its support to the Fusion method. Based in Bristol, close to the HP labs, they have a broad range of consultancy services, covering every stage of the development and implementation of information systems. In particular they are active in the object-oriented, human computer interaction, and business process modeling fields. For more information contact Phil Isham or John Cato:

>   Tel: +44 (0)272 308668
>   Email: sdb_bristol@cix.compulink.co.uk

E-2.5 Advanced Methods and Tools

AM&T is the software engineering division of Knowledge Base Services Ltd. AM&T provides a range of services chosen to provide balanced support for all components of the system development life cycle including specific technology training and consultancy for Fusion. For more information contact John Robinson or Eric Hymas:

>   Tel: +44 (0)274 736895
>   Email: info@acronym.co.uk

E-2.6 Object Engineering

Object Engineering provides consultancy, training, and mentoring in object-oriented design and formal methods. For more information contact Alan Wills:

>   Tel: +44 (0)61 225 3240
>   Email: alan@cs.man.ac.uk

Bibliography

[1] Specification and Description Language (SDL), Recommendation Z.100. Technical report, CCITT, 1988.

[2] The Common Object Request Broker: Architecture and Specification. Technical report, Object Management Group, Framingham, MA, December 1991.

[3] Object Analysis and Design Survey of Methods 1992. Technical report, Object Management Group, Framingham, MA, October 1992.

[4] Open ODB Reference Document. Technical report, Hewlett-Packard, Cupertino, CA, September 1992.

[5] A.F. Ackerman, L.S. Buchwald, and F.H. Lewski. Software inspections: An effective verification process. *IEEE Software*, 6(3):31–38, May 1989.

[6] A.V. Aho and J.D. Ullman. *Principles of Compiler Design*. Addison-Wesley, Reading, MA, 1977.

[7] P. America. A parallel object-oriented language with inheritance and subtyping. In *ACM OOPSLA/ECOOP '90 Conference Proceedings*, pages 161–168, Ottawa, Canada, October 1990.

[8] B. Anderson and S. Gossain. Hierarchy evolution and the software lifecycle. In *TOOLS 2*, pages 41–50, Paris, 1990. Angkor.

[9] P. Arnold, S. Bodoff, D. Coleman, H. Gilchrist, and F. Hayes. Evaluation of five object-oriented development methods. In *Journal of Object-Oriented Programming: Focus on Analysis and Design*, pages 101–121. SIGS Publication, Inc., New York, 1991.

[10] B.H. Barnes and T.B. Bollinger. Making reuse cost-effective. *IEEE Software*, 8(1):13–24, January 1991.

[11] K. Beck and W. Cunningham. A laboratory for teaching object-oriented thinking. In *ACM OOPSLA '89 Conference Proceedings*, 1989.

[12] L. Berlin. When objects collide: Experiences with reusing multiple class hierarchies. In *ACM OOPSLA/ECOOP '90 Conference Proceedings*, pages 181–193, Ottawa, Canada, October 1990.

[13] B.W. Boehm. Software risk management: Principles and practices. *IEEE Software*, pages 32–41, January 1991.

[14] G. Booch. *Object-Oriented Design with Applications*. Benjamin Cummings, Redwood City, CA, 1991.

[15] F.P. Brooks. *The Mythical Man Month: Essays in Software Engineering*. Yourdon Press, Englewood Cliffs, NJ, 1982.

[16] B. Bruegge, J. Blythe, J. Jackson, and J. Shufelt. Object-oriented system modeling with OMT. In *ACM OOPSLA '92 Conference Proceedings*, pages 359–376, 1992.

[17] R.J.A. Buhr. *Practical Visual Techniques in System Design: With Applications to Ada*. Prentice Hall International, Englewood Cliffs, NJ, 1991.

[18] J. Cameron. Ingredients for a new object-oriented method. *Object Magazine*, 2(4):64–67, November 1992.

[19] R.H. Campbell, V.F. Russo, and G.M. Johnston. The design of a multiprocessor operating system. In *Proceedings of the Usenix C++ Conference*, pages 109–123. USENIX, 1987.

[20] M.D. Caroll. Problems with non-invasive inheritance in C++. In *Proceedings of the Usenix C++ Conference*, pages 13–27, Berkeley, CA, October 1991. USENIX.

[21] E. Casais. Managing class evolution in object-oriented systems. In *Object Management*, pages 133–195. Centre Universitaire d'Informatique, July 1990.

[22] P. Chen. The entity-relationship model: Toward a unified view of data. *ACM Transactions on Database Systems*, pages 9–36, March 1976.

[23] E.J. Chilkofsky and J.H. Cross. Reverse engineering and design recovery: A taxonomy. *IEEE Software*, 7(1):13–18, January 1990.

[24] M.P. Cline. Frequently-Asked-Questions for comp.lang.c++. 1992.

[25] M.P. Cline. Object-oriented software engineering and reuse. Course notes, 1992.

[26] M.P. Cline and D. Lea. The behaviour of C++ classes. In *Symposium on Object-Oriented Programming Emphasizing Practical Applications*, pages 81–91, 1990.

[27] P. Coad and E. Yourdon. *Object-Oriented Analysis*, 2nd ed. Yourdon Press, Englewood Cliffs, NJ, 1991.

[28] P. Coad and E. Yourdon. *Object-Oriented Design*. Yourdon Press, Englewood Cliffs, NJ, 1991.

[29] D. Coleman and F. Hayes. Lessons from Hewlett-Packard's experience of using object-oriented technology. In *TOOLS 4*, pages 327–333, Paris, March 1991.

[30] D. Coleman, F. Hayes, and S. Bear. Introducing objectcharts or how to use statecharts in object-oriented design. *IEEE Transactions in Software Engineering*, January 1992.

[31] D. Coleman and D. Skov. Analysis and design for concurrent object systems. Technical Report HPL-93-18, Hewlett-Packard Laboratories, Bristol (UK), February 1993.

[32] W. Cook, W. Hill, and P. Canning. Inheritance is not subtyping. In *ACM SIGACT-SIGPLAN Symposium on Principles of Programming Languages*, January 1990.

[33] J.O. Coplien. *Advanced C++: Programming Styles and Idioms*. Addison-Wesley, Reading, MA, 1991.

[34] J. Cribbs, C. Roe, and S. Moon. *An Evaluation of Object-Oriented Analysis and Design Methodologies*. SIGS Publications, Inc., New York, 1992.

[35] A.M. Davis. *Software Requirements: Analysis and Specification*. Prentice Hall International, Englewood Cliffs, NJ, 1990.

[36] D. de Champeaux and P. Faure. A comparative study of object-oriented analysis methods. *Journal of Object-Oriented Programming*, 5(1):21–33, March/April 1992.

[37] T. DeMarco. *Structured Analysis and System Specification*. Yourdon Press, New York, NY, 1979.

[38] P.J. Denning, J.B. Dennis, and J.E. Qualitz. *Machines, Languages and Computation*. Prentice Hall International, 1978.

[39] R. Duke, P. King, G. Rose, and G. Smith. The Object-Z specification language version 1. Technical report, Software Verification Research Centre, University of Queensland, Queensland, Australia, May 1991.

[40] M.A. Ellis and B. Stroustrup. *The Annotated C++ Reference Manual*. Addison-Wesley, Reading, MA, 1990.

[41] D.W. Embley, B. Kurtz, and S.N. Woodfield. *Object-Oriented Systems Analysis*. Yourdon Press, Englewood Cliffs, NJ, 1992.

[42] W. Wulf et al. *Fundamental Structures of Computer Science*. Addison-Wesley, Reading, MA, 1981.

[43] M.E. Fagan. Design and code inspections to reduce errors in program development. *IBM Systems Journal*, 15(3):182–211, 1976.

[44] S. Fiedler. Object-oriented unit testing. *Hewlett-Packard Journal*, 40(2):69–74, April 1989.

[45] A. Furtado and E. Neuhold. *Formal Techniques for Data Base Design*. Springer-Verlag, 1986.

[46] C. Ghezzi, M. Jazayeri, and D. Mandrioli. *Fundamentals of Software Engineering*. Prentice Hall International, Englewood Cliffs, NJ, 1991.

[47] A. Goldberg and D. Rubin. *Smalltalk-80: The Language and Implementation*. Addison-Wesley, Reading, MA, 1983.

[48] H. Gomaa. Structuring criteria for real time system design. In *Proceedings of the 10th International Conference on Software Engineering, 1988*, pages 418–427.

[49] K.E. Gorlen. An object-oriented class library for C++. In *Proceedings of the Usenix C++ Conference*. USENIX, 1987.

[50] D. Harel. Statecharts: A visual formalism for complex systems. *Science of Computer Programming*, 8:231–274, 1987.

[51] M.J. Harrold. Selecting and using data for integration testing. *IEEE Software*, 8(2):58–65, March 1991.

[52] M.J. Harrold, J.D. McGregor, and K.J. Fitzpatrick. Incremental testing of object-oriented class structures. In *Proceedings of the 14th International Conference on Software Engineering, 1992*, pages 68–80, May 1992.

[53] R. Helm and Y.S. Maarek. Integrating information retrieval and domain specific approaches for browsing and retrieval in object-oriented class libraries. In *ACM OOPSLA '91 Conference Proceedings*, pages 47–61, October 1991.

[54] B. Henderson-Sellers. The economics of reusing library classes. *Journal of Object-Oriented Programming*, 1993. To appear.

[55] J. Hogg. Islands: Aliasing protection in object-oriented languages. In *ACM OOPSLA '91 Conference Proceedings*, pages 271–286. October 1991.

[56] W.S. Humphrey, D.H. Kitson, and T.C. Kasse. The state of software engineering practice: A preliminary report. In *Proceedings of the 11th International Conference on Software Engineering, 1989*.

[57] M. Jackson. *System Development*. Prentice Hall International, Englewood Cliffs, NJ, 1983.

[58] I. Jacobson. *Object-Oriented Software Engineering*. Addison-Wesley, Reading, MA, 1992.

[59] I. Jacobson and F. Lindstrom. Re-engineering of old systems to an object-oriented structure. In *ACM OOPSLA '91 Conference Proceedings*, pages 340–350, October 1991.

[60] R.E. Johnson and B. Foote. Designing reusable classes. *Journal of Object-Oriented Programming*, pages 22–35, June/July 1988.

[61] R.E. Johnson and V.F. Russo. Reusing object-oriented designs. Technical Report UIUCDCS 91-1696, University of Illinois, 1991.

[62] R.E. Johnson and R. Wirfs-Brock. Object-oriented frameworks, October 1991. Tutorial at OOPSLA '91.

[63] C.B. Jones. *Systematic Software Development Using VDM*, 2nd ed. Prentice Hall International, Englewood Cliffs, NJ, 1990.

[64] G.M. Karam and R.S. Casselman. A cataloging framework for software development methods. *IEEE Computer*, 26(2):35–46, March 1993.

[65] M.F. Kleyn and P.C. Gingrich. GraphTrace: Understanding object-oriented systems using concurrently animated views. In *ACM OOPSLA '88 Conference Proceedings*, pages 191–205. ACM, November 1988.

[66] C.W. Krueger. Software reuse. *ACM Computing Surveys*, 24(2):131–183, June 1992.

[67] K. Lano and H. Haughton. The Z++ Manual. Technical report, Lloyds Register of Shipping, 29 Wellesley Rd., Croydon, UK, 1992.

[68] L. Laranjeira. Software size estimation of object-oriented software. *IEEE Transactions in Software Engineering*, May 1990.

[69] D. Lea. Customization in C++. In *Proceedings of the Usenix C++ Conference*, pages 301–314, Berkeley, CA, April 1990. USENIX.

[70] J.P. LeJacq. Function preconditions in object-oriented software. *ACM SIGPLAN Notices*, 26(10):13–18, October 1991.

[71] J.P. LeJacq. Semantic-based design guidelines for object-oriented programs. In *Journal of Object-Oriented Programming: Focus on Analysis and Design*, pages 86–97. SIGS, 1991.

[72] K. Lieberherr. Concepts of object-oriented data modeling and programming, October 1991. Tutorial at OOPSLA '91.

[73] K. Lieberherr, P. Bergstein, and I. Silva-Lepe. From objects to classes: Algorithms for optimal object-oriented design. *Software Engineering Journal*, pages 205–228, July 1991.

[74] K. Lieberherr, I. Holland, and A. Riel. Object-oriented programming, an objective sense of style. In *ACM OOPSLA '88 Conference Proceedings*, pages 323–334, 1988.

[75] H. Lieberman. Using prototypical objects to implement shared behavior in object-oriented systems. In *ACM OOPSLA '86 Conference Proceedings*, pages 214–223, 1986.

[76] M.A. Linton, J.M. Vlissides, and P.R. Calder. Composing user interfaces with InterViews. *IEEE Computer*, 22(2):8–22, 1989.

[77] D.A. Mansell. The pleasures and pitfalls of designing a C++ class library, October 1991, SCOOP Europe 1991.

[78] J. Martin and J. Odell. *Object-Oriented Analysis and Design*. Prentice Hall, Englewood Cliffs, NJ, 1992.

[79] T. Maude and G. Willis. *Rapid Prototyping: The Management of Software Risk*. Pitman Publishing, London, 1991.

[80] B. Meyer. *Object-Oriented Software Construction*. Prentice Hall International, Englewood Cliffs, NJ, 1988.

[81] D.E. Monarchi and G.I. Putchen. A research typology for object-oriented analysis and design. *Communications of the ACM*, 35(9):35–47, September 1992.

[82] G.J. Myers. *The Art of Software Testing*. John Wiley & Sons, New York, 1979.

[83] J. Nielsen and J.T. Richards. The experience of learning and using Smalltalk. *IEEE Software*, 6(3):73–77, May 1989.

[84] W. Opdyke and R.E. Johnson. Refactoring: An aid in designing object-oriented application frameworks. In *Symposium on Object-Oriented Programming Emphasizing Practical Applications*, pages 145–160, September 1990.

[85] M. Ould. *Strategies for Software Engineering: The Management of Risk and Quality*. John Wiley & Sons, New York, 1990.

[86] D.L. Parnas and P.C. Clements. A rational design process: How and why to fake it. *IEEE Transactions in Software Engineering*, 12(2):251–257, February 1986.

[87] C. Pederson. Extending ordinary inheritance schemes to include generalization. In *ACM OOPSLA '89 Conference Proceedings*, pages 407–417, 1989.

[88] D.E. Perry and G.E. Kaiser. Adequate testing and object-oriented programming. *Journal of Object-Oriented Programming*, 2:13–19, January/February 1990.

[89] R. Prieto-Diaz. Domain analysis for reusability. In *Proceedings of COMPSAC 1987*, pages 23–29, October 1987.

[90] D.R. Reed. Efficiency considerations in C++. *The C++ Report*, 4(3):27–30, March/April 1992.

[91] J. Rumbaugh. An object or not an object? *Journal of Object-Oriented Programming*, 5(3):20–25, June 1992.

[92] J. Rumbaugh. Onward to OOPSLA. *Journal of Object-Oriented Programming*, 5(4):20–24, July/August 1992.

[93] J. Rumbaugh, M. Blaha, W. Premerlani, F. Eddy, and W. Lorensen. *Object-Oriented Modeling and Design*. Prentice Hall International, Englewood Cliffs, NJ, 1991.

[94] G. Russell. Inspection in ultralarge-scale development. *IEEE Software*, 8(1):25–31, January 1991.

[95] R. Sedgewick. *Algorithms*. Addison-Wesley, Reading, MA, 1983.

[96] S. Shlaer and S.J. Mellor. *Object-Oriented Systems Analysis: Modeling the World in Data*. Yourdon Press, Englewood Cliffs, NJ, 1988.

[97] S. Shlaer and S.J. Mellor. *Object Lifecycles: Modeling the World in States*. Yourdon Press, Englewood Cliffs, NJ, 1992.

[98] M.D. Smith and D.J. Robson. A framework for testing object-oriented programs. *Journal of Object-Oriented Programming*, 5(3):45–54, June 1992.

[99] M. Spivey. *The Z Notation: A Reference Manual*. Prentice Hall International, Englewood Cliffs, NJ, 1990.

[100] A.G. Sutcliffe. Object-oriented systems development: Survey of structured methods. *Information and Software Technology*, 33:433–442, July/August 1991.

[101] D. Taenzer, M. Ganti, and S. Podar. Problems in object-oriented software reuse. In *Proceedings of the Third European Conference on Object-Oriented Programming, 1989*, pages 25–38. Cambridge University Press, 1989.

[102] J.M. Vlissides and M.A. Linton. Unidraw: A framework for building domain-specific graphical editors. In *Proceedings of the ACM User Interface Software and Technologies '89 Conference*, pages 81–94, November 1989.

[103] I.J. Walker. Requirements on an object-oriented design method. *Software Engineering Journal*, pages 102–113, March 1992.

[104] P.T. Ward and S.J. Mellor. *Structured Development for Real Time Systems*. Yourdon Press, Englewood Cliffs, NJ, 1985.

[105] M.A. Whiting. Workshop: Finding the object. In *ACM OOPSLA/ECOOP '90 Conference Proceedings*, pages 99–107, 1990. Addendum.

[106] N. Wilde, P. Matthews, and R. Huitt. Maintaining object-oriented software. *IEEE Software*, 10(1):75–80, January 1993.

[107] A. Wills. Capsules and types in fresco. In *Proceedings of the European Conference on Object-Oriented Programming, 1991*, volume 512, pages 59–76. Springer-Verlag Lecture Notes in Computer Science, 1991.

[108] R. Wirfs-Brock, B. Wilkerson, and L. Wiener. *Designing Object-Oriented Software*. Prentice Hall International, Englewood Cliffs, NJ, 1990.

[109] J.M. Zweig and R.E. Johnson. The conduit: A communication abstraction in C++. In *Proceedings of the Usenix C++ Conference*, pages 191–203. USENIX, April 1990.

Glossary

abstract class   A class intended to be used by subtyping, for the behavior it describes rather than by having instances.

agent   Entity in the system environment that invokes system operations (by sending events) and receives results (carried by events).

aggregation   A mechanism for structuring the object model whereby a new class is constructed from several other classes and relationships.

analysis   Development of a specification of what a system does in terms of how the system interacts with its environment.

arity   The number of separate classes that participate in a relationship.

attribute   A set of named values associated with an object or relationship.

cardinality   The number of classes that may be associated with each other in a relationship.

class   A set of objects that share a common structure and a common behavior. A class is an abstraction, which represents the idea or general notion of a set of similar objects.

class description   Fusion description of the attributes, methods interface, and inheritance relationships for a class.

collaborator object   Object (on an object interaction graph) that provides some functionality as a server to implement a system operation.

complete   A model is *complete* with respect to another model, or the requirements, if it captures all the concepts of the other model.

consistent   A set of models is *consistent* if they do not contradict each other.

constructor   C++ code to initialize an object once it is created. Often used for resource management (e.g., requesting store for the representation of an object).

contractual model   Programming model where the specification of a method is viewed as a *contract* between the client, which must supply a satisfied precondition, and the server, which must then deliver a satisfied postcondition.

controller object   Object (on an object interaction graph) responsible for responding to a system operation request.

data dictionary   A central repository of definitions of terms and concepts.

design   Development of an abstract model of how a system implements the behaviors specified in analysis.

destructor   C++ code to finalize an object when it is finished with. Often used for resource management (e.g., return store no longer needed to represent the object's internal state).

event   (1) Asynchronous output communication sent to an agent of a system. (2) Input communication with which the environment requests the system to perform an operation.

feature   Eiffel term for entities named in a class interface.

generalization   Relationship between a class and a number of specialized versions of it. See *specialization*.

immutable   Not changeable. Referring to a variable (or slot), means that it cannot be assigned to. For slots, only applies once initialized.

implementation   Encoding of a design in a programming language.

inheritance   Relationship between classes where the inheriting class has all the properties of the inherited class and may have more.

inheritance graph   Fusion model that shows superclass and subclass relationships.

instance   An object is an *instance* of a class if its type is that class or a subtype of it.

interface model   Fusion model that defines the input and output communication of the system.

invariant   An assertion that some property of a system must always hold.

life-cycle model   Fusion model that defines the allowable sequences of interactions that a system may participate in over its lifetime.

member   C++ term for a component of a class, either an attribute or a method.

member function   C++ term for a method; a member that is a function.

message   (1) In the message-passing model of object computation, the thing that is sent to an object to request it to perform an operation. (2) To send such a message.

method (1) Code for implementing an operation on a class, or the operation itself. (2) A development process.

mix-in A class supplied so that it can be inherited from to supply a small piece of functionality. Usually such a class will have no direct instances.

multiple inheritance Inheritance with one class inheriting from several distinct parent classes, as opposed to *single inheritance*, where classes have one parent.

multiple specialization Relationship that occurs when a class is defined as a specialization of more than one immediate superclass.

mutability Access permissions given to the data held by an object.

mutable Changeable. Referring to a variable (or slot), means that it can be assigned to. For slots, only applies after initialization.

object An object corresponds to a concept, abstraction, or thing that can be distinctly identified. During analysis, objects have attributes and may be involved in relationships with other objects. During design, the notion of object is extended by the introduction of methods and object attributes. In the implementation phase the notion of object is determined by the programming language.

object interaction graph Fusion model that shows the run-time messaging of objects to support a system operation.

object model Fusion model that shows classes and their relationships.

object-orientation The computational model that uses "objects," that is, things that respond to methods and have private state, as its atoms.

operation model Fusion model that declaratively specifies the behavior of system operations by defining their effect in terms of change of state and the events that are output.

polymorphism (1) Property of a method that is may be applied to instances of different classes, usually related by inheritance. (2) Property of a variable that it may refer to instance of different classes, again usually related by inheritance.

postcondition A predicate that describes how the system state is changed by a system operation and what events are sent to agents.

precondition A predicate that characterizes the conditions under which a system operation may be invoked.

predicate A list of clauses each of which must be **true** in order for the predicate to be satisfied.

regular expression A way of describing sequences with a restricted form of grammar with sequencing, choice, and repetition.

relationship A potential association between classes.

role Name that qualifies the class participating in a relationship.

satisfiable schema A schema is *satisfiable* if, for all initial values satisfying the **Assumes** clause, there exist final values that satisfy the **Results** clause.

scenario   A sequence of events between agents and the system that is carried out for some purpose. Scenarios are represented on timeline diagrams.

schema   A way of describing an operation in terms of what must be true before it is executed (the precondition) and what is true afterward (the postcondition). Schemata are used in the Fusion operational model.

schemata   Plural of "schema."

slot   A place in a data structure, especially an object, used to hole a value; corresponds to a Fusion attribute, a C++ member, an Eiffel nonroutine feature, or a Smalltalk instance variable.

specialization   Relationship between a class and the class (called its *superclass*) from which it inherits attributes and relationships.

system interface   The set of system operations to which a system can respond and the set of events that it can output.

system object model   A Fusion model that is a subset of the object model. It determines the structure of the state of the system being built.

system operation   An input event and its effect on a system. System operations are invoked by agents in the environment.

virtual   See *virtual inheritance* and *virtual method*.

virtual inheritance   In C++, inheritance where repeated base classes are shared rather than producing multiple copies in the derived class.

virtual method   In C++, a method in a base class that can be redefined in a derived class.

visibility graph   Fusion model that shows the visibility reference structure of classes.

visibility reference   The connection required to an object to be able to invoke its methods.

Index

W